D1200269

SPLIT SIGNALS

COMMUNICATION AND SOCIETY
edited by George Gerbner and Marsha Seifert

IMAGE ETHICS
The Moral Rights of Subjects
in Photographs, Film, and Television
Edited by Larry Gross, John Stuart Katz,
and Jay Ruby

CENSORSHIP
The Knot That Binds Power and Knowledge
By Sue Curry Jansen

SPLIT SIGNALS
Television and Politics in the Soviet Union
By Ellen Mickiewicz

TELEVISION AND AMERICA'S CHILDREN
A Crisis of Neglect
By Edward L. Palmer

SPLIT SIGNALS

Television and Politics in the Soviet Union

ELLEN MICKIEWICZ

New York   Oxford
OXFORD UNIVERSITY PRESS
1988

Oxford University Press

Oxford   New York   Toronto
Delhi   Bombay   Calcutta   Madras   Karachi
Petaling Jaya   Singapore   Hong Kong   Tokyo
Nairobi   Dar es Salaam   Cape Town
Melbourne   Auckland
and associated companies in
Berlin   Ibadan

Copyright © 1988 by Oxford University Press, Inc.

Published by Oxford University Press, Inc.,
200 Madison Avenue, New York, New York 10016

Oxford is a registered trademark of Oxford University Press

Mickiewicz, Ellen Propper.
Split signals : television and politics in the Soviet Union /
Ellen Mickiewicz.
p.   cm.
Includes index.
ISBN 0-19-505463-6
1. Television broadcasting of news—Soviet Union. 2. Television
broadcasting—Social aspects—Soviet Union. 3. Television
broadcasting—Political aspects—Soviet Union. 4. Soviet Union—
Politics and government—1982-   I. Title.
PN5277.T4M53 1988
302.2'345'0947—dc19   88-4200
CIP

10 9 8 7 6 5 4 3 2 1

Printed in the United States of America
on acid-free paper

Preface

In television terminology, broadcast signals are split when they are divided and sent to two or more locations simultaneously. The title of this book refers in part to that technical definition: the recent and massive development of television in the Soviet Union has sent video signals out over a vast area of eleven time zones; they are beamed where they have never before been received and they reach people who have been effectively out of the range of the mass media. This has been a technological and information revolution, and it has taken place with stunning rapidity. Within a short time, less than two decades, television has become the principal source of information—particularly about the West—for most Soviet citizens, and a mass public has been created. It has become pre-eminently *the* mass medium of communication. But there is another sense in which I use the term split signals: the impact of this revolution has been powerful, but contradictory, paradoxical, and unplanned. The split signals affect both ordinary people and elites, both theory and practice. The television revolution began before Mikhail Gorbachev came to power, but he has given it a new impetus and motive power. The most dramatic changes of his tenure have been made precisely in the mass media—television foremost among them—and the effects will be far-reaching. They have been set in motion to a large extent because the Soviet leadership seeks to mobilize its population for domestic economic and social reform and because it recognizes that in the modern world information barriers are porous, that the flow of ideas seeps through with tourists, radios, journals, meetings, the grapevine, and old-fashioned gossip. The advantage, moreover, will always be with the source that first transmits the information. But the Soviet population has changed, too; it is better educated, more urban, and now, through television, much more tuned in to messages emanating from Moscow.

The first chapter of this book sets this new medium of television in the context of changes in the media system as a whole. It looks at new technologies and how television has created new patterns of media exposure. Central to any discussion of Soviet media must be a clear understanding of how they interpret information, especially news. The second chapter looks at the place that the world "out there" has in the Soviet media system. How inward turning or outward looking is the average television viewer in that country? How much do we in the West matter there? We shall find that, paradoxically (another split signal), and to a considerable extent as a *result* of Soviet media policy, there is a virtual obsession with America. Two policy directions substantially altered traditional media practices: *operativnost* (timeliness, or rapid response time) and *glasnost* (openness) are creating new imperatives, though their limits are problematic. In the case of the Chernobyl nuclear power station accident, the new policies were subjected to an unexpected test of huge proportions, and that incident will long be seen as a watershed. We shall also see media guidelines in operation in the work of individual Soviet correspondents.

Chapters Three and Four look at the Soviet news, the single most important program on Soviet television. In these chapters, we look at the Soviet news as compared with American network news. Do these two news agendas resemble each other? Does the huge viewing public in the Soviet Union (some 150 million people) see the contours of the same planet we in the West inhabit, or do we live in different worlds? For this study, we analyzed some 3,695 individual news stories over five months: three in 1984 and two in 1985. Each story was analyzed for over twenty different categories, and the two time periods permit us to compare the news under the Chernenko and Gorbachev regimes. In addition, both American and Soviet newspeople, in extensive interviews, comment on what shapes their decisions and how they look at the coverage of each other. The two news programs use pictures very differently; the role of anchors, the coverage of different kinds of newsmakers, the technical under-pinning of the news: on all of these dimensions, Soviet and American television are distinctively different, yet similarities are very important. But perhaps most important, both interpret the world very differently and see their roles in explaining the news—which could be a haphazard collection of unrelated events—in radically divergent ways. Watching the news is part of watching television. The news is embedded in a day's or a week's programs, and it is important to understand what that context is for the Soviet viewer. Chapter Four also includes an analysis of a week of television programs and discussion of non-news programs of particular interest.

Behind the changes coming on the screen, there have been changes in how Soviet officials and experts think about commu-nication. If television has created the country's first mass public, the old ways of thinking about how people learn about events at home and abroad, what persuades them, and what captures their attention must also change. Even the time honored and doctrinally enshrined practices of millions of ideology personnel have become obsolete. In short, the television revolution is just that: a radical change in a whole system of interrelated processes of information flow and assimilation. Chapter Five examines this complex of components of the television revolution in the light of both Soviet and Western theory, and Chapter Six assesses the impact of television on the Soviet viewing public: how television has changed the way they use their time, for example. Soviet and American citizens reacted to the introduction of television in much the same way. It has affected movie and theater atten-dance, attention spans in school, and reading. Older people, housewives, and the poor are virtual television addicts. But the advent of television on a mass scale has brought more. It has brought the potential for profound changes in the effectiveness of the government's transmission of its messages. It is in this last chapter that we will look at what influences effectiveness and under what conditions it is most likely to occur.

In preparing this study, I have been fortunate to have had access to the Soviet Union's most important national television network: First Program. Emory University has the only research group in the country to receive (and it is received in real time) this network, and I am grateful to Emory for its support.

There are many others to whom I owe thanks. This study was made possible by two grants from the John and Mary R. Markle Foundation, who supported this research from its inception. I thank also the Rockefeller Foundation for its generous grant. These institutions are not, nor are those who are listed below, responsible for the conclusions I reach in this book.

Among those whom I thank, there is one, whose engineering genius made our facility possible: the late Kurt Oppenheimer. I have also benefited from observations provided by George Jacobs, Stephen Hess, Fred Bruning, Vladimir Shlapentokh, and Aaron Ruscetta. I am particularly grateful to the news professionals at the ABC, CBS, and NBC television networks who cooperated most generously with me and provided me with the opportunity to discuss issues related to American broadcast news practices and to observe how they worked. I owe special thanks to those at ABC whose interest and help were very important. In addition, I appreciate the cooperation of Soviet media professionals in the United States and of the USSR State Committee for Television and Radio Broadcasting for the time I spent there with heads of programming and technical departments. The Turner Broadcasting Company has been a most valued and respected friend, whose willingness to assist me in my research is gratefully acknowledged.

I have been fortunate to have had the help of some talented and conscientious assistants: Gregory Haley, Laura Roselle, Nicholas Desoutter, Edward Hyken, Terry Krugman, Marina Teplitsky, and Philip Wainwright. They displayed a commitment to scholarly research and a dedication to this project that I should like to recognize with appreciation.

Atlanta   E.M.
February 1988

Contents

Chapter One: Television in the Soviet Media System   3

The National Networks   5
VCRs: The Newest Entry   11
Communications Satellites   13
Radio in the Soviet Media System   16
Coordinating the Media Market   22
The Soviet Understanding of "Newsworthy"   26

**Chapter Two: Looking Outward: International News
and the Changing Soviet Television Scene**   31

The Salience of the West   32
The Demand for Multiple Points of View: Glasnost in
   International Issues   34
Americans on Soviet Television   51
The New Value of Timeliness   56
Responsiveness, Glasnost, and the Chernobyl Nuclear
   Plant Disaster   60
Moscow Television's Man in Washington   68
The Journalist's Image of the Public: Soviet and
   American   79
Sources for Soviet Newspeople in America   83

Chapter Three: The Worlds of Soviet and American Television News

Chapter Three: The Worlds of Soviet and American
     Television News   85

Countries of the World: The Geography of News   89
Regions of the World: The Geography of News   97
The Geography of News and Elapsed Time   98
Subjects and Stories: The Content of News   104
Subjects and Stories: The Weight of Time   108
The Linkage of Subject and Country   112
Subjects and Format: Talking Heads and Pictures   117
Format and Elapsed Time: How Much Time for Talking
     Heads?   120

Chapter Four: Dimensions of News and Their Setting   124

The Responsibility of Countries and Explaining the
     World   125
Tinting the News: The Use of Loaded Words   130
Emotion and Responsibility: The Total Share   133
Changes in Soviet Leadership Periods   134
Newsmakers: Who Is Covered on the News?   142
The Technical Side of the News   146
The Week on Television: The Context of the Soviet News
     Weekday Programming   150
     America on Weekday Airtime   155
     Weekend Programming   159
     America on Weekend Airtime   162
A Selection of Non-News Programs   164
     Let's Go Girls   164
     The Man from Fifth Avenue   165
     From Chicago to Philadelphia   169
     Space Bridge: Moscow-Kabul   171
     The World and Youth/Twelfth Floor   172

Chapter Five: Television and the Formation of Public Opinion 179

Understanding Public Opinion: Television and Model-Fitting 180
The Hypodermic Effects Model 180
Mass Publics and the Two-Step Flow Model 183
Tracking the Television Audience: The Public as Individuals 193
Gauging Media Effects 201

Chapter Six: The Impact of Television 204

Viewing Patterns 204
The Mixed Impact of Television 207
Assimilating Messages 217
Living with Contradictions 224

Notes 227
Index 265

SPLIT SIGNALS

CHAPTER ONE

Television in the Soviet Media System

IN 1940 THERE WERE ONLY 400 television sets in the Soviet Union. By 1950 there were 10,000; a decade later, some 4.8 million. Then in the five years between 1965 and 1970 the availability of television sets more than doubled. With a crash program, the production of television sets had jumped in the 1970s, and by 1976 Soviet industry was producing seven million sets annually.[1] The economic plan projects the production of television sets at between 10 and 11 million in 1990 and between 12.5 and 13 million in the year 2000.

In 1960 only 5 percent of the Soviet population could watch television,[2] but by 1986 fully 93 percent of the population were viewers, and they were living in areas comprising more than 86 percent of the territory of the U.S.S.R.[3] The number of television sets is calculated by Soviet statistical sources to cover all urban households and 90 percent of the rural households.[4] The rest of the population, roughly twenty million people, are rural residents, mainly in Siberia.[5] Some 50 million receive only one of the two national networks.[6] Why the crash program started so late, or why it started at all, is a matter of some conjecture. Clearly, as one can tell from official pronouncements on communications, the political leaders were slow to grasp the potential of television to capture the attention of the population and therefore to function as an important instrument of persuasion. But perhaps equally critical was the configuration of the country itself, with a vast land mass stretching over eleven time zones. Many areas are thinly populated; many regions are subject to harsh weather and feature terrain not easily penetrated. With the development of communications satellites, however, that sprawling inhospitable territory could be leapfrogged and signals beamed down at relatively low cost. Communications satellites radically altered information diffusion in the Soviet Union. In record time a major new medium of communication has been placed in homes across a vast and linguistically diverse country.[7] For the first time a mass public has been created, as the new electronic medium transmits its message directly to an enormous number of individuals who receive it outside the politically predictable structures of organized groups.[8] Although a system of mass communications had been in place for a very long time in the Soviet Union, it failed in some serious and important ways to reach the number and kinds of people that television has done. Radio, which the Soviets developed in a crash program right after the Bolshevik Revolution, did not reach the entire population, and people who read newspapers (especially the national ones) tended always to be among the better educated. It was precisely because the leadership needed to amplify the range of its media that it developed the institution of political agitation, enlisting millions of Communist Party members in disseminating and interpreting information.[9] But with the advent of television, virtually total saturation of the population could, for the first time, be assured. That meant people of all age groups and all levels of education would be the recipients of standardized messages, and the transmission of these messages would take place with unheard-of speed, reaching everyone nearly simultaneously. That kind of public and those numbers had never been seen before in Soviet mass media. And, as we shall see in Chapter Five, the introduction of a truly mass medium has had a serious impact on the more traditional components of the media system.

Perhaps it should have been foreseen that serious changes would be wrought by such a sudden shift in the way people learn about the world, but the effects of this new medium were, to a large extent, unplanned. And these effects have been rapid and profound. As this and the next chapters show, the television revolution in the Soviet Union, though initiated and administered under tight central control, has created a new and mobilized public, often impatient with the tempo of domestic reform and more than ever attentive to the outside world, particularly the West, and these changes have outpaced the ability of the leadership to manage the administrative and technological demands of control linked to efficacy. As we shall see, this linkage is problematic in any case. Under Mikhail Gorbachev the process of adapting to the new domestic and international information environment and shaping it as well has moved ahead very vigorously.[10] It was in the media that the most dramatic and far-reaching changes first took place.[11] Even foreign policy initiatives, particularly on the critical issues of arms control and security, have been introduced on television and may, in fact, be crafted with that medium in mind. The Soviet media in general and television in particular have a distinctive organizational structure. The development of television is a history of centralized political control in tension with the centrifugal forces of audience demand. The national television network system is a case in point.

The National Networks

In the Soviet Union there are two national networks, called First Program and Second Program. Both originate from the Central Television Studios in Moscow, and all of their programs are broadcast in Russian. Local television stations have their own limited broadcast schedules and also may insert their programming, concentrating on local culture and production campaigns, in "windows" in the national broadcasts. The networks, through delayed broadcasts, reach all the time zones of the country, and local television broadcasters are warned not to compete with the most politically important national broadcasts. In an authoritative statement: "Above all else, the most important social-political programs of Central broadcasts, such as the television program 'Vremya' [the national evening news program, "Time"] . . . must not be 'covered' by local broadcasts."[12] This message was clear very soon after the introduction of the First Program in 1960. Just four years later, a resolution of the Central Committee of the Ukraine called for the elimination of "localism," and "independence" in "issues of the telefication of the republic."[13] Until January 1, 1982, when Second Program was begun, as a result of a decision of the 26th Congress of the Communist Party, there was only one national network. The new network was to feature events which were, on their face, less clearly important (in terms of significant political and social programs) than those of First Program, but which would display more of the lives of the various peoples of the country. In this connection, Second Program was to feature more programs produced by local studios.[14]

Attracting the participation of local television studios is not devolution of authority to the local studio. The question of local programming has been, on the whole, a thorny one for the communications policymakers. As G.Z. Iushkyavichius, a deputy director of the State Committee on Television and Radio, the responsible government agency, noted: " . . . there was a time when local studios participated very actively in our programs, and then 12–15 years ago, their proportion significantly declined. This was explained by [the fact that] the ideological-artistic level and the technical equipment of local TV were lower than on Central Television."[15] That may be only part of the complex administrative problem of those days. Because television signals were more difficult to receive before the widespread development of satellites, local studios did substitute their own programs, and central programming was interrupted for certain localities, with the result that Russian-language transmissions were replaced by programs in local languages. Because of concern about the centrifugal pull of the ethnic minorities, a more centralized direction of programming was decreed in 1970, when television was placed before radio in the title of the governmental administrative body overseeing the two media: the State Committee for Television and Radio Broadcasting (Gosteleradio).[16] The reorganization strengthened central Party control not only over national, but also over local broadcasting, and, as a Soviet official notes: "the party took the entire responsibility for the political, ideological, [and] artistic level of television programs."[17] The intermediate link between the individual studios and the center was abolished, and a central administration for local broadasting was established.

Increased centralization of television broadcasting and the use of Russian on the national networks has had an impact on the linguistic assimilation of the ethnic minorities. Television has reached all of the national republics, and the gaps between them in television ownership have diminished to such an extent that in every republic at least three-quarters of the households have television sets.[18] Local programming is offered at the local level, too, in Russian, in addition to the indigenous language, of which there about forty.[19] But the time devoted to Russian-language broadcasting is actually increasing; in part due to the influence of the national networks, which are expanding their broadcast day and in which only Russian is used.

A study of the republic of Azerbaidzhan, where Russians are fewer than 8 percent of the population, found that even though the number of hours of programming broadcast in Azeri and Russian may result in equal time, it is unequal competition. The native-language programs lack the production values of the national programs; typical programs on Baku television are lengthy performances of Middle Eastern music or programs on industry and production. The music programs are popular, but they do not offer an effective means of language reinforcement—not nearly as effective as the shows and Russian-dubbed foreign imports shown on the national networks.[20]

Soviet studies of patterns of transmission of ethnic values and identity reveal that as, increasingly, native traditions are transmitted not by word-of-mouth but by the mass media outside the personalized settings, those traditions become passive and increasingly remote. Thus, "the traditional ethnic culture is assimilated passively," no longer accompanied by active performance.[21] In the Soviet Union, as everywhere else, differences and traditions are slowly eroding as national television usurps the role of keeper of the heritage. Simultaneously, glasnost has stimulated a demand for more programming in minority languages: a point at issue in the 1988 Azerbaidzhan disorders, a question to which we shall return in Chapter Six.

Second Program, created to bring innovation to network choice, has not worked well. It has not achieved a clear identity or attracted the expected audience, which is less than half the audience for First Program.[22] As an article in *Pravda* noted, First Program carries the most important news, the events of the "highest significance," while on Second Program, the absence of "its own timely, as they say, 'hot' information on international news events, impoverishes the content [of the network]."[23] Second Program plays some repeats from First and airs some broadcasts that for one reason or another did not pass muster on the more important network. Data about the audiences of the two national networks bear out the concerns voiced by the *Pravda* correspondent. In 1985, it was found that the news analysis and commentary programs of First Program were far more popular than those on Second Program, and that "it is from First Program that the audience primarily expects to gain socio-political information."[24] The difference between the two national networks is made greater by the practice of local television studios inserting their own programming into the broadcast day of Second Program, but not into that of First Program. Although there are plans to build television studios in some 67 provinces over the next two decades, the project will be expensive and take time. The chief of the directorate for local television broadcasting finds that in the absence of local television channels, the great majority of television studios in the large Russian Republic insert their programs into Second Program and will continue to do so for some time to come.[25]

The size of audiences for the leading national news and news analysis programs is staggering: an average of 150 million people watch the evening news daily, over 80 percent of the adult population. By contrast, the three network news programs in the United States attract a total of almost 60 million viewers each night, or just over one-third of the adult population. Vremya increased its audience by 20 percent between 1979 and 1984. The figure is so large in part because Vremya is broadcast simultaneously on all television channels. The news analysis program, "Today in the World," shown only on First Program, plays to some 60 to 90 million people daily. "Today in the World" chooses a small number of stories from the daily news, and the commentator elaborates on them, providing analysis, judgments, and additional filmed footage. It is broadcast twice every weekday—around 6:00 p.m. and again at the close of the broadcast day.[26] On Sunday, again on First Program, an extremely influential news commentary, "International Panorama," is watched by over 80 percent of the viewing audience.[27] This program, broadcast at six o'clock Moscow time, serves a menu of international stories, with filmed footage and commentary by some of the best-known newspaper columnists. Once a month foreign correspondents are brought together for an hour on Saturday to discuss international news on "Studio 9." "*Sodruzhestvo*" is a much less popular program devoted to analysis of news about cooperation among the socialist countries. Grigory Shevelev, head of the information editorial offices of Central Television in Moscow, argues that Vremya's "first task is news, facts. And then when there is a good chance to do good problematic material, we do not avoid it. Often this depends on the limitation of minutes. A subject exceeding a minute and a half is a luxury for us."[28] As we shall see later, a story exceeding a minute and a half is hardly a rarity; stories on Vremya have lasted over an hour and a half, when the leader makes a speech.

There are three more network choices for Moscow residents. After a 1965 resolution of the Central Committee of the Communist Party, Third Program was begun. It offers instruction, both for children and adults, and functions as an adjunct to the regular school system and the very highly developed adult education system—a system that includes both instruction in production skills and ideological and political instruction. These programs do not enjoy wide popularity; an audience survey showed that only 5 percent of the respondents said they watched educational programs.[29] Fourth Program, created in 1967, comes on at seven o'clock in the evening and ends its broadcast day after 11:00 p.m. Sports, local cultural events, films, and documentaries dominate the schedule. In 1970 this channel too was "put in order," as central control was exercised over the content and standards of broadcasts after criticism of the "ideological direction and content of many of the programs created on Fourth Program."[30] Finally, the Leningrad channel is also available to Muscovites.

First Program begins its broadcast day at 6:30 a.m. with a live two-hour morning show of news and light fare and continues until some time (it varies) late in the morning, when, except on the weekend, there is usually a break until late afternoon. After the break, programming resumes until 11:30 or midnight, unless there is a late-night show. Two live late-night shows were added in 1987. In fact, the shift in programming policy to live broadcasts is one of the hallmarks of the Gorbachev era. In that year alone over a dozen live programs were inaugurated; in the past only the newscast went on live, and much of that was taped well in advance. The introduction of live broadcasting is based on a belief among Soviet officials that viewers empathize and participate far more fully with live broadcasts. It is part of the campaign to reach the population more effectively. But, more important, this shift to live programming represents a certain relaxation of controls. Taping in advance permits prior censorship and guarantees total control over content; live broadcasts can include the unexpected. This is part of the attempt to enhance credibility and reach the viewers. Very few programs are allocated regular weekly slots and very few programs begin on the half-hour or hour. Even the country's most important program, the news broadcast Vremya, did not have a regular time slot until 1972.[31] Soviet viewers have found it difficult to find their favorite programs, which, although they might be shown several times a month, are impossible to locate without a newspaper listing or the weekly television magazine. The practice of allocating what seems to be random time slots to programs is coming under fire from those concerned with the efficacy of the media. A disgruntled article in *Literaturnaya Gazeta* noted that not a single popular entertainment weekday program had a regular time slot. Take the case of "Cinema Panorama," a very popular show: in 1983, it was broadcast in April and August only. Another show about popular music in foreign countries was shown in January of that year and reappeared only in September and October. To make matters worse, the names of programs will change without notice, as happened to the very popular show "Hello, We're Looking for Talent," which became "Young Voices."[32] To address this problem, on January 31, 1986, a new television program premiered on First Program. Called "Viewer's Companion," the thirty-minute show is broadcast on the last day of each month and covers the new programs and notable broadcasts scheduled for the next month. Keeping track of programs has become even harder, not only because of the lack of predictable time slots but also because of the welter of new programs being generated as the new communications policy takes hold.[33] Executives at Gosteleradio say that the broadcast day will continue to expand for some time. It will begin earlier and new programming will gradually replace the repeats.

VCRs: The Newest Entry

Following on the heels of the television revolution comes its newest adjunct, the videocassette recorder. The production of VCRs is still very slow, though slated for growth in the coming years. About 4,000 a year have been produced, but that figure is set by the plan to increase to 60,000 in 1990 and 120,000 in 2000.[34] The cost of a VCR is 1,200 rubles (about six months of an average salary), and the Soviet-made model, the Elektronika VM-12, is produced in Voronezh, a city about 300 miles south of Moscow. Japanese VCRs sell for at least twice as much, but the demand is so high that, as a man in Sverdlovsk wrote to *Literaturnaya Gazeta*, "We're highly qualified workers; we have money; we would gladly pay three thousand for a Japanese 'Akai' or 'Panasonic.' It would be much better if we paid this money for our cultured leisure than gave it to a wine store."[35] Many foreign VCRs are brought back by diplomats, journalists, and others traveling abroad.

It was in Voronezh that the country's first VCR rental library was started, and until late in 1985 it was the only one. There are VCR rental stores in Moscow and, again, according to the plan, each republic capital will have them, as will some port cities.[36] The stock of cassettes available for rent is very small for a population of over 280 million people. In mid-1985, there were only 250 officially produced cassettes in distribution, but a crash program to record more cassettes was in progress, doubling the output by the end of 1985 and increasing rapidly thereafter. According to Vladimir Olitsky—head of the newly created department for the planning of videotape repertoires, the printing of copies, and the organization of videocassette rentals—the entire stock of Soviet films is being put on cassettes as well as the films from socialist allies. With new repurchasing agreements, films from the West will also be put in circulation in cassette form. In addition there will be theater productions, pop singers (Alla Pugachova is one of the most popular), the circus, how-to cassettes (how to remodel an apartment, how to train your dog, how to drive a car, do gymnastics, and swim). Both Olitsky and Evgeny Voitovich—who directs the film distribution and movie theater construction department of the State Cinematography Committee (the government's administrative body for all planning, production, and distribution of films)—complain that the bureaucracy is unprepared for the VCR revolution. Voitovich recounts how difficult it was to find a place for the Moscow store. Every time he came up with a possibility, he was denied permission; finally, he was assigned a small movie theater (of some 50 seats) in the old Arbat district of Moscow. The problem, as so often happens with something new, is that the bureaucratic lines have been drawn and are ill-adapted to change. Voitovich argues that the only solution would be the creation of an interdepartmental council representing the State Committee on Cinematography, the electronics industry, the Ministry of Education, consumer services, and, because of the propaganda and educational potential of VCRs, the Young Communist League and the trade unions.[37]

The failure to anticipate this newest spinoff of the television revolution (a recurring problem as Soviet policymakers confront an exploding information revolution) has resulted in a rush of illegal imports to fill the void. An article that appeared in the Soviet press in the summer of 1985 urged that production of rental films be stepped up dramatically, since the Soviet Union had fallen far behind "the rate at which the uncontrolled influx, so to speak, is growing."[38] What that uncontrolled influx is bringing in is pornography and films the regime objects to on political grounds. This has become known through the very well-publicized arrests and trials of underground entrepreneurs. The black market seems to have no geographical limitations and the scale is sometimes very large. For example, a sweep of underground operations in the Latvian capital of Riga netted 415 tapes. A movie would be shown in an apartment in the city; each showing would attract about ten people, each paying ten rubles. They watched X-rated movies (*Taxi Girls, The Girls from Paris,* and other pornographic films). The ringleader got one and a half years in prison and a fine of 500 rubles. His partners were also tried and found guilty. The charges included distribution of pornographic materials, illegally arranging paid shows, and "video speculation."[39] In far-away Tashkent, in Soviet Central Asia, Bruce Lee films were being illegally shown by a man who went from village to village charging three-ruble admission fees to audiences of fifteen men. In addition to the flying fists, they showed what the court judged to be pornography. One and a half years in prison was the sentence. The illegal VCR operations can sometimes be very ambitious: a man tried in Moscow advertised, distributed, and sold large numbers of cassettes (many pornographic) and video equipment. He had a whole staff of translators (from some respected institutes). He got money and sometimes goods (automobile tires, for instance) for his services.[40]

The Soviet regime is concerned not only about the economic issues (the flourishing of black market enterprise) and the moral issues involved (the distribution of sexually explicit and hedonistic materials to a rather protected population) but also about the political implications. In the press, they have made a connection between the importation of these contraband cassettes and the attempt by the West to undermine the Soviet regime. It is said to be another example of the West's cultivation of sedition. *Rambo* and *Rocky IV*, runaway hits on the video black market, are particularly worrisome. Even pornography, an article said, "is interwoven with lauding the bourgeois way of life. It goes without saying that this, too, is aimed primarily at poisoning the younger generation's mind."[41]

In an attempt to control the flow of unofficial videotapes, new legislation was enacted making a criminal offense the "making storing, distribution, or showing of films propagating 'the cult of violence and cruelty' "—a crime subject to imprisonment for up to two years.[42] This August 1986 addition to the Russian Republic's criminal code serves as a model for the other republics. The likelihood that this legal solution will be decisive is dim. The methods sometimes leave much to be desired. One man recounted how in the agency where he worked the authorities rounded up all of the owners of VCRs because a search of one owner's home turned up pornographic cassettes.[43] The situation of the rapid development of information sources, the technology that makes them portable and versatile, the increasing salience of the world out there, all suggest that these issues will be difficult to resolve.

Communications Satellites

The Soviet Union launched its first communications satellites in the mid 1960s. Since then, over seventy have been put aloft to relay telecommunications, newspaper facsimiles, and radio and television programs. The early satellites, called Molniya ("Lightning"—launched in 1965), and their later upgrades were really a series of "birds," each carrying the signals for a portion of the day before passing out of reach, as the elliptical orbit took them around to come back the next day. The system is particularly useful for covering the polar regions of the Soviet Union and also carries the Moscow-Washington hot line. In 1975 the Soviet Union launched its first geostationary satellites, the Raduga (Rainbow) system. These provide a fixed focus for antennas, in contrast to the Molniya satellites, which have to be tracked, the antenna finding each bird as it starts its transmission. The footprint of the Raduga satellites covers much of the Soviet Union and Europe. The Ekran (Screen) geostationary satellites were added in 1976 to provide coverage for low-density population areas in Siberia and the Soviet East. A third system of geostationary satellites is the Ghorizont (Horizon), first launched at the end of 1978 to serve the Socialist international communications network as well as the Soviet Union itself. Within the Soviet Union there were, by mid-1986, ninety ground stations in the Orbita system and more than 5,000 for the Ekran and Moscow type combined.[44] The Ekran satellites transmit a strong signal that would interfere with other broadcast signals in populated areas; it can be used therefore only in remote, fairly empty locations. The receiving equipment is quite inexpensive and can be mounted on apartment buildings. The Orbita ground stations use a 12-meter antenna for receiving mainly from the Molniya system, though also from the Raduga satellites, while the Moscow distribution stations use a much smaller antenna—2.5 meters—for Ghorizont satellites. The increase in the Moscow system has been rapid over the past few years, while the Molniya system and its downlinks have not expanded similarly. The Moscow system is more efficient and cost effective. Soviet communications satellite development has been serious, intensive, and very costly; they have the densest network of communications satellites in the world. Robert Campbell concludes that there were more cost-effective alternatives to the strategy the Soviets employed. He finds the ratio of capacity to payload very small by the standards of Intelsat, the Western communications satellite system, and the life of the Soviet satellites relatively short. But the design, whatever its efficiency in technical terms, was chosen, he believes, to maximize the political objectives of the regime: the saturation of the entire population by centralized broadcasting.[45]

The satellites also serve the Socialist international communications network. Intervision, as it is called, is part of the International Organization for Radio and Television (abbreviated as OIRT from the French title). This network is the socialist equivalent of Intelsat, which the Soviets refused to join, although they have participated as observers and cooperated from time to time. About a dozen countries belong to Intervision—client states of the Soviet Union in Latin America, Europe, and Asia. Finland is also a member. According to one Soviet expert, in one year Intervision serves more than 350 million viewers. In addition to members, there are other states that buy time on the Intervision network, and their number exceeds 120.[46] The Soviet Union has attempted to use its international communications satellites for competition with Intelsat by offering cheaper rates—about one-third of the cost of the Western system. This has caused some concern in the United States, but it seems unlikely that Intervision will outsell Intelsat.

The advent of international communications satellites has also raised the opportunity or specter of direct broadcast satellites serving the propaganda or information purposes of one country by intruding on the videospace of another. In particular, the United States Information Agency has raised this possibility, arguing that with the decreasing cost of satellite downlinks and with increasing miniaturization of components, it may become possible to beam American television programs directly into Soviet households—a kind of video version of Voice of America or Radio Liberty. The official Soviet reaction has been similarly strong: inveighing against the information intrusion of the West and linking this behavior to what they call the kind of communications imperialism that motivated the Socialist and Third World countries to argue for a New World Information Order in UNESCO.[47] Spartak Beglov, a noted Soviet expert on communications, wrote that in the beginning of the 1980s, President Reagan got a mandate from "reactionary circles" to develop "unlimited psychological war against the USSR and all the forces of socialism and progress."[48] Whatever the official statements on both sides, there is little evidence in either country that this prospect will become reality in the near term. My discussions with experts both in Moscow and in the United States lead me to the conclusion that this scenario may not be very realistic. Receiving television signals from satellites in most parts of the world is not a simple matter. It is necessary to use downconverters and low-noise amplifiers in order to have an intelligible signal appear on the television monitor. In most countries, though, the purchase of LNAs and downconverters is controlled. It is impossible to purchase an American-style package for a backyard dish, with downconverter and LNA included, and it is also very difficult for the do-it-yourselfers to fabricate them at home. Just building a dish (not a very difficult thing to do) to catch a signal won't work. True, downconverters and LNAs could be smuggled into the country, but unless the illegal operation were massive, it could not supply the entire population or even a very significant part of it. Someday a set may be developed that tunes directly to the 10GHz signal and the downconverters and LNAs won't be needed, but that set has yet to appear. Also, if the satellite were directly overhead and if the signal were very strong, the transmission of television signals would be very significantly facilitated. However, the order of magnitude of the cost of fabricating and launching such a satellite is staggering, and it is unlikely that the mission payoff would justify the expense. Quite apart from technical considerations, which are formidable, there are political and economic considerations. Short-wave radio, unlike television, was designed to cross borders, and when it does so without prior consent it can be jammed (as discussed below). Short-wave radio occupies a small part of the spectrum and has relatively little economic value. Television channels, on the other hand, have enormous economic significance, especially in the United States. The allocation of channels is regulated internationally in order to prevent interference in a very important economic sector. Intrusion, beaming signals without prior consent, would seriously disturb a system created precisely to assure order for economic benefit. Retaliation would be simple: it could take the form of jamming, which is relatively easy or, more serious, intruding in kind. Since American companies are important beneficiaries of the international regulatory system, it is unlikely that they would or should welcome a chaotic spiraling of video band wars.

Radio in the Soviet Media System

When one part of a system of communications changes as dramatically as television has done, it is reasonable to assume that the other parts of the system will be affected. In the United States, the introduction of television has had a powerful effect on radio; both its audience and function have changed substantially. A 1981 Simmons survey revealed that radio was the least used medium compared with newspapers, news magazines, and television.[49] In the Soviet Union, too, radio is not what it once was. In the early days right after the Bolshevik Revolution and up to the Second World War, the policy of "radiofication" was vigorously pursued. By 1940, some seven million sets were being produced annually, and by 1979 there were about 544 sets per 1,000 population—a figure still far below the 2,009 per 1,000 population in the United States, where radios have become so inexpensive that households own several. Not long ago, an article ran in the Soviet newspaper most popular among the highly educated, in which there was a complaint about "screaming loudspeakers" carrying radio programs to outdoor public places. The article conveyed the complaints of a number of letter-writers from various parts of the country. It is not only the noise level that was objectionable, but, more important, the very function of the public dissemination of radio broadcasts for informational purposes was called obsolete. As the correspondent wrote: "In the '30s to hear the radio . . . at all was a pleasure . . . [it was received as] a miracle. . . . In the thinking of some officials . . . . the idea of radio holds the same place in the culture that it did decades ago. But radio has a different role today. . . . It's time to revise our attitude toward radio as a medium of mass communication."[50] A survey published in 1981 (but carried out in the late 1970s) found that urban male workers listen to the radio only nine minutes a day on the average. Female workers listen five minutes a day. Male white-collar technical specialists listen eleven minutes a day; female, only three minutes.[51] This finding contrasts sharply with the statement by the deputy director of Gosteleradio, who asserted late in 1985 that radio is on the rebound, with the average urbanite tuning in more than one and a half hours a day. He credits this growth to the development of small radio sets, higher consumption of automobiles (with radios), and the introduction of stereo sound.[52] The chief Soviet television correspondent in the United States made the comment, when asked about the function of radio in a media system television has so powerfully affected, that "radio passed on to the automobile," particularly since drivers had to listen for weather reports. But, although this is undeniably the trend, and other Soviet media people also bring it up, it surely overstates what might be termed a Soviet Yuppie renaissance of radio-listening while driving in one's private car. There are not enough cars in circulation to account for such a marked change. It is also true that the new radios are lighter, smaller, cheaper, and easier to find. But there is another reason for radio's comeback, one to which Vladimir Pozner (the well-known Moscow radio and television commentator) and other of his colleagues subscribe. The policy of more self-critical, more interesting, and more lively programming (including more up-to-date popular music styles) had been enunciated even before Gorbachev's accession to power. Pozner's point is that radio was much quicker to implement the new policies than television and became, therefore, a much more attractive medium than it had been, reversing the trend in listening.[53] In particular, the news and music program *Mayak* (Beacon), started in 1964, has successfully brought back to radio-listening a population of students, young workers, and scientific and technical specialists. It is the transmitting of fast-breaking news, both foreign and domestic, the round-the-clock broadcast day, and heavy programming of more up-to-date pop music that have attracted a growing audience.[54] Television, with its thousands of employees—10,000 people work just in the Ostankino headquarters in Moscow—its huge plant and greater visiblity, was more cautious. Radio, farther from the centers of power, had greater flexibility.

That shrinking audience that had stayed with radio before the upsurge has very definite characteristics. According to some Soviet surveys, the audience for radio was basically one that had been left behind. One study of mass media in the Soviet Union noted that access to the media depended on five basic factors: health, time, geography, income, and the "semiotic" factor (whether or not the user has mastered the system or code of signs employed in the given medium). In describing the non-audience—the people left out of the media system in general—the focus is on older people—people who do not see or hear well; cannot read quickly and find it difficult to understand newspaper language—on poor people—people who don't have enough money to buy a radio or a television set, especially if they live alone. But it is particularly the semiotic factor, the inability to understand the medium, that characterizes the non-audience in the Soviet Union. In the Russian province of Ryazan, about 20 percent of the people surveyed said they did not read newspapers because they had difficulty understanding them.[55] Another Soviet media specialist concludes that the advantage or strength of radio as a medium in his country is derived from the fact that it embraces those strata of the population not yet embraced by any of the other mass media. It can be received, he observes, under any conditions and doesn't demand total concentration. In fact, according to one survey, almost 70 percent of the people who listen to radio regard it as a secondary activity; the radio is on while they are doing something else. This is especially true for women.[56] The radio audience has been, in sociological terms, an overaged, undereducated, and low income stratum. The three main reasons why radio has retained a following, in the view of Soviet researchers, is because the sets are cheap, the illiterate and poorly educated can be reached, and the programs can accompany work on the job and at home.[57]

In the countryside, radio has remained an important medium—in part because it has taken longer for television ownership to saturate those households; and in part because the function of radio could be directly linked to the utility of its information. Radio provides both crop and weather information that the farmers need. They listen in the morning before going out (between 80 and 90 percent have given this response in different surveys). Daytime radio listening is mainly for women at home, retired people, and children. Some, about one-third of the respondents in surveys, say they keep the radio on at work.[58] Radio does not effectively compete with television; listening is at its lowest during prime time.

In the official mind, among the framers of Soviet communication policy, it is not always clear what role radio is or will be expected to play in the new configuration of the media system in which television is the most attention-getting component. Media journalists, when asked about the "spheres of influence" of the media, cannot easily isolate those of radio. Sometimes the functions seem to merge with those of television in their minds, sometimes with those of the press. Most journalists responded in a survey that with the appearance of television the lines of

demarcation between media are no longer as clear. The chairman of Gosteleradio for the city of Saratov was asked how his
organization gives orders for the division of themes between
radio and television. He answered: " 'I would say that there is
no division, but there is a considered distribution of questions
on one and the same theme'."[59] Practitioners and local administrators do not share a clear common understanding of the spe-
cificities of the components of the media system, and the theoretical literature does not provide much guidance. A book on the
media system states that radio has its advantages and distin-
guishing characteristics: "the spoken word and the acoustically
realistic picture . . . permit direct transmission and a practically
limitless audience." Radio enjoys "ubiquity, maximal timeliness
(including what happens this very minute) [and] always increasing frequency of broadcasts . . ."[60] But "in the scheme of the
entire representation of relations among people—the portrayal
of man in the grand scheme—television has the advantage in
comparison with the press and radio."[61]

The new interest in radio, although it does not nearly match
that for television, does represent a significant change, and it is
likely that the characteristics of the audience have changed too.
The audience that listens to radio in a private car, or is attracted
by the quality of programming, is likely to be more upscale
socially and economically than that enduring audience of people
who use radio mainly as a secondary activity or for weather
reports.

If the policy pronouncements are serious, if rapid response,
getting the story out fast, does become a priority, it would signal
a major reorientation of the media. It is a subject to which we
shall return when we look at the changes taking place in television broadcasting in the Soviet Union. It is a subject that is
critically related to the Soviets' perception of the intrusiveness of
Western radios. For many years, the foreign radios, in particular, the four largest Western broadcasters—BBC, Voice of America, Deutsche Welle, and Radio Liberty—had served as the most
effective window on the West for those who could tune in.

Some of the most urgent concern about intrusive foreign communications is registered by Soviet officials in charge of border
areas. One-half of the population of Estonia, for example, can
receive Finnish television signals, and, as one propaganda offi-

cial noted, "this means that in a certain sense we live in an atmosphere of the constant ideological presence of the West. A new radio program in Estonia broadcasts shows targeted at the youth audience from 11:10 p.m. to 1:30—when Finnish radio and television are broadcasting their entertainment shows."[62] News and information programs on Estonian radio and television have been reformed explicitly because of the competition from the Finnish media; a new emphasis on timeliness can be seen. The head of the Estonian Communist Party has called attention to what he characterized as a barrage of subversive propaganda, and measures have been taken to combat the intrusion. Estonian radio was ordered to offer increased and more timely commentaries on international events, and a new section on international information was set up in the capital, with branches at the city and district levels and in larger factories. The commissions, it is expected, will provide an enhanced capability to "unmask bourgeois propaganda."[63]

At the same time, the jammers are at work to reduce the success of foreign radio. The *Mayak* program described earlier goes out over a frequency used by Western broadcasters and covers their signal with its own. In addition, there is the noise produced by the more than 2,000 jammers operating in the Soviet Union, Bulgaria, Czechoslovakia, and Poland. They are expected to jam foreign broadcasts in the languages of East Europe and the Soviet Union, including those in Yiddish and Hebrew.[64] The jamming process is actually much less simple than it sounds. Jammers have identification signals, frequently transmitted through the noise they produce. Often more than one jamming station operates on the same frequency. One Western tracker of these practices reported that he identified as many as four jamming stations on the same frequency.

The whole process is expensive and often redundant, but it illustrates the importance the regime has attached to limiting unofficial sources of communication.[65] However, as rapid response time entered into Soviet communications policy consistently and effectively, then the perceived threat posed by the foreign broadcasters appeared to be significantly reduced, and it is doubtless a result of this kind of thinking that Soviet propaganda chief Alexander Yakovlev at the Reykjavik summit in 1986 floated the idea that the Soviets would cease jamming Voice of

America (but not other radios) in return for access to American medium-wave radio facilities.[66] That was followed, early in 1987, with an order to cease jamming first the BBC and then the Voice of America.[67] But it is Radio Liberty, which conceives of itself as an alternative domestic service, that most disturbs the Soviet government—and jamming continued. The new policy—pre-empting rather than obliterating incoming messages—is, after all, the logical outcome of the new thinking.

Before leaving the subject of radio, it should be noted that even though the audience is smaller than it once was, and even though the officials and the journalists who are running the system are not quite clear about the place of radio in the new media system in which television is fast becoming the dominant player, radio will always have a critical utility: it is essential for civil defense. It operates around the clock and, as the official policy states, radio frequencies are considered the best "means for notification of the population of a surprise atomic attack of the adversary and on the measures to be followed in such a case."[68]

Coordinating the Media Market

The rapid introduction of television and its virtually instant appeal clearly presents some problems in adusting the other components of the media system. Since they are all state-controlled and highly centralized, it becomes an assignment for officialdom; it is not the market that will sort it out. Centralized administration for all the media takes place simultaneously along two paths: through government administration (Gosteleradio and its subnational branches) and through the Party (the propaganda secretaries and their departments at the national and subnational levels). At the apex of the system is the Party Central Committee's Department of Propaganda. In an early move, General-Secretary Gorbachev put Alexander Yakovlev, a close adviser, into this job, giving him one of the largest departments in the Central Committee. It is charged with mobilizing public opinion and has overall responsibility for the media. As such it has an important voice in the selection of editors, provides regular liaison with editors, and generally communicates to the individual media the appropriate tone and content to be followed. It also allocates budget and determines circulation size.[69] Yakovlev's influence increased rapidly, and within a short time he was promoted to the inner elite, the Secretariat, with an even greater mandate: overseeing all forms of political communication and socialization.

Censorship, another method of centralizing media messages, has changed over the years. The functions of GLAVLIT, the Chief Administration for the Affairs of Literature and Publishing Houses, dating from 1922, have been largely replaced by self-censorship. Authors understand what will be prohibited and seek to avoid difficulties with the authorities, and editorial staffs at newspapers or television studios check the material for deliberate or inadvertent evasions of the censor's guidelines. The powers of officially designated censorship and oversight organizations have clearly declined under Gorbachev. One notable example is in the film industry. Traditionally, the "creative" organization (the Union of Cinematographers, representing the filmmakers themselves) had been responsible to Goskino, the governmental administrative body that exercised the power of approval and distribution of films. When the leadership of the union was toppled in 1986, and Elem Klimov became the new leader, Goskino was stripped of much of its authority. With greater latitude permitted in book publishing, the press, and theater, the role of external censors will continue to atrophy, and the political judgment calls will be made increasingly within the media organizations.

Then, too, the gathering of media professionals into a single union helps to ensure approved messages from approved people. The Union of Journalists has some 85,000 members, about 85 percent of the country's working journalists.[70] The union is governed by a board representing the most powerful and prominent editors and personnel of all mass media. They are leading members of the Communist Party, which is very heavily represented in the union as a whole, 80 percent of whose members belong to the Party. This constitutes a high saturation level, considering that under 10 percent of the Soviet adult population belongs to the Party.[71] Finally, the system of *nomenklatura* powerfully reinforces centralization and control. This is a list of positions, responsibility for which is vested in a particular level of the Party organization. The more important the media post, the higher the level of the Party that must decide who will fill it.[72]

The "public organizations," the trade unions and the Young Communist League, also have a part to play in the direction of the media. At the local level, the role of government is sometimes difficult to determine, even by those officials themselves.[73] The interplay between governmental and Party organizations does not always result in clear-cut lines of authority, although the dominant power of oversight is supposed to be lodged in the Party organization. In the early days of television, coordination was unsystematic and the influence of the Party on it was much less than on the traditional print media. The situation was widespread, and a 1964 resolution of the Turkmen republic Central Committee did not address an isolated instance when it said that the low quality of radio and television programs "in significant measure is explained by the absence of daily, concrete, and qualified direction [by the Party]."[74] Party oversight of the media is supposed to function in a variety of ways, coordinating and directing all the media: First, journalists are informed of the agenda and plans of the Party organization. Then the editorial office of each channel of communication draws up detailed plans to submit to the Party organization for study and approval. Editors are expected to appear regularly at meetings of the executive bureau of the Party organization, and, outside formal meetings, Party officials are understood to maintain personal social contacts with media people and even to write for the media. One of the obligations of the Party organization is to prepare regular reviews of the press, radio, and television programs.

All the media have plans: a long-term development plan (estimated on five years), a shorter-term plan of a year or eighteen months, a still shorter-term quarterly plan (called the "operational plan") and, of course, the plan for the given program or issue. An official at *Pravda* observed that correspondents at his newspaper are given their assignments for the coming week on Friday. The international department, where timeliness is a more critical consideration, gives its assignments one or two days in advance. Quarterly plans are put together during the ten days before the beginning of each quarter. Five days before the beginning of the quarter the departments of the paper pass their proposed plan on to the secretariat, which checks who the authors are and what themes and regions are proposed in stories. The final decision is handed down only on the eve of the new quarter.[75]

The plans of local television studios must not conflict with the major programs of central television. All of these plans are the product of agreement between the studio's editorial board, whose members have been vetted by the Party, and the Party organization at the appropriate level.[76] The increasing attention of the Party to the supervision of television may be seen in the increase in editorials in *Pravda* on problems of television, and the development of new sections on television in the national newspapers. Gosteleradio organizations below the national level have available a quick course (one month) in Party policy and the electronic media for their officials to work more effectively to administer the radio and television studios in their jurisdictions.[77]

The planning process for the Soviet economy certainly does not function exactly as intended. In many respects, plans are merely normative—distant goals providing direction rather than directives. Planning newsgathering is even more elusive, especially for international or foreign stories. To a considerable extent, such planning is dictated by events. For example, *Izvestia*'s Alexander Shalnev, when he was TASS White House correspondent, remarked that if an economic summit were upcoming, he knew he would have to cover it and do some advance stories. Or an important date would dictate certain stories, for example, the anniversary of the Helsinki accords. Although he was on a direct phone line to Moscow, it was rare for story requests to come in. Rather, since TASS is a wire service, large numbers of stories must be generated, whether or not they are used. The situation is quite different for a newspaper reporter, though here too the role of planning should not be overstated. Alexei Burmistenko, Washington bureau chief for the newspaper *Trud* ("Work," the organ of the trade unions, the newspaper with the largest circulation in the world), told me that he does have a quarterly plan in which he proposes not news but feature stories. The international department as a whole submits a plan for about a hundred major articles. From this, the Washington correspondent knows that he will write six or seven features on given subjects. He himself submits his portion of the overall plan, some of it dictated by anniversaries and notable dates (such as the centenary of May Day in 1986) and some generated by his interests. He too maintains that there is little direction from Moscow, that the plans are usually approved as submitted unless there is obvious overlap with a story from another bureau. Outside requests for stories come mainly when Moscow wants to coordinate several correspondents working on different aspects of the same story, for example, the debt crisis in developing countries, or the situation in Haiti, which combined the work of the *Trud* correspondents based in Latin America and Washington. Vladimir Dunaev, Washington correspondent for Soviet television, receives rather few instructions from Moscow, he says—mainly they relate to coverage of notable dates (again the May Day centenary is the example). But Dunaev, as all the other correspondents, is very clear about what is desirable and undesirable, possible and impossible under the guidelines governing permissible stories. He is a veteran correspondent who has worked for thirty-five years as a journalist all over the world. He clearly generates most of his stories and they depend to a great extent on access and what he can put together. Even though these plans are loose, they can exist only if the concept of news, for these stories at least, does not involve timeliness and "hard news." Only soft news, or features, could be allocated in advance. This is an example of a fundamental difference in the understanding of news by Soviets and Americans.

The Soviet Understanding of "Newsworthy"

When a Soviet reporter uses the term "newsworthy" the meaning might not be readily apparent to an American. Each has a notion of newsworthy, but the notions may have little in common. In order to understand how the Soviets use the media at home and abroad, it is important to have a clear idea of what that term means to them and how it governs news selection decisions. The media in the Soviet Union have very distinctive and officially prescribed functions—and also very clear limitations.

The primary mission of the media system in the Soviet Union is the socialization of the person receiving the message. In a broad sense the media are educators, just as are the schools, the courts of law, the family, the individual organizations for youth, women, veterans, and many other groups in society. In fact, the educational mission is *primary* for all of these institutions. According to official doctrine these groups and agencies are first and foremost molders of citizens, and they function because they have *delegated* authority from the state to perform the task of socialization according to established norms. Even the family has no prior right, but a delegated authority to raise its offspring in conformity with guidelines provided by the state.[78] The source of this mission goes back to Lenin and to a revolution that took place before the full maturation of history had been reached, at least that maturation that Marx had envisioned. Marx's notion of the revolution puts it at a time when the ripeness of consciousness was at hand and the great masses of workers would be very near a common ethos, and common social bonds would unite them, thus virtually eliminating deviance, dissatisfaction, selfishness, and acquisitiveness—all those retrograde habits associated with bourgeois life. We are familiar with the way Marx said it would happen—through the growing impoverishment of the expanding armies of unemployed workers, who gradually, in their misery and degradation, discover a shared plight and rise up against the shrinking numbers of obsolete monopoly capitalists.

Lenin's revolution came earlier than Marx's theory had projected, and those habits of mind—that common bond of collective consciousness, selflessness, and class brotherhood—had not been internalized among the disparate groups, mainly peasants, that inhabited the first country to have overthrown its government in the name of Marx's revolution. As a result, as Lenin's writings make very clear, the changes in the popular mentality had to be imposed from above, and all of the instruments of socialization available to the state would be turned to this task. Even the courts, institutions that are not normally associated with the function of persuasion and indoctrination, are in Soviet theory charged primarily with the task of education and only secondarily with punishment.[79] The mission of the mass media was to socialize in another sense, too—that of serving to integrate the sprawling, multi-lingual country that was to be the first socialist state.

The task assigned to the media has two principal dimensions. First, the media must change the ethical and moral outlook of the population. The psychological orientation underlying the society of the future, when full communism has been achieved,[80] requires cooperation and collectivism and eschews selfishness, careerism, greed, and, in general, the development of an individual that might supersede the societal collective. Second, the media must rouse the population to contribute to the economic goals of the leadership. Mobilizing people to meet production goals becomes a critical role for the media. The preconditions for communism, as Marx portrayed them, would be met only when the internal value system of the vast majority had changed dramatically within a context of significantly enhanced levels of economic production. That level of production and the new system of distribution instituted by the revolution must ensure that socially necessary goods will no longer be scarce. This would, of course, eliminate the chief source of conflict in society: scarcity.[81] In advance of that time, as the Russian Revolution was, the state and its agencies must develop those pre-conditions, and the media are agencies to mobilize the labor force.

Because the role and function of the media system in the Soviet Union are grounded in this particular theory, it, as well as the media systems of socialist systems based on the Soviet model, has a distinctive cast. In Afghanistan, for example, one of the earliest moves after the Soviets entered in force, was the reform of the Afghan media system, so that, with changes in personnel and operations, it would look like the Soviet. As a Soviet observer put it: "A new second stage of the April Revolution was begun on December 27, 1979. In the area of the mass media of information, this stage is characterized by the reorganization of the entire newspaper–magazine complex. First, certain publications were closed, the directing cadres of editorial boards were renewed, and the work of radio and television and the *Bakhtar* [news] agency was rebuilt."[82]

Perhaps the most distinctive element of the Soviet media system is the understanding of what is newsworthy. That understanding is not something that the television studio or the newspaper defines for itself; it has already been set by overarching doctrine and Party policy. The denial of plural (competing, equally valid) approaches is derived from the notion that the ruling doctrine is based on science.[83] Lenin's understanding of Marx's "scientific socialism" requires that a new idea or theory be judged correct or incorrect (scientific or unscientific) and that if correct it displace any other that has preceded it. It is perhaps a primitive way of conceiving scientific method, but that dichotomous view of the scientific and the non-scientific is a strong one in Lenin's writing. He considered the co-existence of a variety of ideas simply unscientific. Once an advance is made, the previously held positions must be wholly canceled. To do otherwise would be as frivolous or harmful as, say, according equal validity to the Ptolemaic and Copernican views of the universe. Marxism as science must, therefore, supersede all previous (and unscientific) models of history and society. It is in this sense that the newspaper *Pravda* prints what its name means: truth. As might be imagined, the charge given to the media is education (broadly conceived) in this "scientific" view.

The content of Soviet media shows the influence of this doctrine. Many types of stories carried by the Western media are considered inappropriate. For example, until the waning of the Chernenko leadership, the media were reluctant to cover domestic natural disasters, accidents, crime, or other events tinged with sensationalism. The case of the nuclear power station accident at Chernobyl in 1986 illustrates both the effect of the traditional doctrine and the impact of the policy of glasnost and related changes, as we shall see. The traditional rationale for not covering certain stories was generally presented as follows: dwelling on negative events, the underside of life, would tend to encourage or suggest the wrong kind of behavior and would undermine the positive role models the newspaper or television station must purvey and in terms of which they must educate the population. But this policy has become problematic, as the Soviet leadership seeks to reach its population—a population that demands more information and might receive it from rumor or foreign radios, if necessary.[84]

The kinds of fluff that Western media carry—celebrity doings, horoscopes, social columns—are also out of place in the educational mission of the Soviet media. Advertising is very limited, used not for the creation of needs, but rather to supplement policy (for example, touting fruit juices as part of the campaign to limit alcohol consumption) and steer patterns of buying in order to compensate for snags in the distribution system. The Soviet media are not commercial enterprises, but state-owned and -operated instructional vehicles.

Since the media have been assigned these functions, they evaluate the importance of fast-breaking news rather differently

than do the Western media. Fast-breaking news does not command attention simply because of its freshness. Newsworthy is
what reveals the underlying reality toward which history is tend-
ing. Since history is seen in its Marxist-Leninist interpretation,
that means that the reality toward which history is moving is
already known. Coverage of a numerically insignificant group of
demonstrators opposing a bourgeois government may be newsworthy because in the *future* that trend will become dominant,
according to the theory. Or workers on the Baikal-Amur Mainline railway in frozen Siberia are worthy of coverage as news
because they represent *future* economic trends and their example
is good for the audience to see and, it is hoped, follow. On the
other hand, the traditional doctrine had dictated, the "reality" of
anti-social and retrograde events, such as illegal strikes and riots
or crimes, is ephemeral; they will pass as communism is ushered
in. A study of a national newspaper in the Soviet Union found
that only about 15 percent was devoted to events that had occurred the day before.[85]

But this approach does not enable the government to establish
credibility and reach its audience—an audience that finds these
matters highly salient and often learns about them from unofficial
(foreign or domestic) sources. Nor does the simple expedient of
non-coverage permit the official media to portray the "negative"
event within their own cognitive or explanatory framework. It is
for these reasons that the concepts of glasnost and timeliness
have entered into the Soviet understanding of newsworthy, and
that television has undergone dramatic modification—as we shall
see in the next chapters.

CHAPTER TWO

Looking Outward: International News and the Changing Soviet Television Scene

A LEADING CHARACTER in the Soviet hit movie *Moscow Does Not Believe in Tears* is a trendy young man, and true to the thesis of the film, which catalogues current social trends in the Soviet Union, he works in television. Toward the end of the movie he tells an enthralled young woman that in the future there will be only television—no books, no plays. Hardly less grandiose, and much more serious, were the remarks of a deputy director of Soviet television and radio who ascribed to the influence of television some remarkable effects. He said that television was responsible for lowering the rate of migration away from remote settlements, particularly from the eastern regions of the country, where labor is badly needed for economic development. Television helped people adapt to "harsh conditions of work and daily life." Television helped to keep people productively working on such projects as the Baikal-Amur Mainline—the railroad system built over the course of several years across the inhospitable terrain of Siberia. The influence of television on "the economic and social life" of entire regions could not be overstated, according to this high official. Young people choose their professions under the influence of television—some 70 percent of them, according to the deputy director.[1]

But it is not only on these special groups that television has an extraordinary impact. I described earlier the enormous crash program that brought television into virtually every home in the Soviet Union and the turning of attention away from older components of the mass media system and toward the new entrant. The deputy director cites a study revealing that the majority of the industrial workers and intelligentsia (some 63 percent) find that television is the main source for forming their "views, opinions, [and] spiritual and moral values." The world comes to the Soviet people mainly from the television screen. The head of Gosteleradio found that 90 percent of the Soviet population consider Vremya their main source of information.[2]

In the short time that television news has competed among the media for audience attention, it has had a stunning record of success. For young people, television is the main source of information on issues of international security, arms control, and nuclear weapons.[3] Contrary to the conclusions drawn by an American analysis of former Soviet citizens in the Soviet Interview Project, the Soviet public turns more, not less, to television for news and information.[4] In the United States the process took longer, but it is quite clear that "during the past two decades television has emerged as the most credible and widely used source of news. . . ."[5]

The Salience of the West

How salient for the Soviet people are issues and events outside their country? We have a good deal of information on this, and much comes from studies of newspaper readership. What the studies show is a thirst for information about the world outside the Soviet Union. This thirst, which officials look on with some concern, is probably, paradoxically, the result of official Soviet policy. In every survey of newspaper readers, whether of national or local papers, the strong preference for international stories is both consistent and stable over time.

Most readers turn first to stories about international events, and this interest cuts across all age groups, all levels of education, and all occupations. Even the readers of *Trud* (Work), the trade-union newspaper and the daily with the lowest proportion of college-educated readers (though still well over their percentage of the general population), when asked in what area they would ask for more information, cited international news first. Other areas of newspaper coverage (science, technology, culture, economics, family, youth, etc.) do exhibit the difference in readership by education, or other factors, that international stories do not.[6] In a 1973 survey of the popular national newspaper, *Literaturnaya Gazeta*, it was found that fully 88 percent of the subscribers were attentive to the section "International Life." Different types of stories under this rubric attracted different degrees of interest: the most popular were stories on "the moral system of the bourgeois press, radio, and television" and "the bourgeois image of life." In last place were stories on national liberation movements and the Third World; stories on fellow socialist countries ranked next to last.[7] It is the capitalist countries that attract the greatest interest. For readers of regional papers, a survey found that the most important category of international affairs story was that relating to military conflicts abroad. Some 53 percent of the readers at the regional level were troubled by problems of war and peace and military conflicts.[8]

Even in local newspapers, the thirst for international news is manifest. For example, in a survey in the Perm region it was found that 69 percent of the readers wanted to see more information about foreign countries in the local papers. Similar results were obtained in surveys in the greater Sverdlovsk area. This is, perhaps, a surprising result if one considers that at the level of the local newspaper there are no international correspondents. The secretariat of the local newspaper receives information from the press services of the central newspapers (TASS for hard news and Novosti for features), which have already published it. In addition, only a very small amount of space in local papers is devoted to international stories—about 5 percent. But the West gets the lion's share of this space—over 41 percent of all international stories, while only 30 percent of the stories are about events in communist countries. Under 3 percent are about the Third World. In *Pravda,* too, the United States and its NATO allies claim about 44 percent of the international stories, and Soviet-type systems are given about 31 percent.[9] Soviet television, as well, exhibits this intense interest in the United States and Western Europe. The characteristics of this attention will be examined in subsequent chapters.

To be sure, these stories tend to be negative, containing accusations of aggressive policies of imperialism or depictions of the crises of capitalism—but they do dominate the foreign news. In non-news features there is likely to be more flexibility. The department of International Life of Gosteleradio was created in 1987 to provide a greater breadth of (and balance in) portrayals of life abroad. The central importance of the West is very clear, and concern has been voiced that things may have gone too far. One such opinion stated that "the clear, deep demonstration of the strengths of the world system of socialism, of the camp of democracy and progress, should occupy the leading place among articles on international questions."[10] Viktor Mironenko, head of the official youth organization, viewed with alarm how much young people are fascinated with the West. Addressing a national congress of the organization, he warned: "We can no longer accept that young men and women often know more about events taking place on the other side of the globe than about what goes on in their own region [and] city."[11] The strong preference the public exhibits for international and particularly Western news has clearly become a source of apprehension. Official coverage of the West, which has been so massive and is increasing under the present leadership, is designed primarily to strengthen domestic political support by focusing on a constant and pervasive threat from the West or on its moral and economic impoverishment. That another consequence as well has ensued—a virtual thirst for news of the West—is likely to be an unintended consequence.

The Demand for Multiple Points of View: Glasnost in International Issues

The officials who manage the foreign news have become aware of the public's concern with the way that news is presented. A number of surveys show impatience with a single official point of view. The first *Literaturnaya Gazeta* readership survey in 1973 found that 2 percent of the respondents preferred to see one point of view, but 43 percent wanted more views in stories.[12] The second survey in 1977 developed the issue with more questions and found more dissatisfaction. A majority argued that the newspaper's coverage of stories should acquaint the reader with "all existing points of view on the subject under discussion." They meant by this even wider exposure not just to two opposing sides, but to a wider spectrum of views. As the level of education of the reader rises, so does the commitment to this view. Readers indicated a clear preference for stories based on concrete facts and actual events, rather than for stories couched in general, abstract discourse. Many readers, the majority in fact, think they will get this kind of story if the newspaper were to *reprint* foreign press materials with Soviet newspaper writers only commenting on them, instead of substituting comment for story. But the college-educated readers and those who are long-time readers would rather have no commentary at all.[13]

This kind of public dissatisfaction with a single point of view and their demand for a more complete presentation of information is known not only to the academics who do the surveys but to the operations people as well. On February 3, 1986, in the best prime-time slot, a television program was aired that represented a major departure for the Soviet media. It was a round table discussion of Western reactions to the proposals for total elimination of nuclear arms that Gorbachev had made the previous month. The moderator was Boris Kalyagin, a journalist, dressed modishly, who asked the experts—Vladimir Petrovsky, from the Ministry of Foreign Affairs,[14] Roald Sagdeev, head of the Space Science Institute, and General Nikolai Chervov, head of the legal department of the military's General Staff—to comment on Western views. What was noteworthy and, indeed, innovative, in this hour-long program was the sense in which it was a surrogate for a true debate. It was the beginning of what was to become a significant trend: the presentation of views in opposition to official Soviet policy. At first this presentation, as the account below shows, was confined to an all-Soviet panel relating the opposing arguments. But soon thereafter foreigners began to speak for themselves, arguing with Soviet officials and saying their piece in real, not surrogate, debates.

On this early program, Kalyagin did present Western views for the most part (there were exceptions) fairly and without emotion. Obviously, most of the time was given to the exposition of official views from the participants—there was no rebuttal and no corrective interventions. However, there *were* different views expressed through the moderator and those views *were* reasonably accurate and neutral summaries of Western positions. Kalyagin's remarks began with the theme the Soviets had pressed in many different contexts: the delay in the American response to Soviet proposals for the elimination of nuclear weapons. He then went on to the subject of the Soviet unilateral moratorium on nuclear testing then in force:

KALYAGIN: [on the Soviet unilateral moratorium on nuclear testing] The United States also supports this step—both their social and political circles. The statements of the United States and the White House follow the step of the Soviet Union. The administration says that it [testing] is needed for the modernization of its nuclear forces, which are behind those of the Soviet Union and puts forth the argument that the USSR has finished its planned series of nuclear tests and the next series won't be begun before spring and therefore, the Soviet Union can, so to speak, wait.

Sagdeev and Chervov then challenge this position, citing the number of American tests and arguing that the Soviet moratorium actually interrupted its own series of tests.

KALYAGIN: [on the Strategic Defense Initiative] In the White House, they clearly don't want to reject the program. They declare that it does not constitute a threat to the Soviet Union; that it is not about offensive weapons, but defensive; that they are not directed against people but only against nuclear missiles and those only in the case that they are used as a first strike during launch. What can be said about this, Nikolai Fedorovich [Chervov]?

Chervov responds vigorously, citing Secretary of Defense Weinberger and raising the specter of the threat to populations.

KALYAGIN: Washington has another argument: that SDI is only research and research can't be verified or curtailed; that everyone does research and that this program does not violate the ongoing Soviet-American treaty on the limitation of anti-missile defense; and, therefore, it can't be an obstacle for the radical reduction of nuclear missiles.

After Chervov's answer that the amount of the investment requested for SDI suggests more than basic research and that some components already violate the spirit of that treaty, Kalyagin continues on SDI.

> KALYAGIN: Some leaders in the West say that if the President of the United States, the administration, wants so much to create an anti-missile shield in space, I use their terminology, although, of course it is a means for a strike, the Soviet Union can also build its space shield. There will be two shields. There will be a defined balance and it will be possible in this way to combine both Reagan's Strategic Defense Initiative and the Soviet peace program, the elimination of nuclear weapons, What do you think?

Kalyagin's moderating is, on the whole, direct and unemotional, but his sarcasm here does return two or three times during the course of the hour. Chervov's answer stresses the destabilizing effect of both sides' moving to an SDI program and cites the vulnerability of the program to accidental stimuli, which prompts Kalyagin to put in a few words to the effect that the "*Challenger* tragedy" shows how fallible such plans can be. After Sagdeev's comment that the spin-offs for the civilian economy seem very slight from SDI, the moderator continues with his exposition of the West's positions.

> KALYAGIN: Since we are now studying in detail issues relating to the outcome of the development of the SDI program, I want to bring up another argument, which the President of the United States, himself, expressed. This was the rationale for the space shield. Talking with Soviet journalists, he said, I quote: "It is possible that there could be a situation in which somewhere in the world, some crazy person tries anew to create offensive nuclear weapons to use them for blackmail. In such a case, the deployment of an anti-missile shield would permit all of us to be secure." What do you think of this unexpected argument?

Sagdeev expresses skepticism that such an enormous investment and deployment of weapons would be cost-effective and points to a number of other ways such an individual could breach the security shield—with fishing boats or trucks. After Kalyagin asks how the Soviet proposals relate to the allies of the superpowers, he recounts another Western position:

KALYAGIN: In the West one also hears such opinions: our [Soviet] proposals for complete elimination of nuclear weapons conceal a hidden trap: that if nuclear weapons are destroyed, then the Soviet Union will have an advantage in conventional arms, especially, they say, in the context of Europe. What do you think?

Chervov and Petrovsky both deny this, as might be expected, citing their own numbers for troop strength and weapons that show the opposite to be true.

At the end of the program General Chervov describes the new weapons based on "new physical principles," explaining them methodically and precisely; and academician Sagdeev is asked what the Soviets will do if SDI can't be stopped (Sagdeev says new ways of penetrating any space shield will be devised, but before that happens there is time to come to an "intelligent and sober solution"). Kalyagin then closes the program:

KALYAGIN: Mikhail Sergeievich [Gorbachev] spoke about the necessity for new thinking in the policies of states. He even called the inertness of thinking, its lagging behind the rapidly changing world, one of the real barriers on the road to radical disarmament. In connection with this I want to call to your attention that certain officials in the West have begun to speak about the Utopianism of the Soviet program—that it's hardly realizable in practice. In the past, they say, such proposals for disarmament have already been discussed and each time they were unsuccessful because of their complex character. Isn't such reasoning an indicator of the fact that certain officials in the West don't want to part with old ways of thinking?

Petrovsky reponds that the Gorbachev proposals represent an entirely new step in history.

KALYAGIN: Mikhail Sergeievich, you remember, even said that we are against the degradation of the security of the United States.

Petrovsky responds that for a stable world both sides must be secure, and Kalyagin sums up the program:

> KALYAGIN: Our new peace program is essentially a model of new thinking in the contemporary world. It opens new horizons, a new series of activities for mankind. We hope that the United States will use this unique historical opportunity to meet us half-way for the removal forever of the nuclear threat hanging over mankind. On this, I think, we will end our program. Thank you for your participation, and we thank the viewers for their attention.

Shortly after this program was broadcast, I discussed it in Moscow with Vladimir Pozner, whose rank of political observer and prominence as a journalist much on view in the West make him a very knowledgeable spokesman for Gosteleradio. He brought up the importance of presenting more than one point of view and specifically referred to viewer demand in this direction. He spoke of this program as a response to exactly the same kinds of demands I have described above from the survey results. But he went further and remarked that it would have been even more effective if those who held those differing views had presented them themselves. This was obviously to be the new policy position, since just a few weeks earlier, one of the most famous Soviet commentators on international news, Alexander Bovin, had written in *Izvestia* that there should be live reporting from the West on topical issues and that American officials should debate their Soviet counterparts on Soviet television.[15] The Kalyagin program, aired so conspicuously and heralded by those in the business, was indeed a major departure from the usual violently one-sided commentary; it may be seen as a kind of kick-off for the new policy. It is distinguished not only by the words, but, perhaps, more important, by the dry and unemotional tone of the moderator and, except for General Chervov, of the participants.

I also talked with Pozner about another show—one that he did and one that was another new attempt to show give-and-take, to expose the Soviet public to points of view that radically contradicted the official line. This was a program in the series called "The World and Youth" that aired in January 1986 in the afterschool slot (5:13–5:30). It began with Pozner shown as a guest on the British program "Open Question." For this weekly program, schoolchildren ages fourteen to eighteen are brought into the studio to question a guest. Pozner, in the introduction, calls them the most "knowledgeable and accomplished" of British children and tells his Soviet viewers that these children's questions will reveal how "they imagine us and our country."

The teenagers are combative and sharp in their questioning, asking why the Soviet Union needs such powerful armed forces, and why only the elite can travel abroad. Pozner tells them they are simply misinformed, especially a girl who asks: "How many people this year tried to go over the Berlin Wall?"

Pozner, with some surprise at what he regards as the level of misinformation behind the question, "As far as I know not a single Soviet citizen, but to tell the truth, the Berlin Wall is not located in the Soviet Union."

The same girl gamely continues: "But don't you think that shows the unattractiveness of your country?"

Pozner, less patient now, "I repeat: Berlin is located in the GDR and I live in the Soviet Union. Which country are you actually talking about?"

Same girl, still hanging in: "Your country."

Pozner, harder line, now, "I want to tell you once again the GDR is not the Soviet Union. They are different countries. Do you understand that?"

A fellow student, a boy, breaks in to explain: "She probably means that in general socialist countries are not very attractive."

Pozner responds at some length: he is approaching more closely the theme of the program—sources of what he regards as negative information and images of the Soviet Union. "You know, because occasionally somebody from the socialist countries settles in the West, [that] is being used to a large degree for political purposes. I don't know whether you are aware that in our consulates in various countries, literally thousands ask to come to live in the Soviet Union. We actually do not make a thing of it, because we do not make politics out of it and also because we have a law that every person who lives in the Soviet Union has a guaranteed job, guaranteed housing, free medical care, and we intend to give it to every person who comes here. You know you only see a part of the picture—the political part, which is very much exploited in your country. The fact that anybody leaves the socialist country, you right away draw the conclusion that life in our countries is bad. If you were to ask the 277 million Soviet citizens about this, I think the answer would be a very different one."

There are some other questions, then a shot of Pozner in the studio in Moscow. He, too, has been watching the BBC program with the Soviet television audience.. He turns to the camera and muses: "these are the most informed schoolchildren in England: they are fourteen to eighteen years old.

"And here is such an impression of our country! And all the time I had an inner impression: Who, who is responsible for that? Who is at fault? Somebody has to answer for it, because it can't be that a young person of fourteen or fifteen would have a totally negative impression of an entire country, an entire people. You and I do not have such an attitude toward the English and England. Isn't that right? And when I asked questions, counterquestions, I saw that, and you saw with me, they don't know the answers. They confuse Berlin with the Soviet Union. . . .That means in principle beyond that very thin layer of so-called knowledge, there is total ignorance, total confusion. And generally, however, the desire to learn. . . .And still I come back to the question, who, then, bears the responsibility for such, how would you say it, a way of thinking? In search of an answer to this we shall go together to visit the head of the *New York Times* news bureau in Moscow, Mr. Serge Schmemann. He may help us give an answer to this question."

We see a shot of the plaque on the wall of a building; the *Times* logo is etched in the shiny metal square. The camera moves into the newsroom, with much sound of telex and typewriters. This clacking background noise hardly abates throughout the interview with the bespectacled, bearded Schmemann, who sits at his desk, serious and thoughtful, slowly addressing himself to the questions that Pozner asks and which he answers in very good Russian. This interview, which ran close to seven minutes, is really the first major televised debate on Soviet television in which opponents of official Soviet positions and values are given a considerable amount of time to state their views and argue with their Soviet hosts. It marks a turning point in Soviet television. It is also one of the most concise summaries of the differences between American and Soviet journalistic values.

Pozner holds up a special magazine section of the *New York*

Times. It preceded the November 1985 summit in Geneva and featured two lengthy articles on how the Soviets and Americans see each other. Pozner asks Schmemann: "Why do such a large number of Americans so incorrectly perceive us?" Schmemann's answer is very low key and careful. He says ". . .basically we can say Americans have a little bit less interest and less curiosity. With Russians, it seemed to me, there was a lot more interest in America, but Americans have more information. That means, for those who do want to find out, their opportunities are a little bit wider."

POZNER: So it sounds a little bit strange—there is information, and interest is lacking. . . .[after citing polls showing an uninformed or misinformed American public] I'm trying to dig out, with your help, why it is so?

SCHMEMANN: I don't say there is not interest. I say that there is maybe less interest and less curiosity. Basically we can't force readers to read what we write. So I think there is information and it is flowing and we try to write about everything: culture, how people live, and we transmit as much as we can. But the question is how and who will read?

POZNER: [speaking now with passion] I can't rid myself of the impression which the magazine created, that American schoolchildren (and as it says, pupils of schools at a fairly high level), the overwhelming majority, may have a solidly negative impression about us. And those associations, and the associations that emerge in their heads with the Soviet Union and Russia are negative. You understand? Everything is negative, as though nothing else existed. There's reds, totalitarians, alcoholics—you read it all yourself and you understand, we have our shortcomings. . . . Do you think that there is such a thing as objective information in and of itself?

SCHMEMANN: Certainly, there's no such information, because what we select is already a fact that already forms what we try to say. We say "fairness" [he uses the English word]. I don't know exactly how to translate "fairness." At this point, generally, maybe, the term objectivity may not be quite the right word.

POZNER: [helpfully] "Fairness" [he repeats the English word]—Objectivity is O.K.

SCHMEMANN: So we try to represent simply, honestly, justly, give both sides and simply minimally include one's own, how do you say, feelings, one's prejudices. Try not to interfere with the reader when he sorts it out himself, so that he can draw his own conclusions. "Objectivity" here is a dangerous word, imprecise and impossible.

Pozner refers to what he regards as a constant level—going back twenty years or so—of ignorance about the Soviet Union among Americans. "In 20 years, essentially nothing has changed, even though these are different times. Therefore, I would like to say that without a desire on the part of people who transmit information, it seems to me that we cannot do anything. Don't you agree?"

> SCHMEMANN: I think efforts on both sides [are needed]. On this side one must have more openness; one must try to present a somewhat broader picture of society. On our side, one must try much more to travel, to see, to talk. And making a presentation of a country, one must show all of its sides, and for this, one has to travel more.

> POZNER: [resigned] What can I say? Thank you.

Both of these programs were dramatic departures for Soviet television; both were concerned with the international arena; both were focused on the capitalist West. And both inserted criticisms and charges directed at the Soviet Union that the huge numbers of the Soviet television public had never seen in such bold confrontation. A third example is, perhaps, the most dramatic of all—and the most radical departure from the broadcast past. On February 19, 1986, First Program aired in the best prime-time slot its edit of the Seattle/Leningrad "Citizens' Summit," a satellite link-up (called "space bridge" by the Soviets) of two studio audiences, one hosted by Phil Donahue and the other, again, by Vladimir Pozner.[16] The raw footage of this show, in which the audience in each country questioned the other, was well over two hours. The Soviet version was about 70 minutes, without interruptions; the American version was shown in most markets as an hour program (about three-quarters of an hour excluding commercials).[17] The editing of the raw footage was done separately in each country, and the resulting product is a fascinating double exposure, in which some areas overlap and others are utterly different. For the Soviet audience, what was shown on their version of this program was dramatically different from their usual fare—even under the changed communications policy of the Gorbachev regime.

Without detailing the many variations in the two versions of this space bridge, a general picture can still be drawn.

On the whole, the Soviet show was more serious, in that it eliminated much of the lighter material. For example, it did not show the American questions on General Secretary Gorbachev's wife (an American had asked how much money she made). This started off the American edit and was accompanied by laughter in Leningrad, where the studio audience thought such questions silly and irrelevant. Some of the elements of the American edit were absent from the Soviet version. For example, there was a lengthy accusation from a man in the Leningrad studio to the effect that the United States was threatening the Soviet Union with its missiles in West Germany. The equally strong American response charged the Soviets with an unwarranted military build-up that took place at a time when an American administration was not initiating arms challenges. The exchange was missing. An American in military uniform is shown briefly on the Soviet edit and referred to by Donahue as an opponent of the Vietnam war, but his lengthy remarks about his opposition to war and his invitation to the Soviet military men in the Leningrad studio to meet to protest war everywhere, including Afghanistan, were not carried. An American woman asked about women in the Soviet Union. Her introductory remarks, in which she detailed the double burden Soviet women must bear—work and virtually unaided domestic chores complicated by the shortages of goods and lines—was not carried.

These issues were sidestepped. But many others made it to both edits, though sometimes with different spins. On Jewish emigration, different parts of the debate appeared on the two shows: on the American side, Donahue argues that a large number of Jews cannot leave the Soviet Union. When Pozner challenges the information, saying that those who wish to leave have done so, an American woman says that she has received letters from refusniks and knows that more want to leave. The Soviet edit eliminates this and has Donahue saying that because there has been a decline in Jewish emigration, it must be the result of a government crackdown. A Soviet in the audience argues that those who wanted to leave, have done so, and it is not as a result of governmental policy that the numbers have declined. Thus the emigration issue is raised on both sides, but different elements are put together, and the refusniks who write to America are not brought up on the Soviet program. The question of free speech and right of protest is brought up on both programs in the same way, with the same language. Donahue shows pickets outside the Seattle studio, calls it free speech in action, and challenges the Soviets. A blistering Soviet response, from a man in the studio, points out children among the demonstrators, asks why they should be marching, and argues that they have been poisoned by hatred of the Soviet Union in such films as *Red Dawn*, which educate for hatred and war. He asks the question that Pozner asked of the British schoolchildren and the *New York Times* correspondent: Who profits from this? A soft-spoken man in the American audience replies that it is to everyone's profit to have differing points of view and then goes on to say that the Soviet audience acts as though its government is always right, drawing an analogy to the Germans' thinking Hitler was always right. This American response was reproduced on the Soviet version, except the portion that likened Soviets to Nazis—to the Soviets an emotionally charged and particularly objectionable comparison. As Pozner explained later, that comparison would be so objectionable to the Soviet audience, that the whole program would lose its credibility, and for that reason, he said, it was eliminated. Since the main point of the argument was retained, it seems likely that the removal of this section was, in fact, for the reason Pozner stated. The American challenge to the Soviets to dissent from their government's policies was not moderated or attenuated by its removal. On both edits, the Soviet audience is asked if it can disagree with its government's policies on Afghanistan. On both edits, an American acknowledges that his government has done many things of which he disapproves, "wiping out Indians, supporting Marcos," but that these can be recognized and citizens can work for social change. The Soviet answer: your protests never get anywhere. There are some mild and neutral exchanges that appear in both edits: an American teacher asks what students' dreams are; there is much talk that the two countries needn't be enemies. An American who visited the Soviet Union found it much better than she had expected. A question put to the Soviet audience about racial discrimination receives the reply from a Central Asian that there is none. But the question of the Soviet downing of the Korean Airlines' plane is put on both edits, and it is a very sharp exchange. Pozner expresses sorrow about those killed, but maintains that the Soviets thought it a spy plane. Donahue, on both edits, argues that it was an overreaction typical of the simplistic militaristic response of the Soviet Union. Pozner counters by asking how Americans would feel if a Soviet plane under suspicious circumstances made its way over the United States. The Soviet edit finishes the KAL story here, but the American one goes on to give Donahue's answer: we would never have shot it down. At the end, the closing statements of each side are shown in their entirety to the other, and, again, very sharp challenges are laid down to the Soviet audience. Donahue agrees that Americans do not have as much information as they should about the Soviets, but he also wants the Soviet audience to understand that the invasion of Afghanistan, interference with Polish freedoms, the KAL shootdown, do bespeak fundamental differences. And, he adds, we can complain and speak out, and you can't. Pozner's closing statement is a reiteration of his reaction to the English schoolchildren. He is, he says, sad about what Donahue said. We need to have more contacts to dispel misunderstanding and lack of information, and again he asks: To whose profit is it to have an enemy?

There were, however, many parts of the Soviet edit that were not shown on the one-hour Donahue program in the United States. Pozner, in an article in a major Soviet newspaper, acknowledged that some things had to be cut; there were, he wrote, boring parts, pauses, in short, elements that though part of the live studio interaction would not play well on television. About the Soviet edit, he wrote: "*What* was cut is important. In ours—I, as host and co-author of the broadcast assert—only minor, inconsequential points." On the American broadcast, however, Pozner listed a number of gaps he considered evidence of bias: "For example, two priests talking about the question of religion in our country disappeared. Representatives of the minorities of the Far North [disappeared]. All presentations about our social achievements [disappeared]."[18]

Whether the product of bias or professional judgment about

what makes good television, there certainly were gaps. There was a good deal of talk about freedom of religion in the Soviet Union, conducted by two Russian Orthodox priests. They referred to the training of rabbis in seminaries and the guarantees given for religious freedom in the Soviet constitution. There was talk about the role of sports in solving problems, how children are brought up in the Soviet Union, and health care. On this last subject, a pediatrician in the Seattle studio says that the care of children in America would be improved if less money went to arms. After the piece about disagreeing with one's government and speaking up about policies one thinks wrong, on the Soviet edit only, a writer in the Leningrad studio refers to the protest against the pollution of Lake Baikal as an example on the Soviet side. The Soviet edit is the only one to go into the Star Wars debate and stresses the use of space for "friendship." A Soviet participant asks how many workers are in the American government; the American answer is, they're mostly lawyers. The Leningraders are asked if there are any hungry people in the Soviet Union; the answer states that there are no hungry and no homeless; old people have pensions and rents are low. On the question of emigration and jobs, Pozner states that in the United States, if a person expresses a wish to emigrate to the Soviet Union, "it will be bad for him," and in the Soviet Union, there will be a similar scorn for those who indicate a wish to emigrate to the United States, but to lose one's job for it would be illegal.

The exchanges that appear only on the Soviet edit do not challenge the fundamental doctrines of the Soviet media system. There is little real opposition, and the editing is such that clashes virtually disappear. However, those issues that do overlap seem to come from another world: the exchanges are sharp, and the positions taken on the American side are not communicated with irrational or loud contentiousness—with the possible exception of Donahue himself, whose style is far more dramatic and adversarial than any of his fellow Americans in the studio. On the Soviet side, there are some emotional responses, especially about the effects of war and the threat of the West. The multimillion Soviet viewing public would have seen for the first time such frank and open challenges to their system. It would be an audience more diverse and larger than any for any other medium. The Gosteleradio official responsible for this space bridge told me that it was completed by his department and then presented to the top administration. Several officials had reservations; some wanted to put it on the shelf for a while; some wanted to divert it to Second Program, with its smaller audience. In the end, Gosteleradio chief Aksenov made the decision to go ahead. Gosteleradio estimates that the first showing drew 150 million people and the second, which occurred two days later, 120 million.[19]

The boldness of this early space bridge was new and astonishing for the Soviet public. Others followed, but the editing question was not laid to rest. In a later Donahue/Pozner space bridge the question of editing was dramatically underscored on air in the Soviet Union. In January 1987, First Program carried a journalists' space bridge: Donahue with Soviet reporters in the United States talked to Pozner with American reporters in the Soviet Union. The Soviet viewing audience saw the edit Donahue had prepared for the American audience, with Russian translation over the English sound track. At the end, with music on the sound track and the credits rolling, Pozner abruptly calls a halt to the film, saying, "Stop. This is how the broadcast concluded for American viewers. We want to show you a fragment that was not included, which Americans did not see. It has a fundamental significance." Donahue is shown addressing the American reporters in Moscow (I use the Russian translation). He says that there is pressure on Western, especially American reporters "not to appear soft on the reds. . . .Don't tell me that you guys will transmit positive material from the Soviet Union, because you will look like weaklings, and what reporter wants to look like that?"

The *Baltimore Sun* correspondent denies that his editor has ever dictated such a position, either in Moscow or before that, in South Africa.

Donahue: "So you're saying no, there's no pressure. I think there is. No one's forcing you to be harsh about the communists. I still think such pressure exists. I think such pressure is very real, although it's difficult to perceive. They tell you that anything that may look the least bit good in the Soviet Union is really only a screen behind which lurk problems. And if you talk about good things in your reports from Moscow, it means you sold your soul."

Two more American correspondents in the Moscow studio vehemently deny the charge. One tells Donahue he has a mistaken notion about journalists and how they make decisions.

Donahue: "That's two not guilty. Let me point out to you that in my opinion you are all saying what isn't true."

The program ends on a very problematic note, one that could be resolved only by commitments in future collaborations to joint edits or live transmissions, something that did take place later, with the series of "Capital-to-Capital" space bridges.

The creation of a media public vitally interested in the West has perhaps been an unintended consequence of a policy designed to foster domestic cohesion and legitimate the policies of the leadership. And in a world in which the technology of information diffusion has developed rapidly, boundaries have become porous and the domestic public has to be "immunized." The extraordinary new programs I described above are serious attempts to inform the public as well as prudent measures to pre-empt external sources. In terms of foreign policy, there is a new appreciation of the role that public opinion plays in the West.[20] Even before Gorbachev took over the leadership, a spokesman for the Ministry of Foreign Affairs was appointed. Vladimir Lomeiko was the first to give news conferences (he used the English word "briefing" and said in an interview that "this is a new word here").[21] The extraordinary televised press conferences on the occasion of the downing of the KAL plane (remarkable for the way Marshal Ogarkov, then chief of the General Staff, both accepted and parried more than two hours of questions from the floor—many from hostile Western reporters who were frank and blunt) and the walk-out from the Geneva arms talks, even the regular, though sketchy, newspaper and television coverage of the Politburo's weekly meetings—all suggest the kinds of changes that are related to the emergence of a mass public at home and the recognition of the effect of mass publics abroad. After Gorbachev came to power there were a number of new Soviet media initiatives: when Foreign Minister Shevardnadze went to Helsinki on the tenth anniversary of the Helsinki accords, he and his colleagues engaged in unusually spontaneous, outgoing, and open conversations with the press and other delegates.[22] In Paris, in October of 1985, Gorbachev held a press conference with President Mitterand that was broad-

cast both at home and abroad; and just before, he met with
French journalists in the Kremlin, and this, too was broadcast at
home and in Paris. These two press conferences were riddled
with difficult and challenging questions, of the sort the public
had not heard before, though would hear again in the Donahue
edit. Charges of discrimination against Jews, treatment of political prisoners, the Sakharov case, and many others were raised.
By the end of that month an agreement had been reached which
gave four Soviet journalists the opportunity to interview President Reagan, and the result, accompanied by a full page of
rebuttal by the journalists, appeared in *Izvestia*. The 1985 Geneva
Summit was given very wide exposure on Soviet television, including full coverage of the closing ceremony on November 21.
For the first time, Soviet television broke into its regular programming schedule to pick up the live appearance of the two leaders,
a practice that was repeated and sharply expanded when Gorbachev and Reagan met in Washington at the 1987 Summit. The
new media policy was capped by the simultaneously broadcast
New Year's greetings by each country's leader on the television
channels of the other on New Year's Day 1986. The policy had
begun before Gorbachev, but it picked up extraordinary momentum once he was in office.

Alexander Bovin's advocacy of exchanges of opinion in the
Soviet media[23] was reinforced later that spring when *Pravda*
printed, for the first time, a letter of rebuttal from Richard
Combs, Minister-Counselor of the American Embassy in Moscow. Combs had taken issue with *Pravda*'s assertion that the CIA
was responsible for the bombing of a nightclub in West Berlin
frequented by American soldiers that later led the Reagan administration to engage in air strikes against Libya. Combs' letter,
appearing on May 3, 1986, complained about *Pravda*'s coverage
in very strong terms.[24] At the end of May, *Izvestia* published a
letter from the West German ambassador who complained about
criticism of his country for restricting food imports from Eastern
Europe because of concern about radiation from the Chernobyl
reactor. Although innocuous greetings from foreign countries
had been published in the past, this was the first time that letters
critical of the Soviet media had been so widely circulated in
print. An even more radical move in the direction of permitting
foreign officials to voice their positions to large audiences in the

Soviet Union was the invitation to Secretary of State Shultz to debate his Soviet counterpart under an agreement between NBC News and Soviet television. The invitation, which was issued before the Iceland summit decision had been made, was declined, because, as reported in the *New York Times*, "this is a delicate time in Soviet-American relations and . . . it would be counterproductive to engage in public debate."[25] As it turned out, when Secretary Shultz went to Moscow the next spring, he accepted an invitation to be interviewed by Soviet television on condition that the interview be aired in its entirety. His request was granted.

The arena in which those openly critical of the Soviet Union could reach huge Soviet audiences continued to widen. Although it had been common in the past to show or print comments by Westerners supportive of Soviet policies or decisions, Soviet audiences were now hearing Westerners take issue with Soviet actions. Moreover, these adversaries were being allowed more time to present their arguments coherently and forcefully, instead of the usual packaging in very small bites; and, instead of being confined to the printed pages of journals or newspapers read by the highly educated, these counter-arguments were reaching the Soviet masses through television.[26]

Americans on Soviet Television

The televised interview with the *New York Times* bureau chief in Moscow did mark a turning point. Within months Soviet viewers saw an array of American officials, former officials, and others in public life arguing their positions in an energetic, often adversarial fashion. Just in the six months of the fall of 1986 and the winter of 1987, the following notable Americans appeared on Soviet television: General David Jones, retired, former chairman of the Joint Chiefs of Staff; Jack Matlock, at the time the National Security Council's Soviet expert and later Ambassador to the Soviet Union; former Secretary of Defense Clark Clifford; former assistant Secretary of State Harold Saunders; Ben Wattenberg, editor of *Public Opinion*; former NSC official Helmut Sonnenfeldt; ABC's White House correspondent Sam Donaldson; and James Jackson, Moscow bureau chief of *Time* magazine.

One of the most interesting—and telling—programming decisions could be seen in the special one-hour documentary culled from the many hours of a Soviet-American debate at Jurmala, the resort on the Latvian coast to which the Chautauqua Society brought over 200 people. Most of the American delegation were ordinary citizens, who sat in the huge conference hall together with Soviet citizens listening to Soviet and American current and former officials and people in public affairs debate a series of questions over the course of a week. A large number of Americans presented many different points of view. But, interestingly, in the hour-long special airing on Sunday, October 5, 1986, the three Americans allotted the *most time* were precisely those *most critical* of the Soviet Union—its internal and foreign policies. Jack Matlock, Helmut Sonnenfeldt, and Ben Wattenberg frankly and directly opposed Soviet policies on: the arrest of *U.S. News and World Report* correspondent Nicholas Daniloff, emigration, human rights, religion, Nicaragua, Angola, Afghanistan, "national liberation movements" (called "Soviet imperialism" by Sonnenfeldt), and the use of force outside its borders (Wattenberg read statistics showing that Western European public opinion, by very large majorities, thought the Soviet Union the country most likely to use force to achieve its goals—a finding later reversed by polls in 1987 that showed West Europeans believing Gorbachev to be more strongly committed to peace than Reagan). On the other hand, these strongly worded thrusts were parried by a new breed of media-conscious Soviet officials—relaxed and confident—in tweed jackets and crew-neck sweaters. The responses to the American debaters were far more subtle, articulate, and sophisticated than had been seen in the past; their rhetoric was more low-key, on the whole, and appeared effective and persuasive—to the extent that one can know that without audience surveys. Shots of the audience reaction in the hall reinforced this view (widespread laughter, for example, at certain American assertions), perhaps as a result of the editing process (which appeared unobtrusive) or perhaps because of the effectiveness of the Soviet officials.

Less polarized have been the round-table discussions with foreign reporters. Two editions, one running 25 minutes, the other 30 minutes, were aired in the fall of 1986. Both brought together Soviet and East European journalists with French and

Dutch journalists, the latter two, mainstream professionals in their countries.

In a very unusual move, the Soviets aired two politically controversial American-made programs in their entirety. One was an hour-long Donahue show, with its American audience talking by satellite to Dr. Arnold Lockshin, an American cancer researcher who, claiming persecution by the United States government, took his family to live in the Soviet Union in the fall of 1986. The American studio audience warned Lockshin and his family on the air that the KGB would constrict their activities and freedom of speech and that their standard of living would fall dramatically.

The other was a PBS "Frontline" program, first broadcast in the United States in June 1983. It was an examination mainly of the problems recent Soviet émigrés encountered in trying to adjust to life in the United States, though the people the program featured were those living in only one area: Brighton Beach in Brooklyn. It showed people who were disgruntled and dissatisfied (unable to transfer their social and professional status to the new society), but also some (many fewer) who had achieved some success. When it was first broadcast in the United States, émigré groups protested what they felt to be the unbalanced thrust of the program. It was shown on Soviet television twice in the fall of 1986, both times with advance notice and previews. Although the program was aired unedited and uncut, a wraparound was added, with host Genrikh Borovik suggesting that "American Zionists" were responsible for the death of the series moderator, television correspondent Jessica Savitch. In fact, as Borovik should have known from the ample press reports at the time, Savitch's death was an accidental drowning, with no evidence whatever of criminal complicity.

Borovik's "interpretation" clearly suggests a policy of setting the context for the new opportunities for airing American positions. That context may be provocative and inflammatory, as Borovik's was, or more thoughtful and considered, as Pozner's have been.[27] But whatever the length or emotional temperature of the setting, a new term has entered the equation. Vladimir Pozner said at Jurmala that he thought American views should be given more often on Soviet television. That is happening, and it represents a major departure from the past, a policy championed by Gorbachev himself, whose book written for American readers practically begins with his praise of Soviet-American space bridges and the practice of presenting Americans on his country's media.[28]

The changes are occurring with significant rapidity. Can a large and exceedingly diverse public assimilate and "domesticate" these changes as quickly as they are produced? I referred above to two surveys conducted by *Literaturnaya Gazeta*, the newspaper with the highest percentage of college-educated readers. Those surveys found an increasing number of readers impatient with the presentation of only one point of view. Soviet media innovations suggest that this finding is certainly understood by policymakers. But the television audience is different— it is not as well educated, not as decidedly urban, not as sophisticated or intellectual. The experience of a longtime Soviet foreign correspondent adds a rather different note. He explained that he and a fellow journalist performed an experiment on national radio. They argued about events in Portugal. The next day, they received letters from three different parts of the country, all in the same vein, which he characterized as: "First you iron things out between yourselves and then come to us simple listeners." This correspondent did not deny that the presentation of different points of view was desirable, but rather that if "for decades" the public doesn't hear arguments, then "they don't want them; they're not necessary; they even upset them." Things are changing, he argues, but "it will take a generation or two."[29] When Egor Yakovlev, editor of *Moscow News*, was interviewed on a live late-night show in Moscow, he remarked that those who oppose glasnost accept only a single voice (the Russian word glasnost comes from the word that means voice)—if it pleases them—but they will reject not only the other voices, but also the practice of providing them. The resistance and skepticism of what must be a significant opposition to the new presentation of different points of view could be seen on a later edition of that live late-night show: in the spring of 1987, an irritated viewer protested a 50-minute television interview with Britain's Prime Minister Margaret Thatcher, at the time on a state visit to the Soviet Union. Why was she allowed so much time, as the viewer put it, to spread hostile propaganda?

One of the most powerful expressions of the backlash against the provision of differing points of view came in a letter published in *Izvestia*. Television viewer G.N. Bochevarov expressed solidarity with the Soviet citizens who wrote to Pozner about that "filthy anti-Soviet show organized by Donahue and Pozner." The writer went on to praise the "patriotic anti-American feelings of Soviet people." "Since when," he continued, "did you [the editors of the newspaper] begin to nourish whining, not even veiled sympathy toward an imperialist country, entangled and raised in the force of darkness holding sway over it—in the spirit of shameless anti-Sovietism and inhumanity [and] in the spirit of brutal hatred of all things Russian?" The writer then called Donahue a "political provocateur and saboteur" with a "burning hatred of all Soviet patriots." Finally, his letter concluded with an attack on Pozner: "One question interests me and all my television viewing friends: by whose hand was Pozner made a political observer for Gosteleradio? At this moment elections for leaders are taking place in our country in the localities. And we television viewers have full right to choose for ourselves those observers and commentators, who express our point of view." The reply by the popular columnist Alexander Bovin is curiously weak. It argues that space bridges enable Soviet and American citizens to understand one another, and given the imperatives of the nuclear age and logic of mutual coexistence, these interactive television programs help to alleviate the risk of mutual destruction. But these are well-known, rather bland formulas and Bovin does little to energize them with meaning or passion. It is telling that in the last paragraph of his reply, Bovin acknowledges: "I think that Bochevarov is not alone. Probably there are people who share his position. . . ."[30]

In the concluding chapter, I shall return to the question of the impact of television. Here, I would note the unusually harsh language of the letter, which was, after all, published by a deliberate decision of an official newspaper. It is clearly inflammatory and attacks Pozner, whose formal position of "political observer" accords him the highest status in the profession. The letter virtually accused Pozner of complicity in subversion and sabotage—an extraordinary document and an extraordinary publication decision on the part of *Izvestia*'s editorial board. There is profound concern, and quite obviously not only on the part of an ordinary citizen, but elsewhere in places of power, that tolerance of opposing views has its limits.

Then, too, the provision of opposing points of view is not going to apply to all questions. As a Soviet television reporter remarked, one can't promote objectivity for its own sake; it must relate to moral and ethical judgments—from the perspective of a particular world view. "If you're making a story on the homeless, you can't be objective, you have to be involved. You're saying, 'Look, here, this is awful in your rich society to have no compassion at all, . . . to see people who are mentally retarded just going out in the street in the frost. It's impossible . . . to imagine in the Soviet Union, though we are three times as poor as you are.' . . . You can't say . . . 'I'm showing you homeless, but on the other hand, a lot of people have a very decent living in the United States.' That's bad journalism."

The New Value of Timeliness

Related to the new importance of presenting several, or at least two, opposing viewpoints, is a new emphasis on timeliness, or rapid response time. In the earlier discussion of media effects the point was made that it is more difficult to change predispositions and attitudes than to activate them. The source breaking the story is more effective in setting the agenda; counterpersuasion is more difficult. Soviet communications doctrine never regarded timeliness as a particular value—it was far less important than the educative function of the media, and that is why stories on workers in factories, not particularly time-bound features, take precedence over stories on terrorist attacks or even the taking of Soviet diplomats hostage in Beirut. But timeliness (*operativnost*) has become a new slogan for the Gorbachev regime. Together with its twin, openness (*glasnost*), it is likely that the most important effect of the new policy will be on the coverage of domestic matters. The average citizen is in a much better position to judge coverage of domestic than of international events. Newspapers and television are not the only sources of information—people know about the things around them, through observation, through word of mouth from relatives and friends. There are multiple sources of information and the ability to verify independently. In this situation the news medium operates with less credibility if it either fails to cover events which are known about and taken seriously or covers them in a superficial or unrealistic way. Because of the Soviet policy of simply avoiding many of the stories that profoundly affect ordinary citizens, the credibility of the local media is very low. People say they will not read articles even on subjects that interest them.[31] Nor do they find enough about subjects they care about: they can't find much about crime and shopping, public services and city planning. What they see is full of errors. Ninety-seven percent of the readers of a district newspaper of a city find it usually distorts the events it describes. The closer the medium is to the lives of the people to whom it is addressed, the greater the opportunity to evaluate the coverage independently.[32] Because of the prohibition on stories about deviance and because of the mission to socialize in a single acceptable fashion, the local papers present a certain view of life that is unreal and stilted. Much that is of interest to the local populace simply goes unreported. Other events are portrayed in a way that is so didactic the readers find them unnatural and frozen, or, as one reader put it, "It's not like in life." Television at the local level is no more attractive. Residents of one city said they would rather see resources go into housing construction than into building a new television studio, and they consistently ask that local television studios carry more feature films from a national network than put on, as they do, programs on the local economy.

If stories go unreported, the events do not vanish. Soviet officials appear to wish to occupy the ground they have ceded to word-of-mouth and hearsay. "Sooner or later, truth will come to the surface. However, if the authoritative bodies that are accurately informed about the state of affairs do not employ public openness, the story will come out in the form of gossip, conjecture, and exaggeration. Hence it is in the interests of the cause and of truth to talk to people openly. And to be the first to talk to them, forestalling willing or unwilling distortions of the truth."[33] If this is done, then, a letter to the editor of *Sovetskaya Rossia* argues, "the question 'What are the [foreign] "voices" saying?' will no longer be asked. 'They certainly aren't reporting anything new! Our press has told it all—there's nothing to add.' That's how it should be."[34]

It is in this context that the call for timeliness—or rapid

response—is made. The Washington bureau chief for the newspaper *Trud* observed that the new emphasis should be understood primarily as it relates to domestic news. He remarked that "what Secretary Gorbachev meant by it [openness or glasnost] was the less bureaucracy—ministries and state committees—the more open such things as statistics on crime, more details on negative stories and developments happening in the Soviet Union—this kind of thing. . . .Suppose it's a negative story, something like a gas-pipe explosion in Leningrad, for example, and then you go to the City Council and ask them for details, and they say details are not available, so then you go to the local Party and press council to provide us with those details. Up to quite recently it was quite difficult to press officials to give you those details. I think with what Gorbachev says now, they will be more responsive, less willing to withhold it, and actually they are even talking about punishing those officials who try to whitewash themselves and put a cloak of secrecy or cloak of ignorance on something." He looked forward to the announced changes in the press law—changes requiring officials to provide information. The new expectations are that problems will be discussed more openly and in a much more timely fashion (glasnost and operativnost in action). An example of the problem was related by another journalist in Moscow who found that the people in the architecture-planning directorate of the city refused to cooperate without the permission of the director. It turned out that an order had been circulated in the directorate that no materials be given to the press without the signature of the head of the directorate or his deputy.[35]

Glasnost has significantly enlarged criticism, both on television and in the press. It decrees that, with the exception of the much more narrowly defined area of state secrets, nothing is off limits. However, in practice the limits and opportunities are not always clear, and even among very high-level journalists there is a reluctance to follow stories to high political levels.[36] It is true that the Soviet media have always had a tradition of a kind of investigative reporting, called criticism and self-criticism. This practice, familiar to Western observers, is generated by letters of complaint from citizens. These letters are then followed up by the newspaper or television or radio studio, and the problem presumably corrected. However, the scope of criticism tended to be limited to local rather than national problems, and questions of implementation rather than fundamental policy.

The concern with timeliness actually goes back before Gorbachev became leader. Worry about the power of rumor, the formation of attitudes at odds with the official interpretation, provided the rationale for experiments on television in the Georgian Republic. As a 1983 article in *Pravda* noted, "Suppose that a railroad accident occurred at 12:00 noon in some district. The 'grapevine' reports such incidents quickly. Understanding well that such rumors are harmful, Georgian Television has made timeliness one of the most important principles of public affairs programs. As a result, that same evening you can tune in the regular Today's Interview series and hear the head of the railroad tell what's actually happening. . . . Georgian Television reporters probe the true state of affairs, help the viewers distinguish truth from gossip and try to deprive the magic formula 'they say' of its power to charm."[37] Perhaps the most radical departure in covering a subject never before treated has been the acknowledgment of drug abuse. The netherworld of processing and trafficking in drugs, of addiction and the agony of withdrawal had always been concealed, absent from the official media, and denied by officials. With the tightening restrictions on alcohol—Gorbachev's campaign to stamp out drunkenness—the drug problem widened and the media were called upon to enlist public support.[38] With responsiveness activated, it is hoped, the social problem can be attacked by society itself. The purpose of the new openness is not only to pre-empt the other sources of information, but also to mobilize the population to implement official policy, and that is why the two new media principles function together.

Under Gorbachev the media have clearly gone beyond the limited play of exposé and criticism allowed in the past. But widening the field of permissible criticism can get out of hand, too, as happened in February 1986, when *Pravda* ran an article with excerpts from letters criticizing special privileges for Party members and attacking corruption among officials. It detailed bribe-taking, protection of fellow members who had committed fraud, favoritism, boastful elitism.[39] This went too far, and *Pravda* itself was criticized by the country's second most powerful Party official, Egor Ligachev, at the 27th Party Congress later that month.[40]

A new campaign to instill values of timeliness and openness

can be seen in the kinds of letters published in the major national newspapers: one in *Izvestia* said: "It seems to me that television still does not sufficiently exploit its opportunities, especially when timeliness is involved. . . ."[41] But even more powerful attention to timeliness has been stimulated by the Chernobyl accident. The decision to publish letters critical of the media in *Pravda*, the country's most important newspaper, is a decision to mobilize the public in the campaign for timeliness—to create demands and pressure for rapid response from the bureaucracies with which people must interact in their daily lives and to establish the credibility of the official media, which, in many matters of greatest concern to citizens, have ceded that credibility to the power of rumor and foreign sources of information. But, as Vladimir Pozner put it, what will have to happen, for this policy to work, is that the sanctions applied to Soviet local government and economic bureaucracies for *not* providing information to the press have to exceed the sanctions for reporting bad news. And that may have been the dilemma of Chernobyl.

A new press law is expected to make these boundaries very much clearer and signal to the press corps that investigative reporting of domestic problems will have legal support in the campaign to root out inefficiency and malfeasance. Early discussion of the law addressed these points: codifying the rights and duties of journalists; a more detailed (and narrower) definition of state secret; requirements concerning the duty of officials (most of all people in responsible positions in economic enterprises) to provide information and access to the media; and an understanding of privacy and libel that should expand the journalist's ability to cover individuals.[42] Even before the law came before the Supreme Soviet for discussion, the first warning signals were fired when the K.G.B. took disciplinary action—in a highly publicized fashion—against its own officials for illegally arresting a Soviet reporter who had exposed corruption in the Ukraine.[43] As predicted, the balance of sanctions is changing.

Responsiveness, Glasnost, and the Chernobyl Nuclear Plant Disaster

All of these new moves indicate that the importance of rapid response time is clearly appreciated and that Soviet officialdom understands something of the alienation of the audience from the local media and, perhaps, from domestic reporting in general. To be effective, there will have to be more accurate, realistic, and timely reports both on television and in the newspaper; otherwise, opinions will be formed that will be very difficult to counter. The Gorbachev regime clearly did not expect an early test of its commitment to timeliness, nor, as it turns out, was it in a position to deal with a test of the magnitude of the Chernobyl nuclear power plant explosion in the spring of 1986.

On Saturday, April 26, at 1:23 a.m., an explosion ripped off the roof of the Number 4 reactor at the Chernobyl power station at Pripyat in the Ukraine. A huge fire produced flames as high as 100 feet, and firefighters working to contain the blaze battled high temperatures and several would later suffer the effects of severe radiation poisoning. On Monday morning Swedish monitoring stations reported heightened levels of radiation and, tracking the wind pattern, located the event in the Ukraine. The first official news of the incident in the Soviet Union was given on Vremya at 9:00 p.m., Moscow time, on Monday. The story consisted of a 44-word bulletin read by the anchor and saying only that an accident had taken place at the Chernobyl plant, a reactor was damaged, and aid was being given to those injured. There were no pictures, and the story was buried in the program, after a number of domestic economy stories. However, it should be noted, that sparse as this initial coverage was, it was read in the name of the Council of Ministers and the face of the anchor was grave. Since the Soviet audience is attuned to totally predictable patterns of news-broadcasting, these cues would have alerted them to something of unusual importance. By the next day, the outcry in the West had begun, and with it what would be revealed as grossly exaggerated casualty figures—UPI gave an unconfirmed report of 2,000 dead, which it claimed was relayed on the phone by a witness (she was identified as a resident of Kiev and later denied in the Soviet press having provided this figure). The wire service and the American media that picked it up would be wrong on this, as they would be wrong on the meltdown in the damaged reactor and on the backwardness of the reactor design.[44] On Vremya that night, again after six upbeat stories on the domestic economy, the anchor read another, somewhat longer, bulletin from the Council of Ministers. This provided additional information about the damage to the reactor and efforts to monitor radiation and eliminate its effects. The figure of two deaths was used for the first time. Again the announcer spoke with utmost gravity, and although the coverage was still minimal the television audience would certainly have been attentive to cues indicating the unusual seriousness of the issue. The May Day celebrations soon intervened, and afterwards it was clear that there had been a decisive change in media policy. A high level team had been sent to inspect the Chernobyl plant, and representatives from the International Atomic Energy Agency arrived in Moscow. Television showed these officials, pictures of the plant, pictures of the surrounding areas and of Kiev, the largest major city in the vicinity. The national newspapers, *Pravda* and *Izvestia*, provided extensive accounts of what had happened at Chernobyl. It was not until May 14, some eighteen days after the disaster, that General Secretary Gorbachev addressed the nation—on the evening television news. He stressed certain themes, which the Soviet media had been focusing on: the effort by the West to use this accident to foment panic and disaffection in its irresponsible reporting of large numbers of dead and exaggerating the effect of the accident[45] and the dangers of unleashing nuclear power in armaments. He began linking the Chernobyl disaster to arms control— a linkage he would later put into a proposal for international cooperation in such matters.

Television reporting had been gaining momentum, as man-in-the-street interviews in Kiev were conducted (a happy family out with their baby in a stroller, averring that they were obviously far from panic); produce on nearby farms was checked for radiation; evacuations were described. An officially sponsored tour to Kiev by foreign ambassadors was covered, including interviews with a number of them. Televised news conferences featuring Soviet and foreign specialists were becoming daily events; they were conducted at the highest level, with a Deputy Prime Minister, Boris Shcherbina, who initially headed the official investigation, or the chief science adviser, academician Evgeny Velikhov, often in charge. The one on May 6, though Western-style in appearance, was a carefully controlled exercise: only correspondents from Soviet and other communist publications were called upon to ask questions from the floor. Western reporters were disgruntled and frustrated.[46] Other news conferences were given by the American bone-marrow transplant specialist Robert Gale and the

International Atomic Energy Agency head Hans Blix. A special 30-minute program was broadcast at 3:10 on Wednesday, June 4. Advance notice for the program was unusual in the way that the reporter (one of the field correspondents for Vremya) was described: Alexander Krutov, "in the short time as commentator for Vremya, has been one of the most active reporters. . . . One can always find out something new about the Soviet man from his reports on the program Vremya. He was the first television journalist to go to Chernobyl." Krutov is clearly portrayed here as an intrepid investigative reporter, who, in the best tradition of that profession, kept pushing, from the very first, to cover Chernobyl and transmit the news as soon as possible to the Soviet television audience. The official version is that Krutov was prevented from covering the accident immediately only by fears for his safety. "Krutov asked the editorial staff [of Vremya] when will there be reporting of the basic events? But we were all waiting for it. How can you say that they simply can't let journalists into a dangerous radioactive zone for their own good? But from May 4th on, there was daily reporting."[47] The picture, then, is of a new breed of activist reporter who would have covered Chernobyl from the first moments of the disaster had it been physically possible. This is surely an image that was superimposed retroactively. The Chernobyl special covered the aftermath of the accident and went to Moscow to interview the stricken firemen in the hospital (they had lost their hair from the effects of radiation, but were shown to be in good spirits). The Chernobyl stories were at this point taking up a significant portion of the entire news programs. In Moscow there was even a benefit pop music concert with the famous Alla Pugachova to raise money for the Chernobyl victims.

The Soviet media's handling of the Chernobyl disaster contrasts sharply with the way that its neighbor and ally Poland chose to use its television. Poland stressed the seriousness of the radiation threat and advised people what to do. For Poland this was, it seems to me, an opportunity to try to re-establish the credibility of television, which was the medium most severely compromised by the post-Solidarity crackdown. As Maciej Wierzynski, formerly a journalist for *Polityka*, observed, there were, in the aftermath of the Solidarity period, much more stringent requirements imposed on television than on any other medium. The verification campaign, in which more than 2,000 journalists were fired, established a more powerful system of controls for television than for other media, and in turn the credibility of television was undermined, particularly since more than 400 independent underground publications challenge governmental control of information.[48] The Jaruselski regime had earlier moved with great speed to present its account of the murder of the pro-Solidarity priest Jerzy Popieluszko and to give its warnings about price increases, thus attempting to regain some influence by presenting its own point of view first, a clear advantage in opinion formation. It is an advantage that, once recognized by those in power, sensitizes them to the importance of responsiveness and timeliness.

Chernobyl was probably a watershed for the Soviet media. A policy of responsiveness and openness that had never really been tested and was only gradually being introduced was suddenly in the center of national and international attention. In the past, disasters and accidents in the Soviet Union were generally covered only if word about them had reached the West and the event had been reported there. Then the Soviet coverage was a bare formality, an acknowledgment that the story had broken elsewhere. As we shall see in Chapter Four, the Gorbachev period, even *before* the nuclear disaster, was much more attentive to disaster/accident stories and had begun a policy of considerably more coverage of them. But, on the whole, coverage of these kinds of stories was constrained and fragmentary by Western standards. Chernobyl coverage began in the usual way. Then it took off, and the attention paid to the event, though by no means as open and thorough as Western reporting would have been, was still unheard of in the Soviet communications system. Vladimir Pozner said flatly that for the Soviet media to have waited two days to refer to Chernobyl was wrong. "One of the lessons Chernobyl has taught us," he went on, "is the importance in general of announcing what is happening inside the country." It was, he said, "a mistake not to announce it at all."[49] He said that the reason for the delay was a defensive reaction on the part of the Ukrainian bureaucracy to conceal from Moscow the seriousness of the incident. According to Pozner, only when the commission from Moscow went to the site did the full scale of the disaster become apparent to those in power. On the other hand, a Gosteleradio deputy chief, Leonid Kravchenko, implied that news of the accident was transmitted to the top leadership, that they understood it, but did not act on it for fear of inducing panic among the Kievans. He spoke of waiting until the information could be shown to be "reliable and truthful." "Because it is fast," he went on, "it is not going to be reliable. There will be panic."[50] The control aspect of delaying transmission of information is certainly part of the decision.

It is doubtful that we shall ever know what took place in the Kremlin that spring or who knew about the disaster and when. The official explanation citing lack of information for the delay in coverage, even though we know that vertical communication up through the bureaucracy is not efficient in the Soviet system, is not altogether plausible; Kravchenko's statement tends to contradict it. But the Chernobyl incident did provide Gorbachev with a number of opportunities. He was slow to seize upon them and did not immediately display the political acumen that had been attributed to him by Western observers.[51]

Eventually Gorbachev did see the Chernobyl disaster as a way to separate his leadership from the past and to consolidate his power by reining in the powerful Ukrainian bureaucracy. From the beginning, Chernobyl presented him with an opportunity to assert the innovative departure his leadership could represent for the country. The fall before, he had traveled, with very heavy television coverage, to mix with workers and Party activists, exhorting them to work harder and promising them a new and more pragmatic approach to the future. He would not tolerate, he said, the old ways—the stagnant and unimaginative routines of his overaged predecessor—nor would he countenance the obsequious tributes of fawning lieutenants (he chided an official at the 27th Party Congress in February 1986 for peppering his speech with Gorbachev's name). When the Chernobyl reactor exploded, Gorbachev could have, from the beginning, dissociated his leadership from the entrenched local leaders and put some teeth in his reformist rhetoric. In one move he could have enhanced his credibility, mobilized support and legitimation, and, in the bargain, put his people in more positions at the subnational level. In addition, his much publicized policy of openness and responsiveness would have taken form, with a resultant positive effect on sclerotic managerial practices in the economy—the main target of the responsiveness campaign. But none of that happened for many days. Gradually, however, these political opportunities came to be seen as just that, and the Soviet leadership began to make some moves. *Ogonyok*, the weekly illustrated magazine, quoted the Kiev province (oblast) leader that "a sharp examination of each individual is being carried out. We have already got rid of a few people, including people in leadership positions. They have parted with their Party cards."[52] Only in mid-June did *Pravda* announce the dismissal of the Chernobyl plant director and chief engineer and severely criticize other senior officials whose responses had ranged from passive inaction to cowardly flight.[53] Criticism of poor or non-performance of duties was published in several major print sources, and on July 19, Vremya carried news of the dismissal of ministerial level officials. On July 21, Vremya announced the appointment of Nikolai Lukonin to head a newly created Ministry of Nuclear Power.

The policy of responsiveness was reinforced by publication of letters of citizens who demanded to know more about safety measures and who took the local media to task for not having been more forthcoming at the time of the accident. "I am hurt by our local press," a Chernobyl resident wrote to *Pravda*. He realizes, he writes, that many people pitched in in the aftermath of the accident, some as part of their official duties, others as volunteers, "but you hear about this from friends, [and] neighbors, but in the newspapers and in the bulletins on local radio, you don't find out anything." Another man, whose letter was printed by *Pravda*, is angered that after the accident, "know-it-alls" and the "informed" who "know everything" were quoting "wild figures of the level of radiation," leaving the man-in-the-street at their mercy. The local media were doing nothing to inform people who were bewildered by what the self-appointed specialists were feeding to the rumor mill.[54] The reinvigoration of the local media, recognized as a serious issue, could, equally, profit from the aftermath of Chernobyl. Chernobyl accelerated the implementation of the new media policy beyond what had been anticipated or agreed to. The early decisions conformed to cautious, entrenched policy; the later decisions took a bolder approach and parted with tradition. But it would be a mistake to exaggerate the momentum or ignore the habit of secrecy and defensiveness. A month and a half after Chernobyl, Soviet scientists presented information to their counterparts at a meeting of the International Atomic Energy Agency in Vienna. Western scientists at the meeting expressed serious doubts about the Soviet data and were concerned that the Soviet Union intended to conceal information.[55] Later, however, at the end of August, after their intensive investigation was completed, the Soviet government presented a comprehensive 382-page report to the international body. This candid and detailed document was unveiled at a two-hour Moscow news conference, open and matter-of-fact, a sharp contrast to the carefully controlled, prickly, and defensive one held earlier, on May 5. Consistent with earlier statements, though, the linkage between what had happened at Chernobyl and what could happen as a result of Western insistence on an arms race was made repeatedly. The jagged course of information provision and the initial lag in informing both the West and their own population provide evidence of the strong concern about control and vulnerability so frequently and consistently displayed over the course of Soviet history. We should expect these contradictory tendencies and tensions to accompany any major policy change.

Bold moves have been made; more appear to be on the way. But the momentum into a fuzzily defined new freedom can take the process too far, as *Pravda* learned. In his day, Nikita Khrushchev imposed some far-reaching new policies without assessing their impact. They were later called "hare-brained schemes." The new communications policies have not, as yet, been evaluated in terms of the criteria the regime holds important, and one of them must surely be the orderly maintenance of their own power and the continuing quest for legitimacy. Because these new information policies seem to the West to be positive and to fit our notion of initial steps toward unimpeded flow of information does not mean that they would not bring in their wake dislocations in the system that the officials had not anticipated. In particular, the changes wrought by the Chernobyl incident, the sudden veering of the media toward mobilizing the television audience with respect to domestic events of great moment and concern, remain unexamined in their impact. Yet pressure for a more rapid response time in both domestic and foreign news is being generated by the Gorbachev government with increasing boldness, even before the effects of the changes have been assessed. Most direct was an article in *Pravda* based on readers' complaints. It is an article that has been frequently cited by Soviet media people—an article from which they received their new instructions. They consider it of signal importance. I quote from it here to illustrate the kinds of changes that are contemplated.

> The most important factor in the effectiveness of information is timeliness. It has increased some, as we are again convinced when we watch daily reports from the Chernobyl atomic power station and about the events around it. But the opportunities still have not been exhausted. Often it happens that the greater the occasion for timeliness, the less chance that it will be conveyed by television. This relates to both the domestic and the international parts of the broadcast. . . . One doesn't always sense in the program the "nerves" of the current day—"a few hours ago. . . ," "we just received this communication . . . "
>
> Repeatedly [readers] drew special attention to [the need for] improvement of international information, to the necessity for rapid response and deep analysis of world events. . . .
>
> Information about the capitalist world is monotonous. The journalists' clichés migrate from broadcast to broadcast. Mainly they show political meetings, demonstrations, and protests. Rarely do they discuss the achievements of science and technology, about how, under conditions of capitalism, they turn out for simple workers, about economic and cultural collaboration, about problems of women, old people, the growth of crime and terrorism in the western world, about the problems and successes of the socialist countries.[56]

*   *   *   *

What follows is a picture of the values and attitudes, the approaches and techniques of Soviet correspondents in the United States, including Moscow's chief television reporter in Washington. Theirs is the Gorbachev approach.

Moscow Television's Man in Washington

Timeliness in international news is somewhat different from timeliness in domestic matters. In the next chapters, American and Soviet news broadcasts will be analyzed in terms of the stories they cover and the countries that make up their universe. But the Soviet understanding of news—timely news or hard news—can also be seen in the way a major Soviet foreign correspondent performs his assignment. In this and the next chapters, leading Soviet correspondents tell how they perform their duties in the United States. Through their observations, it is possible to see how they understand what is newsworthy, what is timely, and what changes in the Soviet media system directly influence their work and the expectations of them Moscow holds. We shall also see how they view us—which is how the Soviet media view us and how they want the huge Soviet media audience to understand us. It should be clear from the previous chapter that the purposes and principles of personnel selection for the Soviet media are vastly different from our own. The point has often been made that Soviet journalists work for the state (the media are centralized and state-owned) and do not subscribe to the professional canons of American journalists, particularly in the dedication to unearthing and describing what the government finds uncongenial. Soviet journalists do not disagree with aspects of this portrayal. They acknowledge the source of their employment, but point to larger and larger areas that may legitimately be criticized. As I noted above, the limits of glasnost have yet to be clearly defined and the notion of "responsibility" in reporting is a major limiting factor. These are questions to which we shall return in the concluding chapter. However, two points should be made here. One is that the new medium of television has saturated the country and appears to have an extraordinary impact on the Soviet population. Whoever is presenting information through that medium—under whatever orders or constraints or with whatever belief system—has an immense audience and attention. It is important to see how they do their job and how they understand the world-at-large and America within it. Second, the fact that Soviet journalists differ so much from Western journalists should not blind us to the fact of change. Even though change may take place within—not in opposition to—the system, that change has ramifications we ought to understand, particularly since the whole process of information diffusion has been revolutionized by television.

Valdimir Dunaev was assigned to the United States in 1985. His predecessor as the representative of Central Television in Washington, a correspondent named Druzhinin, did mainly stand-up stories in front of the Capitol or the White House. With Dunaev has come a different technique. A story that aired on the Soviet news on January 8, 1986, showed San Francisco at night. This cinema-vérité piece was shot from inside the patrol car; through the windshield one saw the darkened streets of the city and the lighted windows of Chinatown. Then Dunaev and his camera-man accompany two policemen on their rounds: answering a call about a warehouse burglary, questioning local merchants and the owner of a small Chinese restaurant (without success—we see much shaking of heads and impassive faces); making a heroin bust (the accused is a nineteen-year-old black woman—footage of her with her hands up against the patrol car); investigating the robbery of an old woman living in a barracks-like apartment (she knows who robbed her but is too intimidated to tell—the viewer sees her through the open door as the police question her). There is none of the usual focus on police brutality; on the contrary, there is evident congeniality and cooperation between the police-men, Chuck and Jim, and the crew from the Soviet Union. Com-mentary at the end of the piece warns that drug addiction and the related crime it spawns are the "insomnia of America, its curse, its punishment, its nightmare," even though San Francisco is not the worst of American cities in this respect. This has been a "safe beat"; no gun battles, no deaths. The policemen wish them well, and, again, the streets of San Francisco are seen through the patrol car's windshield.

Dunaev started his career in journalism in 1951, working for the newspaper *Trud,* then Moscow radio, then television. He has worked for years in London and has covered Portugal, An-gola, Saigon (right after the Americans left), and India. His En-glish is good; he is energetic and hardworking. In our lengthy conversation, I asked him how he goes about developing stories, how stories are placed on his agenda. He explains that he took a trip to Boston at the request of Moscow to film a story about Bernard Lown, Nobel laureate and co-founder of the physicians' peace organization. This was, he said, one instance in which Moscow initiated the story idea; most stories are done at his initiative. Dunaev was interested in seeing what else he could do in Boston. His first thought was to interview Massachusetts gov-ernor Michael Dukakis, since he saw Dukakis as sympathetic to the cause of Sacco and Vanzetti. Dukakis was "too busy" for the interview, but Boston's Mayor Flynn was not. Flynn, whom Dunaev describes as "very regressive, very conservative, anti-Soviet" was willing to receive the Soviet correspondent. Then, since he was in Boston and had read about the campaign of Joseph P. Kennedy II for the Democratic nomination for Congress in the Eighth District of Massachusetts, he asked for and got an interview with young Kennedy. According to Dunaev, Kennedy in the interview "said he's going to Moscow and back all the time, buying oil, crude oil, so it was a good story." Dunaev's views of the American electoral system and the values that inform television news stories can be seen in his comments about that Massachusetts House campaign. "I decided to find somebody else in that campaign. It was Mel King, a black gentleman, a progressive guy in Boston [Melvin King, a State Representative for ten years, was runner-up in Boston's earlier mayoral election]. So I compared how they campaigned. One was serious; one was just typical Kennedy: 'I'm Joe Kennedy. Oh, you are Eleanor or Elaine. How nice. I'm from Boston. Could I have your vote? Fine. So long.' He was kissing babies, joking with them, kissing senior citizens. Well that was fine; typical American campaign."

I asked Dunaev for some examples of "hard news" stories for *Vremya*. He referred to Congressional consideration of the President's proposal for aid to the contras fighting in Nicaragua. But he also described, at much greater length, a story he did on Mitch Snyder. Mitch Snyder, who has worked for years to help the homeless, is a well-known figure in Washington. In 1985, CBS made a feature film on Snyder's work. Called *Samaritan*, the film, starring Martin Sheen and Cicely Tyson, aired on May 19, 1986. Snyder, who left his family and a high paying job in New York to campaign for those without political clout, has conducted hunger strikes and street demonstrations. With intravenous feeding tubes and his body reduced to a skeletal form, he was shown on the Soviet television news. In fact, his face appears so often in Moscow that one is tempted to think that his exposure there has helped to put him on the American news agenda, but that is vigorously denied by American media people. As a senior producer at CBS told me, Snyder "has been a player in this town for a long time. . . . Snyder is very aware of what is attractive to television." Since mental institutions have been releasing more people, the homeless are a more serious problem and as a subject, receiving more coverage.

Dunaev's story covered the reception given in connection with the filming of the CBS movie, a gathering that brought together the stars and the real-life homeless who were in the movie. "I asked the cameraman to film the first part as if it were a real reception, somewhere at Buckingham Palace. You see a lot of 'up-ish' people, as they say, a lot of Hollywood stars, ladies . . . with all the candles, their gold, and dishes, like the reception given by the president. And then all of sudden you see the poor homeless people, and they are smiling. I ask them 'Are you satisfied? . . .' [The star, Martin Sheen, is asked about playing someone like Mitch Snyder and says] he's not brave enough in real life to be like Mitch Snyder, but he's smart enough to play him." The story turned up on Vremya as a three-minute story. Snyder enjoys Dunaev's confidence and has captured his interest, and later, in February 1986, his counter-State of the Union message press conference was covered by Dunaev for Soviet news. This story, which took place two blocks from the Capitol, showed poor, homeless, and hungry children—a small crowd around Mitch Snyder.

All of these stories are clearly, in American news terms, soft or features. Except for the contra aid note, none is hard news. But the question should be asked if this is a conscious decision derived from a very different set of criteria for news reporting or if there are other constraints. One of those constraints might be equipment. In fact, equipment is a sore point. At late as 1986, Dunaev was still using a French sixteen millimeter Eclair camera, but expecting to receive a Beta camcorder soon. The Eclair was a fine camera in its day, but American newspeople stopped using it around 1971; news-gathering is done with videotape, not film. Living with film has been difficult. "It's a great delay. You can't send hard news, and you have to buy it—from ABC or CBS . . . " Stories he does himself have to be processed. "It could be done only tomorrow. Then it takes half a day. Then you have to synchronize it. Then you have to edit it. Then you have to combine and narrate it and translate it. Only then can you transfer it onto tape. And only then can you send it to Moscow. So the delay is now about two days, with luck, one-and-a-half." The stories are done in NTSC (the American format for television broadcasting) and put up on Intelsat. In Moscow, the signals are then converted to SECAM (the Soviet—and French—system) for broadcast internally. Dunaev described a story he did when the Potomac flooded. It was before the Geneva summit meeting in 1985 and there were statements at the time on American media that the summit might not actually take place because of intransigent Soviet positions. Dunaev did some man-on-the-street interviews and shipped the film via Lufthansa to Frankfurt and then on to Moscow, but it was somehow delayed in Frankfurt for ten days. When it arrived in Moscow, the summit had been convened and the story was hopelessly out of date.

If there were fewer delays, what would the news agenda include? Dunaev muses about what he will cover. He mentions first a story on a Pushkin symposium. "If they're talking about Pushkin in Russian, that's interesting. That's the event. Americans do know our language. That's the story. They discuss Pushkin in America [though] they have their own Mark Twain." This will create resonance for Soviet viewers; the fact that Americans are seriously interested in a Russian poet is of interest because America is central to their world view. It is a matter of their national self-esteem. He also gives the example of a story he did on a demonstration in Washington, one he calls a "trivial demonstration," of people for and against aid to Jonas Savimbi's guerrilla challenge to the government of Angola. The story focused on the pro-Savimbi demonstration: "On Connecticut Avenue, there were those who were for Savimbi—fascists, just racist, open, they were like Hitlerites; they were shouting; they were crazy. They would have killed me if they had recognized that I was a Soviet correspondent." Other ideas figure in projected stories, once the camcorder arrives, for example, Dunaev wants to do stories about American farmers—both as cautionary tales and as models to emulate. As he says, "Farmers are the nearest I have to the real American, honest American, because they're very good. . . . They have, almost all of them, college education, and they have computers, and they're pretty rich. And they're very successful in the sense that they are miles ahead of us.

They're suffering from being successful: it's the ABC of Marxism; they can't sell what they produce." Dunaev's stories on American farmers will also present models for Soviet farming administration—not immediately or directly applicable, but certainly intended to provoke movement and progress there. That is one of the reasons he wants to do more stories about American achievements—a change from the typical coverage confined to problems and eyesores. As he put it: "Achievement is really a personal computer. . . . I saw a farmer, a dairy farmer, and the farmer, very successful, owned a computer [that] remember[ed] every cow and how to handle it and what kind of grain that cow prefers and that sort of thing. That's marvelous. I love that. I would very much like Soviet farmers just to grasp a bit of it and use it. I'm very happy for American farmers for their intelligence, for their ability. I'm disappointed that they're punished for their intelligence, but that's a different, social matter."

There are achievements, positive sides to Dunaev's agenda for stories. But they relate to the effect of limited, personal initiative—something that can be emulated under the new Gorbachev system. He wants to do stories on managers and how they're trained in business schools, but not on wealth and not on "Mr. Tycoon." He wants to do a story on a small agrofirm that trades, on a small scale, with the Soviet Union—a firm that successfully developed a single product from the crumbling prospects of a failing enterprise. The Soviet audience will see, in this story, "pigs having bath[s]. In Russia they're pretty dirty. In itself, it's very good propaganda." This is exactly the kind of coverage the *Pravda* article quoted above would recommend several months later. The Gorbachev regime will, I think, exploit the Soviet public's keen interest in the United States to present models for emulation, and the new "positive" stories about individual initiative and the diffusion of technology, particularly the computer, will increase in number. They will be stories that show that individual effort can be understood quite apart from the economic system in which it is embedded and that success can be transplanted.[57]

It is precisely in this context that the Dunaev story on McDonald's should be read. This story, airing on "International Panorama" on Sunday November 3, 1986, was an upbeat presentation of the benefits of fast-food operations. Public catering has long been a problem for the Soviet Union. The vast majority of women there bear the "double burden" requiring them, in addition to their jobs, to bear the responsibility for housework and shopping, scarcely shared by husbands and only fractionally relieved by household appliances and fast-food outlets. In 1970 the Ministry of Trade estimated that about 30 billion hours were lost each year simply in trying to buy things and waiting in lines.[58] Most of this time was contributed by working women. But public catering—and, indeed, other kinds of service operations, such as cleaners—is neither popular nor efficient. Even if they were more widely available, they would not be more fully utilized, at least as they are now configured. Surveys find a very high level of dissatisfaction among customers, based on the quality of service, the long waiting time and disorganization, and the "rudeness of the people one deals with."[59] Transplanting the American success story could help to solve an intractable problem; emulating America is always popular. And, as a matter of fact, within months after the broadcast of this story, it was announced that new fast-food operations would be established in Moscow with the help of Swedish and Italian companies.

The more obvious success stories and friends of the Soviet Union are also on Dunaev's agenda: Donald Kendall, chief executive officer of Pepsico, is always of interest to the Soviets. In Dunaev's terms, "he's a common boy who became president of Pepsico." Kendall is not just any success story, but one that sought out Soviet trade. As in the Pushkin symposium story, the connection between the United States and the Soviet Union, evidence of American interest in the Soviets, their history, their present, is immensely gratifying, and important beyond any proportion. Dunaev plans a story on a rural community in Iowa ("very conservative"), where some parents and children decided to learn Russian and regularly traveled 100 miles to take lessons from an American teacher of Russian. The teacher decided she would visit them every other Monday. She assigns homework, and the group makes its way through the language.

It seems to the observer that these story ideas, too, are not hard news. They're still features, with both information and a strong, if much more innovative, didactic thrust, and although the replacement of film by a camcorder helps to get them up on the satellite and into Soviet homes more rapidly, they are not very time-constrained subjects. I asked the question another way: about interviews with leading American officials and hearings on Capitol Hill. Will these be covered? First of all, the whole notion of interviews with powerful figures is not an overriding value. "Television is not about interviews, unless it's Updike or [another] very clever man that could just think aloud. Otherwise it's deadly dull. The man-in-the-street [story] is good, because it's powerful." Alexander Shalnev, TASS White House correspondent, and then *Izvestia* columnist, agrees: "Personally, I think that we know so much about the officials of the other side, I think it's high time we started doing something about the people in the street. . . . And I think it would be much more interesting, and to some extent, easier to show the life of a different society through the eyes of the ordinary people, not only through official writings." Alexei Burmistenko, the *Trud* correspondent, gives a similar view: his readers, he says, are not interested in officials; they would prefer prominent cultural leaders, like Benjamin Spock and Bruce Springsteen. Springsteen is the "perfect hero for the Soviet person." He's a "blue-collar-minded-singer—pro-labor, pro-trade union."

Still one is left with the question of how much access to official America the Soviet correspondents actually have. As a TASS correspondent remarked, on one level, it's very good: "I can go out and walk into the White House pressroom and I can pick up any statements, any announcements, any anything released officially by the White House press office. I could be there at the briefings by Larry Speakes or by the anonymous officials at the background briefings, but if I would like to arrange for some kind of meeting with some White House official for some deeper analysis of what is behind this or that event, this or that speech by President Reagan, it's a kind of iron curtain that's thrown in front of me." He mentioned that he once tried for two and a half months to arrange an interview with a prominent national official. "We failed miserably, and I just didn't have the courage and the interest at all in trying to get any other official to talk to me." But the TASS bureau chief in Washington put a somewhat better face on it. Nikolai Turkatenko said that at briefings of foreign correspondents, if he would like further information, he asks the government spokesman a question; "sometimes they promise to find out things and call back; sometimes they do; sometimes they don't."[60] But he does not feel particularly left out, noting that a TASS correspondent was among the Soviet correspondents who interviewed President Reagan. In fact, access to high-level American governmental officials is a very scarce commodity. The Washington bureau chief for the most influential Egyptian newspaper, *Al-Ahram*, complained that he had "no access to top officials."[61]

An American-based Soviet newspaper correspondent observed: "But you see it's unrealistic to apply for an interview with Weinberger and even if the interview is granted, what will we be talking about with him? Star Wars? A repetition of all those questions? So I never even did attempt to approach these Cabinet Ministers, you see. It wasn't necessary." But some sources are available: Senator Edward Kennedy is particularly appealing to Soviet correspondents, who try to interview him whenever possible, and one correspondent noted that with his office there is a fairly smooth process by which requests are received and responses given. Retired Admiral Gene LaRocque, director of the Center for Defense Information, and opponent of Star Wars, is another accessible person of interest to the Soviets. But, on the whole, as Dunaev said, when asked about his access, "Oh, that's dreadful, you know." This is not the picture that American officials who handle press requests have. They note that in the past it was rare for Soviets to ask questions at briefings or press conferences and they tend not to ask for special access to officials in the Executive. In fact, Jody Powell told me that after he had taken a question from a Soviet journalist at a White House briefing during the Carter administration, longtime White House correspondents told him that this was the first time in their memory that a Soviet correspondent had ever asked a question. When the president gives a press conference, it is rare for any member of the foreign press corps to be granted a question, something about which they complain. One, not a reporter from a socialist country, asked White House spokesman Edward Djerijian when they were going to stop being "second-class citizens." Information is coveted in Washington; time and access are extremely constrained. The Soviets, who had not tried to breach the walls in the past, are experiencing what older hands have learned before. Whether or not it is even more difficult for the Soviets, is not easy to tell, since the margins are so narrow for everyone.

One of Dunaev's most frustrating trips was to Atlanta. On the day before the anniversary of Martin Luther King, Jr.'s birthday, a Dunaev story ran on the Soviet news analysis program, International Panorama. There were shots of Atlanta, the Peachtree Plaza hotel—the familiar cylinder sheathed in a glass skin—shots of black Atlantans, pictures of the Martin Luther King, Jr. Center for Nonviolent Social Change, more street scenes, apartment complexes, a drawing of King in back of a single candle (with a well-engineered sound track of gospel music). All of this was voiced-over by Dunaev. Then the scene changed to the office of Marion Barry, mayor of Washington, D.C., and the rest of the story was an interview about King's life and heritage, in particular about his opposition to the Vietnam War, ending with a note of gratitude from Barry to the Soviet Union for its support during King's lifetime. As far as the time spent in Atlanta, he used film and no sound bites. He found the interview with Mayor Young too general and abstract, and then there was the road. Though Dunaev might not have known about it before his trip, Atlanta had been embroiled in a controversy about an access road for the Carter Presidential Library and the Carter Center of Emory University. The road, as proposed, would be a major highway. It had been vigorously opposed by neighborhood and environmental groups (it would, it was feared, adversely affect a park-like residential area designed by Frederick Law Olmsted); it was supported by business interests, commuters, and those who predicted a heavy traffic pattern for the library. But Dunaev knew none of this and during his visit to Atlanta, late that fall of 1985, was taken to the area where the road was being built (actually construction was suspended by court order at the time). "And then I was brought to a certain neighborhood, saying that there is a fight whether the road should be there or not and that Andrew Young was for that road and now he betrayed or vice versa, and Jimmy Carter was involved, and, as I say, it's not of interest to me, really, you know. I understand farmers; I understand people, businessmen; I understand problems; I understand joy; I understand success. I can't understand people [who are so] *meshchansky* [petty bourgeois], just to discuss forever whether the road will spoil the surroundings or not." He left after two days with no regrets. That Dunaev did not see a story in this is, to a large extent, a product of his way of understanding the American political system. Just as in the story about Joe Kennedy's campaign in Boston, he looked at these differences as only superficial, the surface ripples of a system in which, he believes, power is not shared and to which there is no real access for large numbers of people.

The Journalist's Image of the Public: Soviet and American

It is an interesting question to ask of people who are responsible for news stories what their image of their public is—or if they have one at all. Do they get feedback that tells them to whom they are directing their stories, and how reliable it is? American network television news producers make it a point to say that they know relatively little about their audience and get rather little direct feedback. A good example of this way of thinking is that of a senior producer of network news in Washington: "I certainly think of it [the audience] as diverse and remarkably unresponsive. If we do a story which I think is just a tremendous show, we'll get four calls. Even in Washington, which is a city theoretically attuned, vibrating to nuances, . . . I'm just amazed by how few calls we get, how few letters. . . . we'll have a meeting once every six months or so and talk about how we're doing, and everyone's got opinions; someone says, well, people aren't interested in Washington, and I'll say I think they are interested in Washington; we ought to do more overseas stories; people don't care about overseas stories. . . . There's no evidence. How do you tell?" At ABC, when Vladimir Pozner responded at length to President Reagan's speech, fourteen calls came in to the Washington bureau that day and fourteen the day after. This was considered an extremely strong response. Moreover, the callers identified themselves as people the producers were impressed with as knowledgeable: some were professors; they were clearly better informed than the usual callers. On the whole, the producers consider their news audiences to be occupied with their own lives and that is where their attention lies. As a senior producer at CBS put it, "I have a perception of my audience as not having paid much attention during the day to what the story has been. They've been mostly working, it hasn't been connected to what I'm doing, and they're watching in their homes. There are probably some distractions there, so that you will have to tell the story as strongly, as clearly, and as logically as possible, so that they won't have to struggle with what it is and also because they will only have one chance to look at it." Av Westin, vice president at ABC, sees his audience as having "an attention span that is being interrupted by clattering dishes, dinner conversation, or the fatigue at the end of the working day."[62]

As so many writers have noted, the judgments of other journalists, the satisfaction of those higher up in the organization, and, not least, the journalist's own sense of conforming to professional standards constitute much more important criteria and much more effective feedback.[63] A producer put it this way: "I think the best news program is one that starts with what is essentially a guess as to what the best story of the day is and just goes down the list, 1 through 10, then you go off the air." Because these are the most important sources of validation, there is rather little interest in surveys—in part, because the producers and reporters have little time for them; and in part because not much stock is put in preferences that the newspeople see as lacking a foundation of information.[64] As one producer said, "people . . . [are] not dumb; they're just not terribly interested. I put almost no stock in surveys." One kind of survey, the Nielsen ratings, are talked about. In the morning, each of the networks begins the real work of the day with a conference call sometime between 9:45 and 10:30. All of the bureaus respond to New York and describe what potential news stories could be developed. One such conference call began with New York's reporting of the overnight ratings. But this, too, is a relative judgment—of a network vis-à-vis its two peers. Unlike opinion surveys, the Nielsens identify if the television set is on and the channel to which it is tuned; it does not plumb the subjects that might interest the audience or find its satisfactions and disappointments. The diary method, in which an adult in the household records the family's viewing record, is notably inaccurate. A new form of feedback has the potential to provide a much more qualitatively sound view of the public. The new "people meters" promise "greater accuracy, faster availability of data, and continuous measurements. . . ."[65]

On the Soviet side, one finds the opposite: newsmen who say they are vitally interested in the audience and who are convinced they have a clear picture of that audience. They arrive at that picture primarily through the enormous volume of feedback they get in letters to the newspaper and to central television.[66] The *Trud* correspondent asserted that between 600,000 and 700,000 letters were received annually by his newspaper and that the letters department is the largest single department in the entire newspaper, employing some eighty people full-time and another hundred people part-time. That represents a 30 percent increase in full-time personnel in that department over ten years, while *Pravda* registered a 14 percent increase in only three years.[67] For the most part, letters to the newspapers are concerned with domestic issues, but sometimes letters are received that seek information about international issues, for example, what the Iran-Iraq war is about and who is winning. Alexei Burmistenko even pointed to one letter he received as the source of a story his editor asked him to write. This was a letter from a female student in Elektrostal—about 200 miles from Moscow. As Burmistenko relates it, she asked the following questions: "Can you tell me, please, what's the cost of the dollar or the British pound in relation to the Russian ruble? Who lives better, Soviets or Americans? Can you please compare for me . . . what their salaries are, how much do they pay for a loaf of bread, their rents, their car, blue jeans, and this kind of thing. Not [a] dissident letter, but [a] very simple, sincere and excellent letter."

Soviet television's Vladimir Dunaev, when he was in Moscow, received between thirty and fifty letters a week. Both Dunaev and Burmistenko are well aware that letter-writers are not representative of the population-at-large, or even of their media audiences. But both maintain that the huge volume of the flow is still a valuable indicator, and that what is important is what bothers people, whether or not that group—retired people, for example—is overrepresented. "You have to make certain mental adjustments for that," in Burmistenko's words. Dunaev, when he is in Moscow, finds he gets a sense of his audience from the lectures he gives to ordinary people—not specialists, but white-collar employees at the huge Lenin Library, for example. Soviet sociologists, on the other hand, deplore the situation. They argue that there is a very skewed and clearly deficient sense of the audience, and that there is a wide divergence between audience preferences and interests and what that audience finds in the media. In fact, these Soviet studies find, the chief source for journalists is personal meetings, such as those that Dunaev describes. This is "unsystematic," but so taken for granted that, at the very beginning of the readership surveys for the national newspapers *Izvestia* and *Trud*, "certain comrades, before the beginning of work, said the basic data [about the audience] were well known to them and could be fully received from rich life and practical experience without the use of expensive methods of contemporary sociology." That is why each survey included a series of questions in which experienced journalists and media officials were asked to predict the results of the surveys. The results of the predictions and of the survey were far from congruent. There is concern that only through surveys, scientifically designed and executed, will reliable and important information enter the flow of media decision-making and that the value of surveys must be impressed upon future journalists early in their careers, and that while in college, they be taught the requisite methodological skills.[68] It has become virtually mandatory for officials to say that they use surveys in developing programming, but the survey apparatus for a continuous detection of program preferences is rudimentary and rarely specified. V.I. Popov, a deputy director of Gosteleradio, noted that in developing new shows for 1986, Central Television analyzed "critical articles in the press," letters from viewers, and surveys.[69]

However, the practitioners are not an appreciative audience for surveys. Like their American counterparts, they have little positive to say about them. In fact, the *Trud* correspondent, who has himself taught future journalists in Moscow, observed: "If you properly analyze this flow of letters, I think you will get more accurate results than if you send 1½ thousand questionnaires, as Gallup does. . . . We do not do this kind of thing. I think on a couple of occasions we paid research institutes to do it for us, and we are not very much satisfied. Because what they told us, we knew in advance. They simply confirmed some trivial, general conclusions, which we knew anyway without their studies." Dunaev is not concerned with surveys: "I don't believe in surveys." He relies on his own sense of what makes something interesting. He, like his American counterparts, thinks the television audience is interested for the most part in entertainment and that the main thing is to gain their attention, to interest them. Besides, he argues, his television audience has the legacy of people who dictated a certain kind of fare. A political education program, he said, was prescribed and "deadly dull . . . not because Marxism-Leninism is dull, but because [the] people who were doing them were deadly dull." He thinks the future of Soviet television will be much more in tune with his own values of making subjects interesting. No matter what the subject, he believes, if it is presented in an interesting way, people will watch. "I have my own personal style, and I don't want to rely on what they [the survey people] would tell me what viewers would like to hear more about: Germany . . . [or] Japan." Dunaev knows, he says, what has to be changed on Soviet television, and he doesn't need surveys to tell him. He thinks it will take about five years for the changes to be made, but he is sure the policy is irreversible. But without the surveys, ratings, or competition, one is left wondering how quickly and accurately audience demands will become known. There is no structure sanctioning the articulation of audience demands and no regularized and representative channels in place for conveying those demands. Changes are pouring out from the top, but the reactions of the recipients, known to be less pliant than the leaders had thought, are still obscured.

Sources for Soviet Newspeople in America

Feedback from the public is only one source of information. In order to do their jobs, correspondents must make use of sources of information in the country they cover. The Soviet correspondents in the United States are among the most faithful readers of the politically conservative newspaper, the *Washington Times*. The TASS correspondent, referring to the period of the Reagan administration, put it this way: "that particular paper has pretty close connections to the White House and their reporters covering the White House get exclusives . . . I'm interested in their stories; there are . . . right-wing elements who write frequently . . . who write, as far as I'm concerned, absolutely outrageous ideas, but they're interesting. . . . I'm trying to figure out where they go from this point. How they perceive, for example, our society, our presentation of the news." The *Trud* correspondent calls it a "terrible" newspaper, but "still it keeps me feeling what the extreme political right thinks and does and expresses." The television correspondent also subscribes because the *Times* provides "a great deal of information on the Soviet Union." He reads it simply out of curiosity. But all think it prudent to keep up with what they regard as the influential right, and for them, it resides at the *Washington Times*. They all also use the *New York Times* and the *Washington Post* and the wire services. Daily fare includes the newspaper of the American Communist Party, *The Daily World*. The *Christian Science Monitor* and the *Baltimore Sun* are also referred to, but not read regularly. The newsweeklies and the three networks are on the agenda as much as time permits, and TASS was able to scoop all the other press agencies the day of Robert MacFarlane's resignation as National Security adviser simply by watching live coverage by Cable News Network of the President getting into the helicopter and casually answering a reporter's question.

Less well-known magazines are popular with the Soviet correspondents because there is coincidence of views: They subscribe to *The Progressive* and *Mother Jones*. Dunaev, in addition, likes the *National Catholic Reporter*, a lay Catholic weekly published in Kansas City. This liberal journal has been very interested in the Sanctuary movement, and it is this that attracted Dunaev's attention. He finds that churches provide the safest and most sympathetic environment for "progressive" people, that their protests on behalf of those who oppose the government are legitmated and protected by this agency, both physically and morally. He has observed it, he says, in Boston, Cleveland, and Iowa. "Ministers," he says, "are almost communists."

CHAPTER THREE

The Worlds of Soviet and American Television News

N ATIONS INTERPRET THEMSELVES and the world through the presentation of news. With the era of television, and the concentration of attention on that medium, the importance of television news has increased so powerfully that in the United States it has been credited with (or blamed for) such critical national choices as the election of presidents and the conduct of wars. While we will leave for later, speculation about the effects of television, we will examine here the world of television news that Soviets and Americans receive. It is perfectly obvious, as I noted above in describing the enormous differences between Soviet and American journalists, that news organizations in the two countries, as well as the function and organization of television in general, are profoundly dissimilar. Much has been argued and written about the autonomy of the media in the United States; the Soviet case is much simpler.[1] However, in both countries the audiences are large and television is the most important, often the only, source of information about the other country and the world; in both countries the news is broadcast over the entire country: eleven time zones for the Soviet Union and four for the United States. What is relevant, what is salient, among the countless events and actors on the world scene? Are we, who are so important to each other, drawing from the same or wholly different pools of understanding? To answer these questions we analyzed five months of daily weekday prime-time news programs on both Soviet and American television.

We chose three months in the fall of 1984 and two in 1985. By looking at October, November, and December of the earlier year we could look at some major events, such as the American presidential election, national holidays (Thanksgiving and the anniversary of the Bolshevik Revolution). We could also observe the Soviet news as it was during the regime of Konstantin Chernenko. It was during this period the International Court of Justice decided it did have jurisdiction in the case Nicaragua raised against the United States, and when FBI agent Miller was arrested in California for passing secrets to the Soviets. Workers were striking at Yale University, and the coal miners' strike dragged on in Great Britain. A bomb exploded in the Brighton hotel where Margaret Thatcher and her Conservative Party colleagues were meeting. François Mitterand paid a visit to Great Britain, as did Mikhail Gorbachev; and Helmut Kohl came to Washington. India was beset by crises: Indira Gandhi was assassinated, her son was elected to her position, and the country suffered the tragedy of Bhopal. Svetlana Allilueva, Stalin's daughter, returned to the Soviet Union (from which she would redefect in 1986). The famine in Ethiopia was taking its toll in death and suffering. Ariel Sharon sued *Time* magazine for libel. Americans continued to protest South African racial policies.

The 1985 period—September and October—permits us to look at a new regime in the Soviet Union: Mikhail Gorbachev had come to power in March of that year and moved quickly, as I noted earlier, to use and shape the media in a new way. By the end of our coding period the Geneva Summit, at which General Secretary Gorbachev and President Reagan met for the first time, was still about three weeks off, and the media blitz had not yet begun. Had we included November, our results would have been subject to skewing. During these two months in 1985, the *Titanic* was found, the movie *Rambo* was a pop cultural icon, often deplored, but doing phenomenal business at the box-office; protests and riots broke out in Chile, and the United States ordered some economic sanctions against South Africa. In

Japan there were follow-up investigations of the jumbo jet crash that had taken place at the end of the summer, and in El Salvador, Jose Napoleon Duarte's daughter was kidnapped. Violence increased in South Africa, and the trial of Benigno Aquino's alleged assassins was in its seventh month in the Philippines. In the United States more spy scandals broke. A massive earthquake hit Mexico. When Israeli citizens were murdered on a boat off Cyprus the Israeli air force struck PLO training bases in Tunisia in retaliation. In still more acts of terrorism coming from the troubled Middle East, the Italian cruise ship *Achille Lauro* was hijacked. Vitaly Yurchenko, a K.G.B. officer, defected to the United States and then was to redefect to the Soviet Union, where aged Prime Minister Tikhonov was replaced by the younger Nikolai Ryzhkov.

In the Soviet Union, there is a single authoritative news program: Vremya is broadcast at nine o'clock in the evening, Moscow time, on all channels. Airing for the first time on January 1, 1968, it is and has been the most important program on Soviet television, according to the official directives.[2] However, we did have a choice among the three networks broadcasting the evening news in the United States. It is well known, by observers of "pack journalism," that the major networks do not differ radically in their coverage of events, both domestic and international.[3] But, we did feel that there was a marginal difference. ABC's "World News Tonight," anchored by Peter Jennings, seemed to show greater interest in international events in general, and in the Soviet Union in particular. Because we were looking at such different news systems, we wanted, to the extent possible, to look at "least different cases"; that is, we wanted to reduce, not exacerbate, the very strong differences inherent in the comparison by choosing the network that, even marginally, was most open to and interested in news of the Soviet Union. Certainly, as George Watson, vice president and Washington bureau chief of ABC (and earlier, in Moscow), remarked, "Peter has established a well earned reputation as a reporter and, more recently, an anchorman who has a particular interest in and knowledge of foreign affairs. . . . And I think that's been reflected . . . in the quantity of foreign news coverage that ABC has. . . . [We are] talking about rather small differences, I suppose, but small differences count for rather more when you're comparing three programs which are notable for their similarities and not their differences."

Occasionally, ABC itself has become part of Soviet/American relations. The controversial mini-series Amerika, airing early in 1987, depicted the United States under some hypothetical future Soviet occupation. It elicited sharply polarized opinions at home and received heavy coverage on Soviet television. Just about a year before, Soviet commentator Vladimir Pozner had been allowed to respond to a speech by President Reagan: the response lasted eight minutes and drew the ire of President Reagan's Director of Communications, Patrick Buchanan. The timing of these events, in which ABC was actually inserted into the news, did not affect our analysis.

As I noted earlier, Vremya can be elastic; it can expand to absorb the news that broadcast officials think important—speeches by Party leader Gorbachev, for example. The news begins with national events of great importance—primarily policy statements and directives from the Politburo and the Central Committee and activities of the country's leader. When nothing of this importance has occurred on a given day, the news begins, as it often does, with domestic economic stories. International or foreign stories then follow, and culture or science and the arts. Presiding is a pair of anchors, one male, one female. After the last news story, a new commentator is introduced, who gives the sports news, and then, finally, the weather is shown. We have not included the sports and weather portions of the program. Vremya, on the average, without sports and weather, runs between thirty and thirty-five minutes, with no interruptions. ABC has about twenty-two minutes of actual newstime during its half-hour broadcast. This disparity in time gives Vremya 63 percent more stories for the five months under review. The average length of a story on ABC is one minute, thirty-nine seconds.[4]

In watching the Soviet news, where on one broadcast a single lead story included a complete speech by Mikhail Gorbachev that lasted for an hour and twenty minutes, sometimes one has the impression that, on average, stories are much longer. The statistics, however, tell us they are only thirty seconds longer than the average ABC story. They do, however, vary in length much more: fifteen stories in the five months lasted at least ten minutes. But 90 percent of all stories did not exceed three minutes. On ABC, the upper limit was 6 minutes, 45 seconds, with 90 percent of all stories no longer than 2 minutes, 45 seconds. On an average day, ABC presents 13.5 stories; Vremya, 22. Altogether, for the five months, we viewed a total of 3,695 individual stories: 1,405 on American news and 2,290 on Soviet news. By using such a large data set, we have tried to minimize the effects of individual events. Had we used a narrower time frame, it is much more likely that our results would have been skewed by the sudden peaks and valleys of areas of attention.[5] We looked at each broadcast in real time, receiving the Soviet news on the First Program by satellite.[6] Altogether we analyzed just over 105 hours of newstime, with ABC accounting for just under 39 hours and Vremya, for 66.5 hours.[7]

Countries of the World: The Geography of News

The record of five months of news broadcasts shows us the shape of the planet for the two media systems. One rather clear difference is that on its news, the Soviet Union is much more embedded in the world-at-large than the United States is on ABC. Fully 53 percent of all news stories on ABC were about the United States; 47 percent were international: that is, countries other than the United States figured in the stories, sometimes together with the United States. And this percentage is probably high for American network news. The international outlook of ABC does produce more international stories; a ten-year study of international news on all three networks found the percentage of international stories averaged just under 40 percent.[8] On Vremya, 66 percent of all stories were international.

We can also look at international stories as a percentage of total elapsed newstime. Here, the two news programs resemble each other much more closely. For the five months, ABC devoted 48 percent of its time to international stories, while the figure for Vremya is 56.5 percent. As we shall see in the next chapter, there are significant differences between the 1984 and 1985 time-periods. In part, they relate to what happens in the

United States every four years when a president is elected, and in part, they relate to the new policy on coverage imposed by Mikhail Gorbachev.

There is, indeed, a strong feeling among the American networks that their mission relates first and foremost to the provision of news about the United States. As a CBS senior producer remarked, "if [we have] to make a choice between a foreign and a domestic story, we'll go with the domestic story. . . . We are an American broadcaster, and while we are a world power, and foreign information is so important, when it comes to a jump ball—are you going to run a domestic or foreign story—we tend to go with the domestic story." Av Westin, ABC vice president, observed that the viewer is interested in "my world," "my city and home," and "my wife, children and loved ones." In this scheme of things the domestic story has the overwhelming advantage, especially during elections, when foreign bureaus know "their chances for 'getting on the air' are seriously diminished."[9] At NBC, senior producer John Holland conceptualized the emphasis in a different way, stressing the importance that reaching a basically uninterested public had assumed: "there's probably not a huge appetite for a lot of foreign news on a network television news program. . . . My personal opinion is that the attitude taken by the network news program has changed in the last ten years from—our job is to tell people what they ought to know—to one which is shaped much more to the side of let's tell them what they're interested in."

In November 1985, Politburo member and Party Secretary Egor Ligachev complained about the media, over which, as ideology chief and second in the political power structure, he had ultimate oversight: "The geography of our information is still weak—there are many more blank spots on a television map than on a geographic map."[10] Yet, in the five months of our project, Vremya's universe of countries covered in some way was one-third larger than ABC's, numbering 107 to ABC's 72. Only three countries turned up on the American news and not on the Soviet: Haiti, the Dominican Republic, and Singapore. On the other hand, the countries on Vremya not mentioned on ABC during this period were: Guatemala, Peru, Paraguay, Uruguay, Hungary, Malta, Rumania, Finland, Denmark, Iceland, Equatorial Guinea, Mali, Benin, Mauritania, Guinea, Nigeria, Chad, Congo, Guinea-

Bissau, Uganda, Tanzania, Somalia, Mozambique, Zimbabwe, Madagascar, Morocco, Algeria, North Yemen, South Yemen, Mongolia, Bangladesh, Burma, Laos, Indonesia, and Papua (New Guinea). Almost half are African states.[11]

How do two news broadcasts see the importance of the other superpower? There is no question from the figures that the United States and the Soviet Union are, for each other, the most salient foreign countries. Each receives a significantly greater percentage of news stories than does any other country. The Soviet Union is covered as the most important country in 4 percent of the stories on ABC, and the United States in 7 percent of the stories on Vremya.[12] This is an actual difference of some 42 stories over the period. The countries next in importance for each media system are given only 2 percent and 4 percent of the total number of international stories.[13]

The world, though distinctly bipolar for each news system, is nonetheless populated by other countries. What our figures show is that the news agendas, in terms of coverage of countries, are remarkably similar for the United States and the Soviet Union. Taking all countries that receive at least 1 percent of the total number of news stories, we account for almost 90 percent of all stories on ABC and about 80 percent for Vremya, and this is true whether one counts only one country in a story or includes two. Allowing for two countries in a story permits us to capture more of the international interactions, and we find that sixteen countries are the Soviets' leaders in news coverage, and thirteen, ABC's. From this pool, nine actors top the news agenda in both countries: Nicaragua, Great Britain, France, Italy, South Africa, Lebanon, Israel, India, and the United Nations. Adding the other superpower, they account for 40 percent of all international stories on ABC and nearly the same for Vremya (37 percent).[14] This is a significant identity of interests for both media systems. Before looking further at this common agenda, we will look at the countries which do not receive the same attention on both systems' broadcasts.

News leaders on ABC that do not have that status on Soviet news are: Mexico, El Salvador, and Egypt. Vremya's foci of attention, not shared by ABC, are West Germany, East Germany, Bulgaria, Hungary, Afghanistan, and Japan.[15] It is clear that the Soviet Union's allies and neighbors—East Germany, Hungary, and Bulgaria—are of more interest to it than to the United States, and, similarly, that Mexico and El Salvador, in America's backyard, are of more interest to ABC. But, as we shall see when we look at regions of the world, the Soviet news is, surprisingly, more interested in some of America's allies and trading partners than the American news is. West Germany and Japan were among the most covered states on the Soviet news, and this was certainly not so on ABC during this period. Although Western media often point to the Afghan war as an embarrassment to the Soviets and say that the Soviets only late in 1985 began covering the war itself, from the battlefield or about the battlefield, it is not true that Afghan coverage has been minimal. On the contrary, Afghanistan has consistently been among the countries most frequently covered on Soviet news. Afghanistan is important to the Soviet media, and they mean it to be important to the Soviet population. Coverage has included reports about economic, social, and political changes in the country; about assistance offered by the Soviet Union; about the interference of other countries, most notably Pakistan and the United States; and, of more recent date, coverage of the war itself. In the summer of 1986, there was a special: a satellite link-up, "Moscow-Kabul." This unusual program is described in the next chapter. The new frankness in covering the Afghan war appears to have resulted in a major new attention to television as a source of information. According to one study, between 1984 and 1986 television jumped from sixth place among sources of information about the Afghan war to third. Had the study concentrated on the latter of the two years only, it is likely that the change would have been even more marked.[16] Lacking access, ABC devoted relatively little attention to Afghanistan in the five months of our study; there were five stories.[17]

Turning now to that very large area on Vremya of commonality of focus on international news, we observe its similarity to the Western agenda. Although Gosteleradio has about fifty news bureaus around the world, it lacked representation in many of the countries to which it gives the highest coverage. The Soviet Union does not have diplomatic relations with South Africa or Israel and no correspondents in those two countries, yet they account for a very sizable portion of total international coverage. Coverage of Great Britain is very high: partly because of the tremendous attention given Gorbachev's visit to London, but also because of intense Soviet interest in the long and conflict-ridden British miners' strike. France was the first country Gorbachev visited as Soviet leader. Later, when we look at what kinds of stories are linked to which countries, we shall see the very strong interest in the assassination of Indira Gandhi and the Bhopal toxic poisoning disaster in both countries' coverage of India. Stories about Israel on the Soviet news tend to treat it as a secondary country in a story primarily about another country. Less than one percent of all international stories put Israel as a primary country, but it is accorded 3 percent—a very large share—of the stories about secondary countries. These stories are not about the government and society of Israel; they are not really *about* Israel at all. They are mainly about Israeli actions in the occupied West Bank or in Lebanon. Thus, they are stories about what Israel does that affects other states or the area under its occupation; they are stories about the dynamic of hostility, fear, and misery in the Middle East as a whole.

The Union of South Africa is certainly inaccessible to Soviet correspondents: diplomatic relations were broken when the South African government expelled the Soviets in 1956. It has also become increasingly difficult for Western correspondents to cover what they think important. In 1986 the South African government instituted a regime of censorship so harsh that its own information department virtually monopolized news of racial disturbances and their aftermath. In the United States, where there are economic ties and domestic black populations, where students put up shanty towns at colleges and universities to protest what they regard as economic support of apartheid, the interest of the media is clear. The media have had to accept the very restrictive rules governing coverage, but they have tried to maintain a level of attention. CBS anchor Dan Rather was quoted as saying that "a word is worth a hundred pictures" in this case—that even without pictures, or perhaps, better yet, because of the chance to do backgrounders that are not driven by dramatic new pictures, coverage, far from being crippled, will improve—an overly optimistic reading of the situation. During 1986, particularly with the anniversary of the Soweto uprising ten years before, the government crackdown became so intense that it was difficult to send out any information on important events, and it was all censored, in any case. On the whole, the networks, news agencies, and newspaper bureaus agreed that to stay on, no matter what the constraints, was important. A. M. Rosenthal of the *New York Times* stated that the newspaper was determined to maintain the importance of the South African story and to give it prominence, making sure the story didn't disappear even when there wasn't enough in the story to produce the usual number of words.[18] Even with the best of intentions, the media have not been able to keep the South Africa story as vital and central as it was before the censors cracked down. The number of stories and their prominence declined radically in the nation's newspapers and television.[19]

On the Soviet side, the interest is intense, even without the ties and the apparently greater ability to influence events that the United States has. The Soviet Union regards South Africa as a developing revolutionary situation, for the time being diverted or fractionated by ethnic differences among blacks, but clearly changing in the direction the Soviets regard as progressive. Alexander Bovin, the well-known political commentator, argues that South Africa is at the stage when "subjective factors assume decisive importance in such a period: the activeness and solidarity of the masses, the interaction among the various political factions operating among the 'lower classes' and the correct line, programs, slogans of the political vanguard."[20] Bovin is saying here that even if the repressive and seemingly solidly entrenched political elite, with all of the instrumentalities of the state, maintains itself with little real change, the revolution can, nonetheless, be moved forward by the will, the activism, the apparently spontaneous acts of resistance of the repressed *if* they are guided and unified by the proper Party line. Soviet interest in South Africa is undoubtedly related to its strong support and sense of community of interest with those who are pursuing that African revolution. The African National Congress as a body and Oliver Tambo, its leader, are frequently shown or discussed on the Soviet news. The Soviet Union regards itself as a champion of what it calls a revolution, not only to appear as the friend of the non-socialist repressed everywhere, but also because of a sense that it can be a major player in a different South Africa. Although the Soviet Union does not maintain diplomatic ties with the Union of South Africa and there are no Warsaw Pact embassies in the country, Soviet presence in the area is assured by diplomatic legations in Botswana, Lesotho, and Mozambique. The U.S.S.R. has supported the African National Congress militarily, as well as diplomatically. As a study of Soviet–South African relations notes, ". . . only the Soviet Union has consistently championed the plight of the oppressed population with guns and money. This fact has been duly acknowledged by the UN unit on apartheid and other international organisations concerned with South Africa."[21]

The United Nations is much more important for the Soviet Union than for the United States; it receives a great deal of coverage as an entity, in addition to its role as site for the expression of policy of individual states. Partly, the strong interest in the United Nations is related to the fortieth anniversary of that body, which, in the fall of 1985, attracted the participation of heads of state and foreign ministers. President Reagan spoke, and the new Soviet foreign minister, Eduard Shevardnadze, made his maiden speech. The United Nations is presented as a genuine world forum for the resolution of conflicts and the amelioration of the human condition. It is shown as a body of many differing political and social systems, most of which are generally in agreement with each other and with the Soviet Union, which is shown to generate many of the resolutions that form the agenda of the international organization. The United States is portrayed as either an obstacle to progress in resolving conflicts and bettering the life of the world's population or as merely irrelevant to the dynamic thrust of world events. For Americans, the United Nations has become a problem in international relations: the balance of voting and alignments has swung drastically away from the preferences of the Western founders, as the world has changed and new nations have entered. Majority policies of the United Nations have increasingly diverged from policy objectives of the United States, whose leaving UNESCO was only part of a larger dissatisfaction. In fact, as a United States Mission report concludes, most of the world voted against the United States most of the time.[22] As the salience of the United Nations has declined for the United States, it has risen for the Soviet Union. During the five months of our coding project, the UN was the primary "country" seventy times on Vremya and eight on ABC. It was second country sixteen times on Vremya and six on ABC. When ABC covered the UN, it did so mainly (75 percent of the cases) in connection with the United States and its NATO partners, or the Soviet Union (13 percent) or Central America (13 percent). The Soviets made virtually the same connection, though less focused on themselves and their allies (just under half). But the Soviets expanded the linkages reported through stories on the UN, covering South and East Africa, the Middle East, and Asia as areas of UN discussion and resolutions. In terms of agendas, the Soviets take the UN much more seriously by presenting a wide array of issues in which the UN takes an important position: space and science, media, legislative issues, political violence, civil rights, intelligence operations, law, arms control, economic issues, and many others. ABC focuses on very few issues, thus implicitly reducing the salience and significance of the world body: formal national and international politics, economic issues, and arms control and military issues. But there is one subject for which ABC considers the UN relevant and Vremya does not: the disaster story. Clearly, Vremya prefers to show Soviet contributions and those of its allies in assisting countries stricken by famine or earthquake, while downplaying the role of multilateral cooperation through the international body.

Serious Soviet attention to the United Nations reached a new high in the fall of 1987, when, in a turnabout, it agreed to repay its nearly 200 million-dollar debt to the international body, thus making the United States the top debtor. In addition, the Soviets advocated larger authority for the United Nations. As the discussion of Soviet media coverage clearly shows, there are many important dimensions, building over time, on which the Soviet Union considers its interests to be consistent with United Nations activities.

The importance of Nicaragua is obvious, but it is interesting too for what it suggests about its neighbor. Nicaragua is not the only Soviet friend in the Western hemisphere. Cuba helps Soviet foreign policy interests with manpower and internally has patterned itself far more decisively on the Soviet socialist model. There is considerable movement of people—students, teachers, vacationers—between Cuba and the Soviet Union, and the annual meeting of COMECON, the international communist economic organization, was held in Havana during the period of our analysis. But Cuba receives three-tenths of one percent of the total number of news stories; it is not invisible, to be sure, but hardly a major interest either.[23] In my view what makes Nicaragua far more important than Cuba for the Soviet media is the involvement of the United States. It is a developing and not a settled situation; it is a conflict that is really more about the United States and its foreign policy process than about the embattled Sandinista neighbor, and it is for this reason that the Soviet media are so concerned with a country that is far from its borders and which it has assisted, but cautiously. It is really another example of the extraordinary centrality the Americans have for the Soviet Union.

There is another country that is curiously absent. Greece under Prime Minister Papandreou made headlines in the American press because of its opposition to American foreign policy interests. Papandreou's anti-American rhetoric and accommodating stance vis-à-vis the Soviet Union provoked some concern among his NATO allies. There was, however, little spillover into the Soviet news, which devoted less than half a single percentage point to Greece, some three-tenths of a point more than ABC, but quite distant from the countries of marked Soviet interest.

Regions of the World: The Geography of News

Coverage of regions of the world shows us the bulges and blank (or barely colored) spots in the attention of the news broadcasts of the Soviet Union and one American network. We looked at the individual countries making up the news leaders for each media system; now we will look at the world as a whole, to see where the attention of the public is drawn. The table below displays the newsmap of the world, with regions as a percentage of total news stories, with countries in each region (or, as in the case of the countries of NATO, political region) as primary (most important) countries in a news story.

The asymmetry of focus is striking: the United States and its allies in NATO are far more central to the Soviet news than is the

Regions: Percentage of Total Stories

	ABC	VREMYA
US/NATO	77	18
USSR/Warsaw Pact	5	51
Caribbean	—	1
Central America	4	3
South America	1	2
Non/NATO West Europe	1	3
Non/Warsaw Pact E. Europe	—	—
Central and West Africa	—	1
South and East Africa	3	3
North Africa	—	1
Mid-East (incl. Egypt)	4	4
Indian Subcontinent	2	5
Asia	2	4
South Pacific	—	—
Other	—	4

Note: Total does not add up to 100 because of rounding.[24]

Soviet Union and its Warsaw Pact allies to the American news. The centrality of America and the strong interest in the countries of Western Europe are clearly shown. Even those Western European countries not in NATO are of greater interest to the Soviet Union than they are to the United States. The regions of the Monroe Doctrine are also greater claimants of attention on the Soviet news, which devotes a larger share of its program to South America and the Caribbean. Central America is of greater interest to ABC than to Vremya, but not by much. A good deal of Africa is blank for ABC news, and Asia receives only half the attention it does on Vremya.

The Geography of News and Elapsed Time

To round out the picture of news coverage and blank spots on the globe, we should look at the amount of time devoted to regions and countries. As we noted above, stories may vary in length. Again, we look at how much the superpowers show of each other. ABC and Vremya spent exactly the same percentage of total elapsed time on the other as *primary* country: *5 percent,* but that translates into a total of *1 hour and 55 minutes* that Americans viewed stories principally about the Soviet Union on ABC and *3 hours and 15 minutes* that the Soviet public saw stories mainly about the United States on Vremya during the five-month period.[25] If we look at stories for *two countries* covered, then, the American viewer saw the Soviet Union as the primary or secondary country in 10 percent of the newscast (totaling 4 hours), while Vremya featured the United States in either position in *12 percent* of the newscasts (slightly over 8 hours). The Warsaw Pact countries without the Soviet Union account for so little time on ABC that they take up less than a single percentage point of airtime. The NATO countries, however, even when the United States is excluded, are given 5 percent of Soviet airtime as primary country: that is, over five hours.[26]

Time devoted to other countries is rather different for the two news broadcasts. Vremya tends to spread its time over many more countries: ABC bunches up its time to concentrate on a few countries: Mexico, Great Britain, France, Italy, South Africa, and India—all of which got at least 2 percent of airtime (or 46 minutes) over the five months.[27] Four countries were given 2 percent of Vremya's airtime: Great Britain, Bulgaria, India, and the United Nations. But another nineteen received 1 percent (or 40 minutes) of Vremya's airtime over the five months, compared with eight for ABC. Of the eight, all except two are also the greatest consumers of percentage of stories. The two newcomers are the Philippines and Ethiopia, and only Ethiopia is a common concern—of both ABC and Vremya—in terms of airtime. Vremya misses the growing problems in the Philippines. The rest of the countries that are given at least 1 percent in Vremya's column include several newcomers not part of the group receiving the largest percentage of stories. If one excludes allies and neighbors of the Soviet Union (Cuba, Poland, Finland, and Mongolia), the list has some interesting additions: Chile, Libya, and North Yemen. We will see later the (negative) importance attached to Chile. The leader of North Yemen, as we noted, paid a state visit to the Soviet Union and was the target of very concentrated attention to buttress the Soviet position in the area, even before the cracks appeared in South Yemen, the Soviet ally that erupted in rebellion the next year. The importance of Libya was also related to a state visit by Colonel Qaddafi. In fact, as a percentage of stories, cover-

age of that country turns out to be slight: only 0.4 percent over the
five months.[28] This suggests that while the attention and ceremony are turned on while the state visit is in progress, a sense of
continuing involvement with that country has been absent from
Soviet television. When President Reagan ordered a military
strike at Tripoli in 1986, the Soviet Union deplored the move but
did little else.

A study of the coverage of international affairs on American
network television news found that the location of news bureaus
was a strong predictor of news coverage.[29] Is this why Eastern
Europe receives so little coverage, or are events there (or anywhere else in the blank spots) simply not newsworthy by American criteria? In fact, ABC does have a bureau in Poland. The
bureau was started when Solidarity ignited the Polish political
scene, and at that time coverage was extensive. It is not heavy
anymore because the events are rarely considered newsworthy.
After the decline of Solidarity it became a skeletal operation,
with the correspondent, who used to live in Warsaw, based in
Rome and traveling to Poland from time to time. George Watson, bureau chief in Washington for ABC, remarked: "I suspect
that if there were stories of significance and general international
interest in other East European countries [other than the Soviet
Union], we would certainly cover them, and depending on the
size and magnitude of them, establish bureaus there. . . ." Some
years ago, after his stint in Moscow, Watson did a good deal of
work on Eastern Europe, doing "evergreen" (not immediately
perishable, not hard news) stories, with trips to Eastern Europe
from his London base. "At the same time," Watson concluded,
"I rather suspect that when you looked at what you might do
and went to Hungary or Czechoslovakia, you'd have a tough
time selling the story, getting the executive producer to say: yes,
it's worth spending time [and] money—in the expectation that it
would get on the air." It would be difficult, because it would be
soft news, a feature. Watson had seen a story on Soviet pressure
on Bulgaria to energize its economy and had thought it an interesting idea. But, he said, if the executive producer were ap-
proached with it, the answer would be that with Nicaragua,
Central America, the Middle East in turmoil, terrorism—and the
cost of the Bulgarian idea—it could hardly compete.

If one asks American network television newspeople what

they would do if the newshole were larger, if there were more time to do whatever they wanted, their first response is that they would do more intensive, rather than extensive, coverage. They do not immediately think of expanding the number of countries they cover, but rather of spending more time on a story with the mix they have. It is the straitjacket of time that bothers them. One senior producer at NBC spoke of the incredibly difficult job of paring, editing, reducing to fit the one minute-forty-second format and said if he had more time, he would make stories longer. Brian Healey, senior producer at CBS, concurs: "I'd want to add longer, more in-depth stories that you can't do as well as you'd like to do in a framework of 2½ to 4 minutes. More '60 Minutes'-type stories on a given subject. Now when we do that we're forced by circumstances to spread it over 5 days." What the producers with whom I spoke at all the networks would not favor is an increase in the *number* of stories. George Watson put it this way: "I think there are probably two models one could imagine—*USA Today,* faster paced program with even more elements, everything in 30 minutes [and] the other is like *The Wall Street Journal,* [which takes] a couple of stories and [does them more deeply] and compress the rest into headlines." If there were more newstime available, he would not just double the number of stories he can fit in the 30-minute news program. ABC was on its way to the second model, he pointed out. On April 2, 1986, "World News Tonight" went more than halfway through the program on the single story (though from several angles) of the terrorist bomb that exploded on a TWA airliner.

In answer to my open-ended question about what network people would add if they had more time (and there was not much conviction that the local markets would yield more time), all said they would use the time to do the same mix of things they were currently doing, but allocate more time to explore the issues in depth. No one volunteered the notion that the extra time could be used to cover more of the globe. They speak from experience; they know the odds. There are a good many stories that died on the shelf: for example, the ones at one network about the Hungarian economy and Scottish devolution. They were held nine months or more, never able to compete with the rush of more critical news, and eventually expired. Given the definition of news and the assumptions about the interests of the American viewing audience, most of what goes on in the rest of the world is not newsworthy, unless, as we shall see below, it concerns disasters or coups. One network producer described his irritation with the constant attacks by Third World spokesmen on American news selection. At a conference he responded to complaints from an official from Senegal by saying: "Most of what happens in your country . . . does not interest most Americans; it will not get on the air . . ." Though he later tried to mollify his questioner, and though he admits that there is virtually no coverage of the Third World, he finds that the basic question is one of newsworthiness: "you will not," he told the Senegalese questioner, "get on [the air] with ups and downs of your GNP."

Foreign countries may come alive for the viewer if there are pictures, and, consistent with ABC's far greater preference for pictures, more stories are presented through pictures (either by the anchor's voice-over or by correspondents in the field) on ABC than on Vremya. On the average, just about three-quarters of the stories on ABC about any region of the world will be aired with pictures, and there is not a great deal of variation in percentages.[30] On the average, on Vremya, only 59 percent of the stories are presented with pictures; the rest are talking heads: read by the anchors or commentators, or interviews. However, on Vremya, the region where the story takes place does make a difference. Only 1 of the sixteen stories on Central and West Africa was accompanied by film. Only three of the eleven stories on North Africa were filmed. Just over two-fifths of the Asian stories had film. But two-thirds of all stories on the Soviet Union and its Warsaw Pact allies came with film, and two-thirds of all stories about non-NATO Western Europe. Stories about the United States and the NATO countries were more likely to have film than talking heads, but not by much (55 percent were filmed stories). Of course, it is much easier for Vremya to cover domestic stories and stories about its neighbors on its borders with pictures. But ease of electronic newsgathering is not the sole explanation for the differences in the proportion of pictures or the vividness with which a region is shown. The region of South and East Africa is shown through pictures in 53 percent of the stories, not much different from the American/NATO stories proportion. Clearly, newsgathering is not easy for the Soviets in one part of this area: South Africa. Yet, by far, the largest number of stories about this region are South African stories. In 1984 there were almost as many stories from Ethiopia (which, as a friend of the Soviets, made newsgathering easier), but, by 1985, South Africa was the focal point of all stories emanating from the region.[31] There is no Soviet news bureau in South Africa; the two countries do not even maintain diplomatic relations. Although the footage is never identified, it is clearly of non-Soviet origin. Soviet interest in this part of the world is very high and, as we shall see, increasing, and it is presented with pictures even when those pictures are purchased.

The People's Republic of China accounted for 18 percent of the total number of stories on Asia on the Soviet news.[32] Of the thirty times that Soviet viewers received news of the PRC, all but three stories were read by anchors. The three stories on film were not from a correspondent but were voiced-over by the anchor, and all were about official political matters, such as Party, economic, or diplomatic issues. Relations between the Soviet Union and the People's Republic of China have been improving, but slowly. There have been high-level exchanges of officials, but still below that of head of state; new agreements have been concluded that will stimulate trade and cultural contacts. But fundamental change is slow; deep differences remain. Nonetheless, as we will see in the next chapter, when one separates the Gorbachev period from the period under his predecessor, China enters as a country of significant coverage.[33] It is a reflection of his active interest and policy initiatives in Asia and the Pacific. The chief of news programming at Gosteleradio indicated to me that news bureaus would open in China and Australia.

PRC stories are low-key during these five months. Picture stories are, as we have noted, rare. PRC stories are also very short. The average is 45 seconds. However, in the summer of 1986, a new kind of story began appearing. China had mounted a trade fair in Moscow, and Vremya covered it at length at the end of the program, with pictures, and sympathetically. The camera panned in a leisurely fashion over Chinese products: ceramics, silks, and small appliances, and the Chinese official in charge gave an interview in fluent Russian; a small change, perhaps, but one that accords with the increased attention in that country.

Subjects[34] and Stories:
The Content of News

The Soviet news shows a clear preference for the formal processes of national and international politics, which take up 43 percent of the main, or primary, subject—we were able to look at up to three subjects for every news story.[35] In contrast, ABC, even in a period in which an American presidential election was included, devoted only 19 percent of its primary subjects to these two themes.[36] What this means is that the Soviet viewer is shown the official visits and the sessions of the Supreme Soviet, the country's legislative body, the operations of Party organizations, the decrees of Party and government (often read in full), while even during an election year, the American viewer sees much less of the formal and often formalized routines of his or her government. Take official visits: these are visits by high-ranking official representatives of a foreign government. Most of these events would simply not be considered news by the American networks. They are not linked to some event that is unusual or critical, and as photo opportunities they lack drama. It is this predictable, undramatic ritual that is staged over and over for the Soviet viewer. It is a celebration of Soviet status, as the foreign visitor is shown arriving in his plane, standing with the Soviet hosts at the airport during the playing of *both* national anthems, reviewing the massed precision of the Soviet honor guard, riding in a forbidding file of black limousines through the streets of Moscow, and, finally, being received at the Kremlin. It is also a celebration of the state, as such. The emphasis on the making of news by the state itself, by officialdom, is an acknowledgment that the source of movement, of dynamism, of direction lies in Moscow and with the organs of power. During the period of our study, some 112 stories on Vremya covered official visits to the Soviet Union from 32 countries. On ABC, there were nine stories about visits to the United States of officials from eight countries.[37]

If anything, the American news networks are increasingly wary of the official Washington story. At CBS the producers told me a legislative hearing or an announcement of a significant change in governmental policy would be linked to the man-in-the-street. Whereas in the past it was enough to cover a hearing on the Hill from the committee room with some voice-over, that is now seen as inadequate. The story may be generated by the hearing, but the issue as understood by and affecting Americans "out there" can become the subject of the story. This trend has been called "Sauterizing the news," after the former president of CBS News, Van Gordon Sauter, who "came to New York [from a background largely in local television] convinced that the networks were out of touch with the rest of the country, that CBS in particular had to become less tradition-bound and more with it. . . . Rather than cover the institutions of power, CBS would explore how those institutions affected ordinary people."[38] After Sauter's resignation, CBS began "hardening" its news. As one observer noted, the CBS Washington bureau was "reanointed."[39] But the aftermath of the Sauter period is not so clear. CBS did provide complete prime-time coverage of the 1986 elections, but its ratings plummeted and it was decisively beaten by the competition. The new reality of increased network news competition and the pressure from local affiliates and their very lucrative game shows playing to increasingly large audiences have made the choices more difficult. Some newspeople, such as a senior producer at NBC, were always skeptical of the softening news trend. About taking governmental institutional stories out to the people he said, "That's not a myth, exactly; it's almost a conceit. People always said when working out of Washington, well, the way to do that story is to take it out. It seems to me that a lot of the most important things that happen in Washington can't be done that way, because there is no sensible—without really straining it—extension to everyday people's lives. . . . A lot of important Washington goings-on are just not susceptible to that kind of treatment." Even when the president is away and Congress is in recess, Washington, in his mind, remained the center, and whether the issue is contra aid and battles on the Hill or the FAA investigation of the TWA bomb explosion, the story is often a "Washington kind of story" and disguising it or contorting it doesn't make sense.

For ABC's "World News Tonight," space and science (including health) made up the single largest cluster of stories, accounting for 15 percent of primary subjects, outdrawing formal national politics. Stephen Hess notes that increasingly nongovernmental news is claiming news space, with three subjects likely to gain as coverage of official news declines—business, religion, and science/medicine.[40] For ABC the last is already on the way. Economic issues, though, were first when secondary and third subjects of stories were considered, gaining 11 percent and 14 percent of the stories, respectively. On the Soviet news, three subjects take up 60 percent of all primary subjects: formal national politics, formal international politics, and economic issues each account for about one-fifth of the total. Typically, the stories about economic issues are placed in the first part of the program and deal with the domestic economy, usually in an upbeat fashion, although under Gorbachev the problems and tensions in the economy received considerably more notice. This has been a hallmark of Gorbachev's leadership; the volume of criticism and questioning of mid-level management increased significantly. It is part of his campaign to achieve economic growth through reducing corruption and mismanagement, and it found a loud voice on television, both in news and non-news programs.[41]

Stories about political violence are important to both news programs, with political violence on ABC accounting for 11 percent of the stories and on Vremya, 9 percent.[42] While political violence is important for both news programs—and more important for ABC than for Vremya—nonviolent political protest is much less important for ABC. Nonviolent demonstrations and marches make up some 3.4 percent of the primary subjects on Vremya, while ABC has 1.1 percent. That adds up to seventy-eight stories on Vremya and sixteen on ABC. A typical protest story on Vremya might show a demonstration either against the military policies of the United States or the repression—political or economic—of the demonstrators' own government. A viewer might see a sequence of demonstrations around the world—in Chile against Pinochet, in Great Britain against the Thatcher government's economic policies or its willingness to accept American weapons, in Norway and Japan against American nuclear weapons, in South Africa against apartheid—a *tour d'horizon* of American culpability or the discontent of oppressed peoples. American newspeople do not consider these events to be inherently newsworthy. Unless the demonstration exceeds some intuitive threshold of numbers or unless it is linked to an event they are covering extensively (such as a summit), it does not qualify for coverage. The numbers game is really central. George Watson, ABC Washington bureau chief, observed that they covered a pro-abortion march because the organizers had made a conscious attempt to exceed the numbers of the Right to Life march, and there was, in his words, "a vast number of people. . . . if there are 25 people marching in front of the White House pro- or anti-abortion, so what? But if there are a hundred thousand, sure." The other reason he gave for a decision to cover a peaceful demonstration is freshness of subject. This is why demonstrations on the "Amerika" flap and on animal rights got on the air: the subjects were different and new and merited some attention. The kind of political protest story that Vremya does so often would not meet these guidelines.

There is a great difference on the two countries' newscasts in the coverage of natural disasters and accidents, on the one hand, and crime, on the other. As the discussion of Soviet media theory in Chapter One pointed out, in that political system the calamities of life, be they inflicted by human beings or by nature, generally have not been considered to be inherently newsworthy. Quite the contrary, they were usually associated with sensationalism, rapaciousness, and other traits inappropriate to the communist society of the future, and dwelling on them, the official theory pronounced, tended to nourish precisely those elemental tendencies that the state is attempting to transform, if not eliminate. Some of these are not arguments peculiar to the Soviet system, as those who warn the Western media against cultivating copycat criminals or terrorists well know. Stories on natural disasters and accidents as primary subject make up 8 percent of all stories on ABC and only 2 percent on Vremya. An even greater difference is seen in stories where crime is the primary subject: 8 percent on ABC and 1 percent on Vremya. But the Soviets' non-reporting of an event that is important to people does not simply suppress the news. News is then passed around a human chain of observers and participants through hearsay and rumor. As we noted in the previous chapter, the new concern with the effects of the rumor mill and the enhanced credibility it gives to the foreign radios has resulted in policy moves toward more timely reporting of events. Perhaps the most spectacular test of the new emphasis on timeliness was the official reaction to the Chernobyl nuclear reactor accident in May 1986.[43] As we shall see in the next chapter, the differences between Gorbachev's policy and that of his predecessor are particularly strong in this area.

Another predictable difference between Soviet and U.S. news programs concerns that category known as "human interest" and activities of celebrities, which together with sports, accounted for 6 percent of the primary subjects on ABC and 0.2 percent on Vremya.[43] In part, the difference is accounted for by a difference in format. On Vremya the sports news runs after the news proper has finished, and that and the weather have not been included in this analysis. Still, when a sports event of tremendous interest, such as the Karpov-Kasparov championship chess match, takes place, it will break into the news part of the program, but it happens rarely. Light human-interest stories, often the last upbeat story on an American news program— it may be about the shortage of frogs' legs in France or the raising of llamas as pets in California—simply don't exist for Soviet newspeople. Their last stories are also upbeat, but with heft: Soviet news usually ends with one or more stories on culture and the arts, not necessarily high culture, but always officially sponsored culture, whether folk dancing, folk crafts, or opera. Stories on these subjects made up 3 percent (68 stories) of all stories on Vremya and 2 percent (26 stories) on ABC.[45]

Subjects and Stories: The Weight of Time

Nearly three-fourths of the total time on both Vremya and ABC is accounted for by subjects allotted more than 1 percent of total news time.[46] There are eighteen such subjects on ABC and twelve on Vremya. Of these, five can be found on both ABC and Vremya: national elections, official visits, arms control, space achievements, and arts. These are the subjects that together take up 17 percent of ABC's and 25 percent of Vremya's total newstime. The official visits, in addition to the kind of story noted above, included, in this period, Gorbachev's visit to Paris and Foreign Minister Shevardnadze's to Washington, both of which received heavy coverage on both programs. The rest of the time, the mix of subjects is very different, with ABC devoting a very large share of its time to terrorism, disasters and accidents, and nature and the environment. Vremya favors economic progress stories and stories giving official governmental pronouncements and national ceremonies (such as anniversaries and commemorations—National Rocket Forces Day is an example), and operations of Party organizations. The most important subjects and the time they are given on ABC and Vremya are given below.

% Newstime for Selected Primary Subjects (Over 1% for at Least One News Program)

	VREMYA	ABC
Government Policy	8	1
Elections	3	9
National Ceremony	6	1
International Negotiation	1	2
International Meeting (Intergovernmental Organization)	3	1
International Meeting (Nongovernmental Organization)	2	—
Official Visit	14	2
Formal Diplomacy	1	2
Arms Control	2	2
Operations of Party Organizations	8	—
Terrorism	1	8
Military Issues	1	4
Intelligence/Spying	—	3
Space Achievements	3	2
Science/Health	1	11
Media	4	1
Economic Progress	17	1
Economic Problems	1	2
Economic Issues (no evaluation)	—	3
Disaster/Accident	1	8
Nature/Environment	—	2
Crime	1	7
Sports	—	3
Arts	3	2
Total newstime (percent)	81	77

Nearly half the time (47 percent) on Soviet television news is taken up by four kinds of subjects: official governmental policy and pronouncements; official visits; activities of the Communist Party; and economic progress. The last is usually a domestic story, a staged visit to a farm or factory to show the strides being made by ordinary workers and responsible managers. A number of stories about the economy—some five or six—will often begin the evening news. The top five subjects on the American news account for 43 percent of total newstime: national elections, terrorism, science/health, disasters/accidents, and crime. On Vremya, as compared with the American news, the sense of the state, of the center, of the political elites is a far more obvious, powerful, and coherent theme.[47]

Certain subjects emerge when a second subject in the story is considered. For ABC, four subjects became important as tied to other, primary, subjects. They are: the legislative process at the national level (workings of parliaments at home and abroad) and the softer subjects of religion, ethics, and family issues. Civil rights and civil liberties enter as a major claimant of time as secondary subject on ABC and on Vremya. Many of these stories on both programs are about South Africa. Two secondary subjects stand out as most important in the allocation of time: economic progress (13 percent of the total time) and arms control (12 percent). No other subjects on Vremya or ABC even came close to using this much time. The importance of arms control and nuclear issues as tied to some other subject is evidence of something we shall explore later: portrayal on the Soviet news of the underlying reality of the nuclear threat drawing together the nations of the globe into a coherent whole. In fact, as the third subject in a story on Vremya, arms control takes first place in consumption of time.[48]

Stories about economic problems are more important as secondary than as primary stories, both for ABC and for Vremya. On ABC, neutral economics stories—reports neither about problems nor about achievements—are given more time as primary story and problems in the economy take up more time as secondary subject. On Vremya, progress and achievements take up most time, both as primary and secondary subject, but the problem stories move from 1 percent of the total time to 5 percent (considering the length of the Soviet news, a significant difference). It is the story on economic problems that comes closest to investigative reporting, Soviet style. A striking example of a story devoted to an economic problem was aired on Vremya in October 1985. This story showed an inspector from Moscow castigating the director and deputy director of a factory. They had accumulated unsold products (fittings for nuclear power plants). The inspector—long black leather coat and clipboard—stood outside with them in front of piles of pipes overgrown with weeds. He interrogated them, first reading figures from the documents he had brought with him, then waiting impatiently for their self-absolving, waffling explanations. The inspector asked where the money for these unsold products had come from. The answer: from "credits." "Credits" were clarified by the inspector to mean the operating funds of the factory, including the wage fund, which was debited to account for the unsold inventory. The managers were sharply asked what they thought the workers were going to say about the fact that their wages were prevented from rising by these faulty managerial practices. The answer: "The working class can't say anything good about it." The managers, sweating profusely, eyes darting, visibly uncomfortable, promised to fix the whole thing within a year. Not good enough, the inspector retorts and announces that the ministry will have to deal with this one. This story—trial by television—was clearly part of the swelling Gorbachev rhetoric that the economy was each person's responsibility and changes in the way people related to their jobs would be high on the agenda of the 27th Party Congress in 1986. A 1986 story in *Pravda* took a critical look at Vremya and asserted that the news is meaningful insofar as it touches the everyday interests of the public. Those kinds of stories are seen more frequently on Vremya, it went on, but it is still rare to name names and place the responsibility squarely on the shoulders of the guilty. More often, some abstract cause is cited.[49] Not so with this story, which had no hesitation in blaming its squirming prey, and that is what official policy is calling for. This story was part of the new look. Its hard-hitting investigative reporting style has entered the broadcast day in a new program that debuted in 1987. "Spotlight of Perestroika" comes on every day for ten minutes right after the news. It is a prime-time spot for this mini-"60 Minutes" show. Individuals are charged with breaking the law; people who carry out illegal acts are questioned about their blind obedience to orders; the practice of accusation by anonymous letter is stigmatized. In short, the topics and treatment—all relating to daily life in the Soviet Union—make it one of the most widely watched shows on Soviet television.

The Linkage of Subject and Country

What kinds of subjects define individual countries or regions? How does the viewer see a country—in terms of what kinds of stories? ABC sees much of the world as the site of political violence and natural disasters and accidents. South America, for example, is shown in two-thirds of all stories on that region as a locus of political violence, political protest, and crime. Over half of all stories about the Middle East deal with political violence. Central America is seen in just under 90 percent of all stories on the region as a place for political violence, natural disasters and accidents, and military issues.[50] Rather different is coverage of non-NATO Western Europe. Although it does not receive very much attention, it is seen mainly in terms of the more "normal," everyday processes of domestic politics, international politics, and the arts, which together account for three-fourths of all stories. Coverage of domestic issues in various regions of the world is not a high priority for ABC. During the five months of our analysis, about one-third of all stories about the Indian subcontinent were related to the domestic politics there; that was the largest percentage of stories on the domestic politics of any region in the world, and it occurred because of the assassination of Indira Gandhi and the subsequent election of Rajiv Gandhi. Although many regions of the world are identified primarily with violent events, the largest share of the political violence stories actually takes place at home. Half of the total number of stories on political violence take place in the United States and the NATO countries. For the rest, the political violence stories are found next in the Middle East (just over one-fifth); Central America (11 percent), and the U.S.S.R. and Warsaw Pact (5 percent) and South Africa (5 percent). Disasters and accidents, one of the most popular subjects on ABC, are found mostly in the United States/NATO cluster (about two-thirds of the total number of disaster stories are here) and then Central America (18 percent), South and East Africa (6 percent), and the Indian subcontinent (6 percent). But even though these stories are found so often at home, they are balanced there with other kinds of subjects that define the operations of a mature state. As we noted above, there are regions of the world which are defined almost exclusively by disruptive and anomic events.

For Vremya, most regions of the world are portrayed as acting in predictable ways: engaging in official visits, having elections and administering their economies, negotiating, and generally following patterns of governance at home and interacting on the international scene. Much more emphasis is put on the institutional procedures of domestic and international politics everywhere in the world. These two categories account for over two-thirds of all the stories on Central and West Africa, over 80 percent of the stories on North Africa, two-thirds of the stories on Asia, two-thirds of the stories on non-NATO/non-Warsaw Pact Eastern Europe, two-thirds of the stories on non-NATO Western Europe, over half the stories on the Caribbean and almost half the stories on the Indian subcontinent. There are still some regions, though, which are seen almost exclusively as arenas for turmoil, disaster, and violence: South and East Africa (and in this grouping, South Africa accounts for the heavy coverage of political violence, while Ethiopia is the scene of famine and drought), Central America (Nicaragua figures heavily here, as does Mexico, with considerable earthquake footage), and the South Pacific (because of the revolt in the French possession of New Caledonia).

The political violence stories on Vremya focus principally (and almost equally) on the United States and its NATO partners (22 percent of all political violence stories—much less than ABC's 50 percent) and South and East Africa (mainly South Africa—20 percent—much more than ABC's 5 percent); then the Middle East (15 percent—not very different from ABC's); Central America (12 percent—virtually the same as ABC's); the Indian subcontinent, which includes Afghanistan (11 percent); and South America (8 percent). The last two are a very small proportion of ABC's agenda of political violence stories; Vremya leaves the Soviet Union and the Warsaw Pact countries off its list.

Disaster and accident stories, one of the most popular categories on ABC, appear on that network mainly in connection with domestic news and news of the NATO countries (about two-thirds of the total number of disaster stories). Central America provided another 18 percent of these stories. Just under two-thirds of Vremya's disaster stories were identified with Central America and the United States and the NATO countries (31 percent and 30 percent, respectively). Vremya is attentive to natural and man-made problems in the United States—covering hurricanes, forest fires, explosions of fuel depots—very often with pictures. Crime, both on ABC and on Vremya, is mainly a phenomenon related to the United States and its allies: relatively little coverage goes beyond this group of countries on either program.[51]

As for coverage of each other, the linkage between country and subject for the two superpower clusters is rather different. ABC looks at the Soviet Union and its Warsaw Pact allies mainly in terms of six kinds of subjects: formal international politics (about one-fourth of all stories); citizenship (civil rights, emigration, immigration—13 percent); political violence (10 percent); arms control (10 percent); formal national politics (domestic institutional procedures—9 percent); and sports and human interest (7 percent). Vremya's list is both more institutionally oriented and more security focused, giving formal international politics first place (17 percent); then formal national politics (for example, coverage of the American presidential election—15 percent); political violence (10 percent); political protest (10 percent); arms control (8 percent); military issues (non-nuclear questions, such as conventional arms deployment and production and military budgets)—7 percent; media stories (coverage of the media of other countries) are used very frequently as a legitimating source, and the coverage of Gorbachev's interview in *Time* was very heavy—7 percent; and crime (5 percent).[52] It is a picture colored by security threats, conflict, and violence.

Both Soviet and American media people complain about the coverage of their country by the other. Both argue that few subjects are covered and that the pattern is repetitious and negative. We will look later at the degree to which each news broadcast actually produces opinionated newswriting—the clear and unambiguous use of emotionally loaded evaluations by the anchor or correspondent. Here we look at the range of subjects: is it too narrow, is it a fair approximation of the reality the correspondents see? When Alexander Shalnev was White House correspondent for TASS in 1985, he saw in American television coverage of his country: "three or four topics: drunkenness is one; then [the] dissident movement, second; or what is going on in the higher echelons of the Communist Party or the government of the Soviet Union and . . . problems in the economy, all these long lines outside shops. Agreed, we have problems . . . but [we] have achievements, too." In Shalnev's four years in Washington he couldn't remember a single story on Soviet culture. Vladimir Dunaev, the correspondent for Soviet television in Washington, agrees:

> Quite honestly I think your coverage is bad—all three networks . . . What people are doing, coming to Siberia and making a story for ABC, for the party congress, that's really cheap. [They] cover it like cowboy[s]; . . . Siberia is a prison place where you keep camps. . . . Well, probably because they're followed, accompanied by a Soviet comrade or somebody, they're annoyed by that. I think that Russia should be shown not as a communist paradise, but as a big, interesting, changing country, with lots of problems, with a lot of shortcomings, but like America. Could you find something typical for America? I don't think so, because everything is typical for America. America is rich, is noble, is proud . . . is desperate, and is poor.

Washington-based Soviet newspaper correspondent Alexei Burmistenko put it in comparative perspective. He is not far off the pattern that shows up in the analysis of the five months of the news:

> I think your media, in general, are guilty, as well as we here [are] guilty in covering American affairs to Soviet audiences, in stressing the negative sides and playing certain favorite stories: dissidents versus unemployment, totalitarian state versus high rate of crime . . . So I think both sides do not present a balanced and objective picture . . . It's difficult to do something about it: we have our pressures; your people in Moscow have their pressures.

American television producers I talked with suggested that potential stories about the Soviet Union, as all foreign news, must compete to get on the air. Given the networks' preference for domestic over foreign news, that competition is intense. ABC Washington bureau chief George Watson observed that anyone with a particular interest in a particular country is unlikely to find sufficient coverage on the network news.

> Our problem is that we have a limited quantity of time and the Soviet story is in competition with all of the domestic stories and all the foreign stories . . . on a given day the competition for airtime is intense. . . .

But there is another dimension to the problem: American newspeople all say that the restrictions governing news coverage in the Soviet Union make it very difficult to produce stories that would be competitive in the scramble for airtime. If the access of Soviet newsmen to American officials is defined as limited, the access of Americans in Moscow is also extremely slim. There are also logistical problems: Watson noted that the ABC bureau in Moscow is too small to permit coverage of more than Moscow. With only one correspondent, one producer, and half a camera crew (cameraman but not sound technician), they are reluctant to pull everyone away from Moscow and leave it uncovered. Thus, news tends to be "Moscowcentric." Roone Arledge and a number of his senior vice presidents tried to make the case for expansion and went to Moscow for that purpose, but these are matters that involve reciprocity and bilateral diplomacy. The ability to move around the country with more personnel could result in more "slice-of-life" stories, as Watson put it. This kind of coverage has found its way into special programming, but often founders on the definition of newsworthy. These stories are essentially features and, as such, would come up against fast-breaking hard news stories at home and abroad. The real question for the American media people is how to reduce restrictions on hard news stories that would be able to compete for space on the evening news. Again, in Watson's words:

> If one had access and ability to look at the Soviet space program and ask and answer some of the questions we are doing of our own space program, and compare and contrast, I guarantee you that piece is going to compete successfully with others struggling to get on the air.

CBS producer Brian Healy said some things were improving. Only two or three years ago it was difficult to find English-speaking Soviets in the United States who would appear on American news and public affairs programs. "Now they're all over the place. Somebody over there got smart." He argues that the network does as well as can be done, given the restrictions, but changes will be only cosmetic as long as the severe restrictions within the Soviet Union prevail. But even there, he sees improvement.

To some extent, the new Soviet attention to the foreign press and international information might usher in some very real gains. If the practices of press conferences and briefings were complemented by reductions in the restrictions governing news-gathering, the "Soviet story" would become much more competitive on the evening news. The lifting of restrictions might also permit a different kind of coverage. Some Soviet correspondents in Washington did a study of American coverage of the 27th Congress of the Soviet Communist Party in February 1986. They found that although the media showed a welcome upsurge in interest in the Soviet Union, the packaging was, in one correspondent's words, a "sort of soap opera," featuring Gorbachev as a young, upcoming man. They objected that coverage of personalities slighted the substance of the issues—his changes in economic and other domestic policies. The human interest/entertainment element of the American television news, the need to reckon with the interests of the audience, does, as we have seen, encourage dramatic and personalized stories. On the other hand, the impediments to ferreting out harder stories are often so formidable that alternative coverage is often impossible. That is what Schmemann was trying to convey in his careful talk with Pozner on Soviet television.

Subjects and Format: Talking Heads and Pictures

The way subjects are portrayed, the vividness or drama of the format, should tell us something about the way the broadcasts might be received and assimilated. American newscasts favor pictures wherever possible. Every subject cluster is accompanied by pictures in the vast majority of cases. The only subject that is much under 75 percent pictures is the one on economic issues. This category, when primary subject, is shown with pictures 57 percent of the time (because of Dan Cordtz's commentary on the economy on ABC). When economic issues are tied to some other subject, the usual preference for pictures obtains. Some subjects—arms control and citizenship issues (immigration, emigration, and civil rights)—are broadcast about two-thirds of the time with pictures. The rest run from 71 percent to 92 percent for pictures.[53] Thus, with the exception of the analysis of economic news (done with a talking head), the news on ABC is shown with pictures most or almost all of the time.

On Vremya, that is not the case, and there is a real difference between which subjects are chosen for picture stories and which are relegated to talking heads reading the text. On the whole, Vremya opts much more for the more controlled and conservative presentation of the news-reader. For example, stories about crime are presented by the anchors alone more than two-thirds of the time. But there are five subjects that are unusual, in that pictures are used more than 75 percent of the time.[54] This is in strong contrast to most other stories, which are presented with pictures only 21 percent to 58 percent of the time. If a story is about space and science, it is very likely to have visuals (81 percent). Here are some of the greatest achievements of the Soviet Union, and they are extremely important to those who program the mass media. We should not think of the Soviet space program as in any way peripheral to their image of themselves or as problematic. The stories are majestic and compelling and feature footage that is sometimes breathtaking, as, for example, when they filmed the crew during lift-off, from the inside of the capsule, responding to mission control on the ground as the engines fire and the crew, dwarfed by the huge apparatus on which they are perched, makes its way into space. The re-entries are covered in detail, and since contact is made on land there is a sudden enormous puff of dust as the capsule hits the vast brown plain of Central Asia. Stories include coverage of scientific experiments in space, cosmonauts' observations upon return, medical evaluation of the cosmonauts. These tend to be long stories; the cosmonauts are humanized—they speak modestly and simply. Space stories were given very marked status several times by being placed among the leaders in the sequence of stories for the nightly news—in our coding period, a space story was the lead story one night. Given the rigid and inflexible order of the Soviet news, with governmental pronouncements first, then economic stories, then international stories, and only then science and arts stories, this signals extraordinary attention to the space program.

A second story for which the Soviet preference for the spoken word is reversed relates to disaster stories (81 percent in pictures). Many of the disaster stories in the period we analyzed were about the famine in Ethiopia, and they tended, increasingly, to become stories not so much about the famine itself as about Soviet assistance to that country. There were many pictures of Aeroflot planes bringing food to the hungry (and Soviet news indicated that at least three-fourths of all food deliveries were made by Soviet transport). Since the delivery system was Soviet—and conspicuously Soviet—it is not surprising that the American contribution of foodstuffs was underplayed. And it should not surprise Americans, who were so active in the relief effort, that they got relatively little credit. Many of the Soviet news stories covered the official Ethiopian reaction to assistance from all sources, and in one, at Ethiopian leader Mengistu's press conference, he angrily dismissed what he referred to as the American desire to buy people with their dollars.

The political protest story is very likely to be a story with visuals (77 percent). The peaceful march or demonstration is, as noted above, not very frequent on American news, but it is on the Soviet news, and it is dramatic. The footage is sometimes provided by a team in the field, but often bought from an international source, rarely identified. It is often unclear how many people are demonstrating; sometimes the groups look thin; sometimes they are more densely packed. Leading activists are interviewed, but more often these are pictured and narrated events. There is usually a sequence of stories strung together, example after example of people massed to protest American weapons on their soil or what are identified as American-backed domestic oppressors—a band of discontent and anger spanning the globe.

Stories on the economic issues are likely to have pictures

rather than talking heads (80 percent). For the most part, these are stories about the Soviet economy; they are placed in the front part of every news broadcast and form a sequence of stories, often upbeat and staged. The stories move from one region to another, from industry to agriculture. In each, workers are shown proudly discussing their new methods and equipment, and reciting the progress they have made—how many more pipes have been fabricated, how new computers have brought automation, how cattle feed has been stored. These stories, with obviously memorized responses, are in sharp contrast to the international stories, which use footage that appears spontaneous and dramatic. The economy stories are a very large proportion of Soviet television news, making up about one-fifth of the total number of stories.

Finally, the arts are almost always covered not by talking heads but with pictures (81 percent). Here, too, the audience sees what are considered to be the strengths of the Soviet Union in an area accorded high prestige by the regime. The importance of the arts is not merely lip-service, nor is it only for export, where the Soviets compete effectively with the West. The arts, from folk to classical, are key to the self-image of the Soviet Union. The creativity not only of professionals, but also of amateurs, not only of Russians, but also of the national minorities, not only in Moscow and Leningrad, but all over the country, is shown again and again. Although, on other programs, the viewer will see pop or rock music, the features at the end of the nightly news show the more pedigreed forms of art and clearly indicate the regime's preferences.

Format and Elapsed Time: How Much Time for Talking Heads?

The importance of pictures for American television news is obvious to anyone who has watched the evening news or who has observed life in the newsroom. For the five months of our project, we found that ABC devoted 88 percent of total newstime to stories with pictures: the stories could show a correspondent in the field or filmed footage, which the anchor narrated. Occasionally a story will be shown live from location. Most of the film stories will be of the first type: the field correspondent. This type of story makes up 83 percent of the total newstime. The rest of the pictures will have a voice-over by the anchor. The Soviet news broadcast is less likely to show pictures. Only 69 percent of its newstime is allocated to pictures. Vremya splits the visual stories, with correspondents in the field generating 38 percent and voice-overs accounting for 31 percent.

The voice-over, which CBS calls the tel-op, is an interesting format, and the reasons for using it are not as simple as one might expect. In some cases a voice-over is used when a crew is not on the spot and the network acquires the footage from a service. That happens far more frequently on the Soviet news than on ABC. As we saw, the Soviets are intensely interested in areas where they cannot place their bureaus, and therefore they must purchase the footage from international suppliers. The voice-over must then be used to provide the narration. It is also the case that the Soviets have economic constraints that limit how many correspondents they can put in the field and what kind of crew can be assigned to them. Until the mid 1980s, when massive cost-cutting and downsizing hit the American networks, it did not seem to be an American problem. When Vladimir Dunaev worked in London, Moscow did not provide a Soviet crew and was having difficulty paying for a British crew, which was charging about 200 pounds per film. Dunaev was desperate for pictures and worked out an arrangement with Visnews, the international service. Visnews would permit Dunaev to go out with its crew and, at the end of a session, would give him one minute for his own story. For this they would charge the equivalent of about ten dollars a story, but the events and the schedule were entirely up to Visnews. One day, Visnews called to say they were going to cover a war-games championship. Dunaev observed, talked to people, and found one participant, a British officer from Ulster. He sat with him and talked about Northern Ireland, about the Bogside troubles, and that was his story. All in all, he worked with Visnews to produce twelve stories, and all because there was no money. It was, he says, the most valuable lesson in journalism he ever learned. Had he followed his own bent, he would have covered "something revolutionary, strikes, singing [the] International . . . It's one color, but [this way] you have the whole picture." Going out with

Visnews pulled him into a view of Great Britain that he would never have got and enabled him to see far more than his earlier narrow vision would have permitted, he says, so that, he recalled, "when I got my money I was already thinking differently."

Anchors also do voice-overs on American television when the pictures come in very short segments, say, fifteen seconds, or when the picture speaks for itself and there's not much else to say. As an NBC producer remarked, "Sometimes there's simply an arresting picture, like someone falling off a balcony somewhere. There's nothing more you can say about it than it's simply arresting and you'd run that." Sometimes, too, when the network is following up on a story that needs to be finished off, it will do a voice-over. Chris Wallace of NBC was quoted as saying that " 'They decided at the "Nightly News" that they were tired of the [Margaret] Heckler story [about her removal from the Department of Health and Human Services and appointment as Ambassador to Ireland] . . . so they will [do] just a brief piece of voice-over, with Heckler and the President talking, which Tom . . . [Brokaw] will narrate. They didn't want a standup piece on it tonight.' "[55]

But there is still another reason for voice-overs, a reason that suggests that they have an important role in assuring comprehension and coherence. One producer told me that "there's a theory . . . that the more the anchor does, the better . . . that people know who the anchor is and you can get their attention better if he does something other than simply lead in and lead out of pieces." In that way, people will also understand the stories better.[56] ABC's Washington bureau chief observed that this is something the anchors continually press for. "From time to time the executive producers have done that [decided to have voice-overs instead of correspondent pieces] in all the broadcasts in an effort to involve the anchor more, so [that] the anchor is not just a traffic cop introducing correspondents, but . . . has a more visible and meaningful role in the program. The anchors are always keen to do this . . . [and] are looking for ways to expand their role in the program. . . ." Eliminating the field correspondent altogether also saves money and is another powerful justification for the voice-over. As the networks downsized in the 1980s and bureaus closed both at home and abroad, the rationale was heard more and more for concentrating on the anchor and a few "star" reporters.

On Vremya, where coherence and a particular type of intelligibility are considered essential, the heavy reliance on voice-overs might make of an economic and political necessity an advantage in persuasion. That would be so especially if the anchors exhibited the personalized "propriety" over the news that their American counterparts have. The impassive, faceless Soviet anchors do not regard this overlay of personality as professional, and that surely limits the degree of confidence and emotional attachment the audience experiences. Even less effective is straight reading; the anchor reading the news from a paper on the desk is no match for pictures.[57] As *Pravda* wrote, the onus should be on the anchor for *not* providing pictures. Our analysis shows that the anchor alone, reading the news, takes up, on the average, over a *quarter* of the entire news broadcast, in contrast to a mere *6 percent* for ABC.[58]

In the next chapter, we will look at other dimensions of news in the Soviet Union: the particular context that provides the explanatory framework and sample some important and innovative individual programs. Additionally, we shall look at the rather marked differences that occurred when Gorbachev took over the reins of leadership.

CHAPTER FOUR

Dimensions of News
and Their Setting

News sometimes bears a heavy load. This "freight" is the weight of opinion, the biases and views, of the broadcaster. It is the temperature of emotion. The history of American newsgathering is well known—as it moved through "yellow journalism" to value objective, impersonal reporting, whose sway was to be challenged in the sixties by the new reporting that put emotion and an often ideologized context back in the picture. The dominant mode is still the appearance of objectivity. I say appearance, because every news program must be selective in what it chooses from the millions of events that happen "out there" in the world. Choosing which events to report necessarily skews the relationship to reality.[1] By their choices, news programs make sense of the world and attempt to form the agendas of their publics. George Gerbner has written that "all news is views," and he is right in that our media function within the context and constraints of the system in which they are embedded.[2] These are subtle but important ways to understand objectivity as it functions within our media system; it involves fairness—the inclusion of opposing points of view; it rejects overt evaluation and judgment on the part of the anchor or correspondent. That is the style of our news presentation, but it does not eliminate the powerful role the media play in shaping political opinions through the selection and presentation of events.[3] The situation is radically different in the Soviet media system, where interpretation is clearly and openly a part of the broadcaster's function. Nonetheless, different as they are, both systems do attempt to make the world intelligible to their viewers. In the previous chapter, I showed the kinds of subjects associated with countries and regions. A story may be negative if it shows a one-sided picture of the reality it covers. This is the principle of selection. However, there are still other ways of explaining the world to the huge audience of television viewers. The two most important methods by which stories are inserted into a coherent cognitive grid are responsibility and affect. As with so much else, in the Soviet and American contexts the use of the tool of opinionated newswriting will also be quite different.

The Responsibility of Countries and Explaining the World

The Soviet political doctrine, as we saw in Chapter One, does impose the requirement of coherence. The world, teeming with events, past and present, must be a coherent place and follow a discernible path. The key to the understanding of what may seem chaotic and random happenings has been provided by Marxism and its later Leninist variant. It was Marx who, through his painstaking study of the empirical data of his time and the overlay of grand theory, claimed to have founded the scientific study of human interaction and to have grounded it in the "real" world of human history. Thus he made the world explainable, and the Soviet news, imbued with this principle, suggests to its vast audience that what it portrays, no matter how varied and disparate the events, is generated by the unfolding of known and knowable laws.

On one level, both Soviet and American news programs aim for coherence. After all, both want their audiences to understand and remember what they have seen and heard. The way that the American networks do this is by making of each story a kind of drama and by clustering stories into packages with some thematic relationship.[4] Because audiences for television are much larger and more heterogeneous than are audiences for any other medium, the requirement for clarity and comprehensibility is that much more critical. According to one media researcher, "producers apparently act on the intuitive assumption that this packaging [of items into clusters from the same category] of isolated events into more meaningful combinations makes them more readily learned by the audience. . . . this reasoning would seem to be fallacious. The attempt to arrive at simplicity and clarity by packaging items into one category of news may in fact represent one of the fundamental reasons why people forget the news that the television organisations, at tremendous expense and effort, have prepared and distributed."[5] The point here is that, as other media scholars have noted, "recall of news stories often shows a meltdown effect, where elements of one story merge or are confused with elements of other similar stories."[6] It may be the very similarity of the stories—or, more accurately, the narrative flow that forces a similarity on stories that may co-exist only in a strained way (I have in mind the cluster that combined a freighter run aground on a posh Florida beachfront estate and the commissioning of a nuclear submarine in Connecticut)—that hinders recall and learning. Therefore, " . . . while it may be useful to draw similarities between stories, providing distinctive features for stories is also important. Unless distinctive features, which may be used as retrieval cues at recall, are present in stories, misremembering news items may be likely. . . ."[7]

Although the American networks rely primarily on this narrative flow and the imposition of a sense of coherence through packaging, there is a more direct and, for the Soviet news, a much more important tool. In Soviet thinking, the clearest and most powerful way that the news reinforces a sense of coherence is by imputing responsibility. For the Soviet news, this is the key to explaining the world. From Vremya there emerges a network of responsibility: there are certain actors who exert decisive influence in parts of the world beyond their borders. In some cases, the influence is exerted through the activities of secondary, or proxy, actors.[8] This is not a factor that detects emotional loading or affect; the assignment of responsibility can be presented as a matter of evident logic and very matter of factly. Later, we will look at emotional coloration—the anchor's or correspondent's use of clearly inflammatory (or laudatory) judgments. During the five months of our analysis, the assignment of direct responsibility to a country for an act or event outside its borders was made in only 0.1 percent of all international stories on ABC and 18 percent of all international stories on Vremya. ABC declared in two stories that two countries were responsible for manipulating events elsewhere. They are: South Africa and Iran. Specifically, Iran was said to be fomenting terrorism in Lebanon, and South Africa was embarking on a campaign (in September of 1985) to influence the American Congressional vote on sanctions.

Two stories contrast vividly with the 265 cases of responsibility that Vremya assigned during the five months. Even though Vremya covered some 107 countries on its broadcasts during this period, only twelve are assigned responsibility. Over *three quarters* of all responsibility stories implicate the United States.[9] The state actor most responsible for the negative events occurring all around the world is the United States. The culpability of the United States is shown in stories about a variety of subjects: formal national and international political processes, arms control, political violence, political protest, military issues, espionage and intelligence operations, stories about the media, economic issues, the legislative process, civil rights and immigration/emigration, disaster stories, law and crime stories. It is a menu of subjects that is larger than that of any other "responsible" country—the range of issues in which the United States meddles elsewhere in the world is shown as much broader than that of any of the other eleven countries identified as guilty of interference in the affairs of others.

A smaller cast of characters is identified as countries responsible for events in another country, but perpetrated by a third country. Here, too, the United States bears most of the responsibility, followed by Israel, Pakistan, and Japan.

There is a particular kind of glue that attaches many of the responsibility stories to the United States and creates American involvement in every part of the globe. Orthodox Marxists might expect at this point to see the impact of economic issues: world imperialism, monopoly capital, impoverishment of the proletariat. But that is not the case for the Soviet media in the latter part of the twentieth century. The specter of the United States is not drawn primarily in the frock coat of the bloated capitalist ensnaring the dependent world. The image has changed to the United

States as the keeper of nuclear hostages. This was the image used by General Secretary Gorbachev in his keynote address to the 27th Party Congress in 1986, and it is the most forceful representation of the United States on Soviet television news. It is, moreover, the issue which to a very great extent provides a unified and unifying view of the world. The key issue of arms control, disarmament, and nuclear strategic themes is one for which the United States is held uniquely responsible. It is American obstructionism that prevents reduction of the nuclear threat; it is the American obsession with strategic superiority that fuels the spiraling arms race. It very often links one story to another by its position as second subject, tying many different subjects to the underlying concern with nuclear issues. In the very frequent stories about the official visit to the Soviet Union of heads of state or other high officials, one of the most important issues raised between host and visitor will be the looming nuclear threat to the entire world and the role of the United States as responsible. The official visit story makes up 40 percent of all *secondary* subjects of American responsibility.

The imputing of responsibility to the United States is, in a very significant way, unique. Only the United States operates on a global scale. There is really only one *global actor*, one global force creating turmoil and misery, and that is the United States. Only the United States reaches beyond its region to interfere with the processes of development and progress all over the world. This portrayal on the Soviet news gives by implication tremendous reach and tremendous power to the United States. The other actors, no matter how harshly vilified, tend to be confined within their regions. The United States, unlike all those other countries, cannot be caged. This makes the United States *the* other global power; the sense of bi-polarism on the Soviet news is very marked.

But there are still some eleven other countries which do meddle and manipulate what goes on in other countries. Only one exercises a positive influence or responsibility: Syria is praised for its influence in dampening the civil war in Lebanon. The remaining ten countries are forces of negative influence. They are: Israel (second to the United States in culpability), South Africa, Pakistan, Thailand, Great Britain, Canada, France, West Germany, South Korea, and Japan. Most often these states are linked to stories on political violence, although South Africa, Great Britain, and Pakistan are also involved in stories about formal domestic and international processes. Most of these stories and most of the charges of manipulation take place within the region of the responsible actor. Israel, which is very often judged guilty of interference, affects events in Libya, Syria, Lebanon, Jordan, and Tunisia. Pakistan supports the guerrillas (called bandits and terrorists) in Afghanistan and the Sikh separatists in India.[10] Thailand is responsible for sedition and violence in Laos and Vietnam; South Korea threatens North Korea; South Africa is linked to events in Tanzania, Angola, and Zimbabwe. Japan is linked to militarism in the East and, as American ally, unhelpful in the quest to dampen the arms race, but it receives none of the emotionally charged epithets that most other "responsible" countries do. Great Britain is guilty of malign influence in the affairs of the Republic of Ireland and, of course, Northern Ireland. West Germany is called revanchist for not accepting the postwar "realities" of Europe. Only two countries are portrayed as guilty parties for events outside their regions, but one involves a former dependency—France is blamed for actions taking place in Chad. Canada is charged, in a story from the French wire service and reported on Vremya, for secretly providing the "pro-American regime" of South Korea with information necessary for production of nuclear weapons.

The notion of responsibility, of the puppetmaster pulling strings around the world, is the single most important method by which Soviet news imposes intelligiblity and coherence. Such an overlay of culpability is rendered necessary particularly because, as we saw earlier, the news agenda is so significantly Western. Had the Soviet news been able to be so selective that nothing but welcome news entered its arena, the need to explain the world in its terms might not be necessary. But that degree of selectivity is not possible in the modern world. There is a clear sense, on the Soviets' part, of the permeable boundaries through which information flows and of the need to set its own agenda with its population, before another is formed. The alternative is, therefore, to explain and relate all those hostile or retrogressive events in terms of a knowable reality based on familiar doctrine. The new term in the equation—that of the nuclear age and its threat—has become the most important term.

Tinting the News:
The Use of Loaded Words

Responsibility can be assigned to a country in the guise of factual reporting. It can be quite separate from emotionality in presenting the news. We also took account of opinionated newswriting, stories in which the anchor or correspondent quite clearly used loaded words—positive or negative—about individual countries. For inclusion in this category, I should emphasize, we required deliberate and very clear emotional loading. A flick of the eyebrow or an inflection in the voice was not enough. Nor did we include the many stories on the Soviet news in which a negative side of America or another country was covered—if it was covered as news and in an apparently factual way without the intrusion of vituperation on the part of the representative of state television, the correspondent or anchor. Soviet wording that did qualify for inclusion in this category were adjectives commonly used for Israel ("criminal"), Chile ("fascist regime"), and South Africa ("racist regime"). Not surprisingly, we found very few instances of affect or emotion on ABC; it runs against professional canons. In fact, we found only one case that comes close to emotional loading in the entire five months; it occurred in a story on the fifth anniversary of the Soviet invasion of Afghanistan. The correspondent described the Soviet methods of warfare and remarked that they are using aircraft "for what's been called the campaign of migratory genocide."[11] It is not quite as direct as Soviet language would be, and it wears a cloak of objectivity by asserting that the highly pejorative term has been advanced by others, not the reporter himself, but it is, in fact, an example of evaluation by the broadcaster rather than his sources.

On Vremya, however, we found that a total of 250 stories put forth a clearly emotionally tinged reading of the news. That makes up 17 percent of all international stories—almost the same percentage of stories that assign responsibility.[12] About a quarter of these stories present a positive view of a country in a story; the rest are negative. Some countries are given only a negative or only a positive treatment; others are mixed. Vremya gives unmixed positive evaluations to nineteen countries: Cuba, Argentina, Switzerland, East Germany, Rumania, Bulgaria, Yugoslavia, Finland, Ethiopia, Mozambique, Angola, Algeria, Iraq, South Yemen, North Yemen, India, Mongolia, Kampuchea (Cambodia), Vietnam, and Japan. The vast majority of these countries are allies of the Soviet Union or have important trade or other ties to the Soviet Union. Most are considered, at the very least, to be friendly to the Soviets.

The Soviet Union is Argentina's most important commercial partner, and it is a relationship that is expanding. Beginning in the 1970s, the U.S.S.R. began to absorb increasing amounts of Argentine agricultural exports, dramatically increasing its trade commitments as Argentina's relations worsened with the United States because of the military junta's human rights violations and its war with Great Britain over the Malvinas, or Falkland Islands. Even though the military junta cracked down on domestic leftists, it did not ban the Communist Party (PCA), and Moscow gave rhetorical, if not material, support to the generals' ill-fated attempt to dislodge the British. By the end of 1980, Soviet grain purchases from Argentina had increased enormously, owing to the embargo the American government had imposed in retaliation for the Soviet invasion of Afghanistan. After the military junta had been deposed, relations developed on other fronts as well, with Aeroflot flights to Buenos Aires, new multiyear trade agreements, direct contacts between the Soviet Union and several Argentine provincial governments, and a visit by President Alfonsin to Moscow in 1986. Still another agreement allowed for exchanges of visits by military officers and the posting of military attachés in Buenos Aires and Moscow.[13] Clearly, Argentina occupies a very important place in the list of countries which maintain large-scale interactions with the Soviet Union. That Argentina is in the Western Hemisphere only adds to the salience.

North Yemen was much praised on the occasion of a state visit to Moscow by its leader. Moscow clearly wanted to extend its influence beyond its socialist friend in South Yemen. The relationship with North Yemen has been see-sawing in a delicate balance for several years. Fearful most of all of aggression from South Yemen (a closely bound Soviet client), North Yemen has over the years received American arms through Saudi Arabia as intermediary and banker. These sales have been carefully circumscribed in the amounts and kinds of weapons North Yemen has been allowed, while its ambitions and demands—and most of all—its increasing restiveness under the patronage and, it feared, increasing control of Saudi Arabia, spurred a turn toward the Soviet Union for both arms (which have been increasing), and advisers, much to the consternation of the United States. It is a precarious state; North Yemen has counted on Soviet friendship and arms to hold its southern neighbor at bay, while attempting to limit the Soviet presence.[14] Yugoslavia, after years of fierce independence under Marshal Tito, is, once again, a more congenial friend to the Soviets. Preoccupied as it is by internal economic problems and the danger of political fragmentation, it is unlikely to pursue a course the Soviets judge ill-considered. Switzerland, as host to arms control talks and the summit, got a warm nod from the news. There is one country that also was, surprisingly, the subject of two stories, both of which used very positive language. Japan is not a compliant friend of the Soviets and then Prime Minister Nakasone's calls for increases in the military budget deeply concerned the Soviets. Japan is, as we saw above, one of those responsible for negative events in the world. However, its responsibility is portrayed in neutral, unemotional language. That responsibility is imputed without emotionality is undoubtedly a reflection of a deep ambivalence in Moscow's attitude toward Japan: on the one hand Moscow displays a serious interest in prospects for the trade it badly needs, and on the other, deep concern with Nakasone's defense build-up.[15] The positive language about Japan is the result of a visit to Moscow by the leader of Japan's Socialist Party in September 1985, a visit that was accorded very high-level status and symbolism, with Gorbachev filmed sitting with his advisers across the table, a scene reserved for serious high-level discussions.

There are also countries that come in only for negatively laden, in some cases abusive, emotional terms. These countries are: El Salvador, Paraguay, Chile, Uruguay, Great Britain, France, Italy,[16] South Africa, Israel, People's Republic of China, South Korea, Pakistan, Thailand, and the Philippines. This is not to say that every mention of these countries carries negative emotional freight. That is hardly the case, considering that less than a fifth of all news stories carry emotional baggage, but when there are emotional terms associated with these countries, they are always negative. In the case of China, as the previous chapter notes, a

later, 1986 story was unusual in that it was not about formal
political issues, but the attractive elements of Chinese consumer
goods on view in Moscow.

There are also three countries that are given mixed emotional
signals, sometimes vilified, sometimes praised. They are the
United States, Lebanon, and West Germany. But the weights of
positive and negative certainly are not equal. Ninety-six percent
of the emotion-laden references to the United States are negative. In fact, references to the United States account for almost
two-fifths of all the emotionally colored stories. Four other countries are loaded with considerable emotional baggage: Three
have negative evaluations: South Africa (which has 10 percent of
the affect stories), Israel (20 percent), and Chile (5 percent); and
one, India (6 percent), has a distinctly and warmly positive loading. Together with the United States, these countries account for
two-thirds of all the unambiguous and blatant emotional output
of the Soviet news. The United States, South Africa, Israel, and
Chile account for *three-quarters* of all the broadcaster's negative
emotional vocabulary on the Soviet news.

Emotion and Responsibility: The Total Share

Roughly a fifth of the stories assign responsibility, mostly negative, and another fifth uses clearly emotionally loaded words,
such as "barbaric act," "criminal occupation," and "racist fascist
regime" (for the negative side), and "positive," "progressive,"
"humane" (for the other side). In order to arrive at a clear notion
of what share of the international news stories is given to this
clearly heavily armed exposition, we remove those cases in
which responsibility and affect are found together in the same
story. We find, then, that one-third of all the international news
stories on Vremya give clear directions from the broadcaster.
There are many more stories, as I noted, that because of the
material they broadcast (homeless in Washington, mothers pro-
testing American nuclear installations in Great Britain, the Afghan government awarding irrigation rights to poor farmers) we
would consider clearly slanted—positive or negative—because

of the one-sided nature of the story. The balanced story, as Americans understand the term, does not carry the same value for Soviet media people, administrators, and correspondents.[17] Then, too, there are stories—usually TASS bulletins—which are simply announced: a meeting of NATO, a bomb explosion in Brussels, an election in Portugal. These stories—the neutral bulletins and the programs in which the newsmakers provide the commentary—are rather different from the one-third of the international stories with affect or responsibility where a clear evaluative framework and instructions have been provided by the broadcaster. These last attempt to impose a cognitive schema on the disparate events of world news—a schema of great simplicity and highly repetitive and consistent over time. The number of actors is relatively small; the evaluations, unmistakably clear.

Changes in Soviet Leadership Periods

The five months we viewed the Soviet news were divided into two periods: three months in 1984 and two in 1985. During the first period, Konstantin Chernenko was in power and during the second Mikhail Gorbachev had been in power for about six months. Doubtlessly, during the last days of Chernenko's leadership, Gorbachev had been an increasingly powerful voice. There are changes, clear and dramatic shifts, in some areas of the news. Perhaps the most significant is the change in coverage of the United States and its NATO allies. Coverage rose from 15 percent of the total number of stories in the Chernenko period to 22 percent in the Gorbachev period.[18] Two other regions of the world increased their share of Vremya: coverage of South and East Africa (over half of which in the Gorbachev period was devoted to the country of South Africa)[19] rose from just under 3 to over 4 percent; and non-NATO Western Europe, from 2.5 to almost 4 percent. An increase of even one percent is large—amounting to some 23 stories. If these regions gained a larger share of the news, there were some losers, too, and one of them was the Soviet Union itself and its Warsaw Pact allies. Coverage of these countries fell from almost 52.5 percent to just over 49 percent.[20] The biggest loser was the Indian subcontinent, coverage of which fell from 4 to 3 percent.[21] But this drop is probably not due to a cooling of interest, but rather to an unusually high volume of stories the year before, when Indira Gandhi was assassinated, Rajiv Gandhi was elected, and the Union Carbide gas leak in Bhopal took place. Comparing the rank-orders of intensity of coverage of regions of the world between the two periods shows the disappearance of COMECON (the Socialist economic organization) and decreased coverage of the Soviet Union and its allies, while a concomitant rise in coverage of the West takes place.[22]

In terms of the coverage of individual countries, some dramatic changes occur in the Gorbachev period, and the most significant is the elevation of coverage of South Africa. Whether one figures in terms of a single country in a story or two countries, the coverage of South Africa more than doubles in this period. Mexico becomes a leading newsmaker only in the later period, as does Poland.[23] In part, this is related to the devastating earthquake Mexico suffered at this time, but quite beyond this event, the increasing visibility of Mexico has been marked: the Soviets' largest newspaper, *Trud* (organ of the trade unions), moved its Latin American bureau from Lima to Mexico City in 1986, and Vremya's Mexico City correspondent has been featured live, commenting on negative reactions to such American initiatives as nuclear testing not far from Mexico.

In general, under Gorbachev, a larger group of countries is given a significant portion of the total number of stories, as Hungary, Austria, Italy, and the People's Republic of China are added.[24] On the other hand, two countries fall below the one percent of total stories threshold and do not show up in the latter period: Israel and India.[25] The countries of heavy coverage over both the Chernenko and Gorbachev periods are: Nicaragua, Great Britain, France, West Germany, East Germany, Bulgaria, South Africa, Lebanon, Afghanistan, Japan, the United Nations, and, of course, the United States. Coverage of the United States even increases in the Gorbachev period.[26]

In terms of *elapsed time*, the picture is somewhat different. The share of time Vremya devoted to the United States and to its NATO allies remains remarkably stable across the two leadership periods—with five percent for each in each of the two periods.[27]

There are also changes in the kinds of subjects that make up the Vremya broadcast. The most radical change is the drop in stories on economics, a category that accounted for slightly over 22 percent of all stories under Chernenko (and was the leading subject category) and fell to just under 17 percent under Gorbachev (falling as well to third place in the rank-order of subjects covered).[28] Economic achievements as a subject contracted from 20 percent to only 13 percent of total newstime. Another loser is the story about the legislative process. The greatest gains were registered by formal international politics coverage, arms control issues, military issues, space/science, and disasters/accidents. Coverage of official visits was dramatically expanded in time— going from 12 percent (already a hefty slice of total newstime) to an enormous 18 percent. Much of this was related to the activities of the new Soviet leader, whose trips were seen as an important legitimating factor. Second to this subject in total newstime was another that was stunningly increased: operations of Party organizations, which rose from 3 percent of newstime under Chernenko to 16 percent under Gorbachev. As early as the fall of 1985, preparations were being made for the Party Congress the next February. However, the very sharp increase related not only to that event but also to the new Soviet leader's preoccupation with fundamental and critical problems of the role of the Party. The Communist Party was to be the guiding, though not intruding, economic force as well as the leading socializer, though often guilty of corruption and the stifling of initiative within its ranks. The recognition of these faults and the search for the reorientation of this critical elite did become a major emphasis of Gorbachev's media policy.

The disaster story got more coverage under Gorbachev than his predecessor, going from near zero as a percentage of total airtime to a significant 2 percent. Most of the total number of disaster/accident stories are about foreign countries: the Bhopal chemical poisoning, the Ethiopian famine, and the Mexican earthquake, to cite the biggest stories. It is the coverage of accidents or natural disasters at home that the Soviets have always rejected. The repugnance for the disaster story, so deeply rooted in the Soviet notion of newsgathering, was reversed very dramatically on October 14, 1985, when the news provided coverage of the earthquake in Tadzhikistan. The day after the event the news had filmed footage of the area. The story began with the anchor, a map behind him, reciting the facts of the quake: its place on the scale and the location of its epicenter. Like the later Chernobyl event, it was defined as an *avaria* (the dictionary definition is disaster, accident, wreck). The story then shifted to the scene, as the anchor narrated and showed the rubble of houses, government buildings, and economic enterprises; huge cracks in the pavement and the land; officials and workers digging through the rubble and inspecting the area. Food, clothing, blankets, and other supplies were unloaded as the anchor announced that there had been deaths (number unspecified), and the injured were receiving the necessary medical care (virtually word for word the formula used in Chernobyl). After the film, the anchor expressed the sympathy of the highest organs of the party and government and promised that they were taking all measures to help those affected and remove the effects of the quake. Two days later, an even bigger story on the earthquake was aired. This time, the anchor went to a local (judging by the accent) correspondent, who showed people digging in the rubble, removing bodies (dozens were said to have perished), shown covered by sheets. The homeless were shown—children, women, entire families living in tents or on the street. Supplies were shown, contributed, it was said, by the whole country. This kind of coverage was unique in our entire five-month period. But the Gorbachev period went further and covered two other cases of natural disaster at home. In one case, it covered a disaster that didn't happen, although it was a very close call. In October of 1985, the *Mikhail Somov* steamed into Leningrad, after having been trapped in the arctic ice. The situation had been dangerous; the ship was shown to have been damaged, and the crew had undergone severe hardships. In still another case of domestic natural misfortune, a story at the end of October of that year showed a region in Belorussia, where rain had flooded potato farms at harvest time. The correspondent on location showed combines stuck in mud; fields under water; volunteers and farmers—many of them women in boots—slogging through the submerged fields to uproot potatoes by hand. All of these, none of which we saw during the earlier Chernenko period, are examples of the changing techniques and, to a considerable extent, the changing communications theory underlying practice.

As we saw earlier, that change was tested, challenged, and eventually accelerated by the disaster of Chernobyl.[29]

At the same time that the previously constrained disaster story was making its way to the forefront, the previously hallowed arts story was declining, its share cut in half by the Gorbachev agenda, from 4 to 2 percent of total newstime.

Underneath the rise and fall of the varied subjects, there is a pattern: the Gorbachev regime has initiated greater coverage of issues outside the U.S.S.R. at the expense of domestic coverage. The drop in stories about the economy is the key. Most of these, though certainly not all, are stories about the domestic economy, and many looked artificially staged. The legislative issues category is also largely about the Soviet Union. In fact, the only *domestic* story to receive increased coverage in the Gorbachev period is about space and science. As noted earlier, the disaster/accident story also registers an increase under Gorbachev.[30] The rank-order of subjects shows international politics in first place under Gorbachev, replacing economic issues, in first place under Chernenko.[31]

It may be that we should not be so quick to call these changes in the Soviet media system. Perhaps they simply reflect the changing contours of the world of news "out there." The news line-up is never entirely and uniquely the product of a closed system unresponsive to the real world. Since, however, we cannot posit an objective and complete world of news against which to compare the changes in the Soviet news output, we shall have to look at comparisons between Vremya and ABC to see how another news agenda has responded.

As expected, the events of 1984 in India—the Bhopal tragedy, the assassination of Indira Gandhi, and the election of Rajiv Gandhi—did create a more than usual interest in that country, not only in the Soviet Union but also in the United States. ABC devoted almost 2 percent of its stories to the Indian subcontinent in 1984 and not even half a percentage point in 1985.[32] As we saw, Soviet coverage was halved. This is one case where both were probably responsive to the same changed news environment. Similarly, it is likely that the events in South Africa made a difference to both news programs. There was more news out there in 1985, as troubles and conflicts mounted. ABC's coverage of this part of the world almost doubled, going from 2 percent to almost 4 percent.[33] The increase in Soviet coverage, though absolutely greater, did not quite double. In these two areas, then, it is likely that the news opportunities in the real world—a real world of interest to both the Soviet Union and the United States—influenced both news programs in much the same way, though ABC's reaction was more volatile and swung more sharply.

On the other hand, there were two significant areas of the world where ABC's interest markedly increased in 1985 but Vremya's did not. Coverage of Central America on Vremya showed no percentage change, but ABC's coverage went from 3 percent to 5 percent.[34] Coverage of the Middle East on ABC doubled over the course of the two periods,[35] while Vremya's coverage of the region actually declined in percentage terms. America's growing interest in Central America and the Middle East was not matched by the Soviets. America's involvement in Central America, though important to the Soviets, as we saw above, does not seem to them to be increasing in importance. Perhaps that is their understanding of stalemate. The relatively declining importance of the Middle East on the Soviet news doubtlessly reflects many factors. One must surely be the frustration of being excluded from the political processes they would like to affect directly rather than indirectly, through Syria. After all, in those areas where Soviet and American coverage both increased, the Soviets had as much, or more, capability to influence the course of events as did the United States: In India, clearly the Soviets, as well as the Americans, were major players. In South Africa, although the Soviets have no relations at all and no capability of influencing a very hostile government, they have highly publicized ties to the opposition African National Congress and its leader Oliver Tambo, who is often shown in Moscow. It is the present or perceived future ability to influence events that creates the difference for the managers of the Soviet news.

I noted that the news under the Gorbachev regime displayed a much greater interest in the West and reduced coverage of the Soviet Union and its allies. There is a reciprocal movement at ABC. On World News Tonight, coverage of the United States and its NATO partners declined from 80 percent to 73 percent of the total number of stories, while coverage of the Soviet Union rose from just over 2½ percent to just over 7 percent.[36] This is

still less than the almost 7.5 percent of the total number of stories
Vremya devoted to the United States under Gorbachev (up from
just over 6 percent from the Chernenko period),[37] but a very
considerable increase for the American network. Two factors
operate here. The more important one is the American presidential election, which had a strong impact on coverage in 1984. The
return to a more "normal" time in the later period also began
leading into coverage of the upcoming Geneva summit, which,
though still three weeks away by the end of our period of analysis, reinforced the trend toward coverage of the other superpower. In terms of elapsed time, the weight of international
stories on ABC shifted markedly: in the 1984 period they accounted for only 41 percent of airtime, but a year later, the figure
was 60 percent. It has often been remarked that election coverage has been increasing virtually exponentially over the years.
Whether it is desirable effectively to shut off the rest of the
world's news with considerable frequency is a real question.
Expansion of airtime would be a solution, but not, perhaps, a
likely one.[38]

ABC's menu of subjects also changed: there is an enormous
drop in stories on formal national politics as primary subject,
from 18 percent in 1984 to 4 percent in 1985. Although the networks may insist that they want to relate what happens in national politics to the lives of individuals, during an election year
the focus is certainly more on the macro-system and less on the
impact for individual Americans. The other side of this change is
a more outward-looking view of the world, with a rise in stories
on formal international politics from 4 percent to 11 percent.
Only four other categories of primary subject registered any
substantial change over the period, and they were all increases:
stories on political violence (from 9 percent to 13 percent); stories
about civil rights, emigration, and immigration (from 1 percent
to 3.5 percent); disaster and accident stories (from 7 percent to 10
percent); and arts stories (from 1 percent to 3 percent).[39]

In a parallel movement, both the Soviet Union and the United
States display more internationalist and less parochial orientation to news coverage. But it is unlikely that they are responding
to the same stimuli. In the American case, the change is a result
of a quadrennial affair that focuses attention as no other event
does.[40] Once it's over, the pattern changes drastically. In the

1984 period of our analysis, almost 59 percent of the stories on ABC were domestic stories; by the next fall, that figure had dropped to 43 percent. In the Soviet Union there is a clear move under Gorbachev to lessen coverage of domestic issues and increase coverage of international ones. On Vremya, domestic stories were only 36 percent of the broadcast in 1984 and dropped to 30 percent the next fall. The figures tell us that the changes have taken place independently of a "world news agenda."

But the changes also involve a certain narrowing of perspective, both for ABC and for Vremya, across the two years. In terms of elapsed time, there is shrinkage of range on both programs. Under Chernenko, the number of countries (excluding the two superpowers) receiving at least 1 percent of total newstime was twenty-three, and it became eighteen under his successor.[41] ABC narrowed its focus from thirteen to eleven countries. Very few countries are durable enough to claim attention over the long haul. For ABC they are: El Salvador, Great Britain, France, Italy, South Africa, and Lebanon. Vremya maintained a high level of interest across the two periods for a much larger number of countries: Nicaragua, Great Britain, France, Poland, Austria, Hungary, Italy, Bulgaria, Ethiopia, Lebanon, Afghanistan, Japan, India, and the United Nations. Other countries come and go, when earthquakes and assassinations take place or when heads of state succeed one another in line for official visits and extensively covered rituals. Both Ethiopia and India, where disasters or political violence made them newsworthy in 1984, were of relatively little interest to ABC the next year, but both still continued to claim very significant amounts of time on Vremya—another illustration of the different notions of newsworthiness held by the two media systems.[42] South Africa, which figures so prominently among the most heavily covered countries in percentage of total stories, becomes a heavy claimant for newstime on Vremya only under Gorbachev. Israel and Egypt both become notable claimants of newstime only under Gorbachev; time allocated to them was negligible in the earlier period. Only about a quarter of the total newstime on Vremya is taken up by stories involving a third country, and Israel is by far the most heavily covered third country. It is another indication of the manipulative role assigned to it; it exists for the Soviet news not as a nation-state where the processes of politics and society, culture and economy, are played out, but rather only as a very frequently cited source for disturbance and turmoil elsewhere in the region.

The news on Vremya has moved, under Gorbachev, to a more international focus and has also become more lively and, the professionals no doubt assume, more convincing. Pictures are used more.[43] Our 1985 period had just over 71 percent of total newstime in pictures; while the earlier three months in 1984 had just over 66 percent. That increase is the result of a greater interest in securing filmed footage of international stories, whether or not accompanied by a correspondent on location. In fact, the share of pictures on the Soviet news taken up by domestic Soviet stories fell by 1.5 percent.

The data indicate that policy was changing well before publication of the *Pravda* article that called for a much greater use of pictures in order to increase the effectiveness of the news: "By most accounts television is not suited to the reading of news from papers. . . . Maybe the time has come when television journalists are obliged to explain to the audience why 'we weren't able to show you . . .' anything except the reader."[44]

Newsmakers: Who Is Covered on the News?

Stories on the news are about countries and issues, but they are also about people. The broadcaster's choice of people shown or cited in stories tells us about certain important values: to what degree do political elites, or a country's leader, dominate the news? How often are representatives of certain institutions, such as the military, identified? Does the public see scientists and scholars, and how much does it see just ordinary people? For the five months of our comparative analysis of ABC's World News Tonight and Vremya, we looked at the people who make the news in each country.[46] The country's leader is of critical importance to the news, but how pervasive are references to that leader? Is the news leader-dominated? Is there a "cult" of leadership on the news, exercising a kind of proprietary and controlling right over the events the viewer sees every evening?

If we look first at a news broadcast's coverage of its own country's leader, we find that overall, taking the entire five-

month period, the President of the United States accounted for
6.5 percent of all people shown or referred to in a news story on
ABC. For the same period, the Soviet General Secretary was
given *9.5 percent* of all such coverage on Vremya.[46] As we might
have expected, given the much more strongly statist thrust of
the Soviet news, and the history of personality cults, their leader
is much more central than is the American president on ABC.
However, as we also might have expected, considering the asymmetry in attention to each other, the American leader takes up
more than twice the share of the newsmaker references on
Vremya than the Soviet leader does on the American news.
However, the American elections do make a difference at home.
During the 1984 period of our analysis, the President was given
7.4 percent of the entire coverage of persons, which was reduced
to *5 percent* the next year. This was primarily a drop in the weight
of the President in domestic news. During the 1984 portion of
our study, when there was an election, the President represented *9 percent* of all people covered in domestic stories; the
share fell to just under *3 percent* in the 1985 period. On the Soviet
side, the change in coverage is also very marked between the
two periods. There is perhaps no more visible indicator of the
political weakness of Konstantin Chernenko than the amount of
television coverage allotted him: he occupied *8.5 percent* of all
references or coverage of people in the Soviet news in 1984, but
his successor the following year was given almost *12 percent*.
Considering the very large base of the total number of people
shown or cited on the news, this is an extremely significant
increase. Since our definition of people in the news specifies that
they may be included if they are shown or mentioned, Chernenko's increasingly frail health would not have prevented references to him or precluded anchors from reading his speeches.
He did not have to perform in front of the cameras in order to be
a part of the news. Our data indicate that his physical health
had, quite obviously, affected his political health. Moreover, the
pronounced increase in coverage of Gorbachev results from a
much greater projection of the General Secretary into *international* stories where the Soviet Union interacts with other countries, and it is in this arena that the new Soviet leader was most
active, meeting with foreign officials at home and abroad, and
enunciating new Soviet policies (for the most part using televi-

sion to do so) on nuclear issues, chemical warfare, conventional arms, cooperative agreements, United Nations questions, and many others. The new General Secretary would move the Soviet Union much more actively into an articulation with other countries. If we allow for the anomalously low visibility of Chernenko, we see that in general there is a much greater emphasis on leader-driven news in the Soviet Union—an important difference between the two societies. The later Soviet figure also shows a much more canny use of the medium of television, a factor that is likely to be characteristic in the future, as well.

How much is the leader of the other superpower referred to or shown on the news? Here, we find the characteristically greater preoccupation of the Soviets with Americans than of us with them. For the five months of our analysis, the Soviet General Secretary was a figure in only *1 percent* of the total number of newsmakers on the ABC, while the American President was a figure in *2.5 percent* of the Soviet news. The conclusion of the presidential elections in the United States (and a more outward-looking view) and the accession of a new leader in the Soviet Union (with even more pronounced interest in the United States) produced important changes. In the 1984 portion of the analysis, the American news covered the Soviet leader as *0.4 percent* of all people covered, but after the elections, and with a new Soviet leadership, that figure rose to *1.5 percent* in 1985. On Vremya the coverage of the American President rose from slightly under *2 percent* in 1984 to *3.3 percent* in 1985. It is a movement from already asymmetrical interest in the other superpower to an even greater concern with us and with the person of our President.

The country's leader is certainly the primary figure or person on the news in both countries, but the news broadcasts show a dramatically different mix of elites and ordinary people, of political officials and other citizens. The Soviet citizen is much more likely to see the world of political officials on the news than is the American. The news is official; it is made by officials; it is transmitted through official pronouncements and official presentations.[49] Though Marxist doctrine bases its validity on movements of large classes of people in contradistinction to the activities of leaders or individuals, the Leninist development of that doctrine, as I noted earlier, stresses the role that the state must play in bringing about the preconditions for the communist society. Fully *64 percent* of the people covered in some way on the Soviet news are officials; for Americans, it is *37 percent*.[48] In fact, the American lack of interest in officials is understated by this figure. The election year made officials the bearers of news in 41 percent of the total coverage of people; but by the next year, that percentage had dropped to 32.

The frequent presentation of economic leaders on the Soviet news actually increases the weight of officialdom. Whereas on the American news economic leaders are most often corporate heads or officers or trade-union leaders, on the Soviet news the counterparts to leaders of private industry would be the directors and officers of enterprises and the chairmen of state and collective farms. This is a group that is generally in the official job list, called *nomenklatura*, that requires party approval or appointment. These people make up 4 percent of the Soviet news and 3 percent of the American.[49]

But there are other people on the news—both elites and ordinary people. The table below shows what kinds of people in these other categories fill the news broadcasts.

There are four types of people in this list to whom Vremya accords much more coverage than does ABC: they are the military, astronauts and cosmonauts (many of whom are in the military and whose programs are closely linked to the military), agricultural workers, and people in the arts.

Selected Categories: People in the News[50]
(Percent total people covered)

	ABC	VREMYA
Scientist, scholar[51]	8.8	2.6
Lawyer	1.8	—
Physician[52]	2.1	0.2
Military[53]	2.6	3.6
Religious leader[54]	2.0	0.3
People in arts	1.4	4.2
People in sports	2.1	0.1
Journalist	2.5	1.1
Astro/cosmonaut	0.2	1.0
Activist/dissident	1.1	0.8
Agricultural worker/farmer	0.2	1.3
Ordinary people[55]	29.1	13.7

The Technical Side of the News

News decisions may be constrained by technical possibilities. Equally, what may seem to be a decision attributed to technical constraints may be really a policy decision. In order to sort these out, since the manner of the presentation of the news is a key factor in its impact, we turn to what the news looks like.

Earlier, in the discussion with Moscow television correspondent Vladimir Dunaev, the problem of equipment surfaced.[56] Soviet foreign bureaus often must buy expensive filmed footage, and when they wish to transmit their own footage by satellite, it is frequently necessary to buy time on a Western satellite, whereas their own would be a much less expensive option. Any studio work in Washington, or other Western capitals, substantially increases the expense. The round table of correspondents in world capitals, a new feature on Vremya, entails these additional expenses.[57] One of the most ambitious was aired on July 25, 1986. The segment, called "Studio 20," picked up the correspondents in Bonn, New York, London, and Mexico City.

The money problem has plagued newsgathering operations in the West. Dunaev did not have money for studio or crew in his early days in London. In Washington, he uses a very small, fairly inexperienced studio to prepare his tapes for the satellite. The financial constraint and the equipment problem present real limitations in television news coverage from the United States. However, as the previous chapters have shown, the fundamental difference between the Soviet and American notions of what is newsworthy and how it should be covered are not necessarily attributes of the technical environment. They go much deeper, although they may be moderated as the technical environments of the two countries approach each other.

When a Westerner watches Soviet television—both news and entertainment programs—he or she is soon aware that when the sound track is in another language, the Russian translator's voice-over is pegged virtually at the same sound level. I am not speaking here of the practice of dubbing feature films, but rather about what happens when a foreigner is interviewed or gives a statement in his or her language and a Soviet commentator provides a Russian translation for the television audience. This results in the viewer's hearing simultaneously two sound tracks in two languages at roughly equal volume. It is a practice that is puzzling to Americans, who in our own television programs expect the English translation sound track to be much louder than the original foreign language track, so that the latter recedes into the background and one hears one's own language without the distraction of a competing sound track. During one press conference in Moscow on the Chernobyl incident, the usual Soviet practice was followed, and one American network told its viewers that there were sound problems in Moscow, and left the Moscow coverage. Are these technical problems or does this puzzling practice have a policy rationale?

It is certainly not a technical problem. Adjusting the level of the two sound tracks is done by mixing. It is a simple procedure, and the equipment that the Soviets use in Moscow and in the field has this capability. In Washington, Dunaev does the mixing himself. It is a simple matter to hold one track down and increase the volume on the other. It is a policy question, not a technical problem, and the policy is embedded in history and concern with the efficacy of media and the alienation of the audience. Keeping the two sound tracks at what are to Americans, at least, disturbingly similar sound levels, is done deliberately. It is done in order to enhance the authenticity of the broadcast and the credibility of the medium. The statements of the foreigners are important legitimating acts. Foreign sources, as we saw in the previous chapter, are often cited (selectively) as indications of global approval of Soviet actions. Legitimation is undercut if the audience is skeptical of the communication. And the audience has reason for skepticism, since, according to one Soviet correspondent, in the past journalists did not hesitate to "put [their] words in somebody's mouth." Even if only a few in the television audience can follow the foreign sound track, there may well be the sense among many more that the statements attributed to others can be verified independently.

In the spring of 1986, Vremya was given a facelift. The opening graphics were radically changed, as were some of the effects used for transitions. In the past, Vremya began with a picture of the Kremlin and then the Kremlin clock tower. Letters rolled across the bottom of the screen announcing the news information program. The camera slowly zoomed in on the red letters of Vremya, to the right of the clock tower. Stately, vaguely martial music accompanied the graphics. The new opening shows a comet-like red star streaking from behind the globe. The graphics and music are upbeat and deliberately modern. They also represent a technological departure from the past: computer-generated graphics have come to Vremya. They are used in the opening of the news program and to introduce several of the stories. The digital devices that the Soviets have begun to use are not as complex or sophisticated as their American counterparts. They tend to have a flatter, more two-dimensional quality, unlike the graphics generated by equipment in the United States which can take a flat map and wrap it around a globe or even a spindle. One Soviet news story on agricultural production in Tadzhikistan began with a map out of which smaller sections— or submaps—sprang forward out of the larger map and then zoomed into the background. Inside one of these smaller maps, filmed footage gradually emerged in a clock-wipe, leading into the story itself. In order to do this, multiple layers of effects have to be produced. But the number of layers, or generations, is less than would be considered acceptable in Western news graphics. Still, suddenly and clearly, in 1986, the look of Vremya, its logo and identity, became deliberately and unarguably modern.

In a system that is developing, that is introducing modern techniques and equipment, change does not happen all at once. Certain areas have not changed very much and seem clearly outmoded by Western standards. The lettering used by Vremya is still produced by a very simple character generator. The viewer sees only one color, as compared with American lettering, which can add several colors and shadows, as well. American lettering devices are microprocessor based; the Soviets are much more limited in the number and size of the fonts they use.

Standards for editing Vremya are often rather different from those required by American broadcasters, local and national. The transition from one story to the next on Vremya is sometimes slow, with a cutaway from one story, some two or three seconds of silence, and a new shot into another story, for example, an interview, and at its conclusion, a cutaway, another few seconds of silence, and a new shot. This editing would not be considered tight enough by American standards, which would require closing the silences and more artfully arranging transitions. Transitions may also be rather abrupt; there is almost never a leadout (the correspondent's practice of identifying himself or herself at the end of the story and inviting the viewer back to the studio) and stories simply end. Sometimes a number of stories will follow one another, without introduction by the anchor. The viewer knows that change has taken place by the change in correspondent and locale.

Jump cuts are used far more frequently than they are on American news programs. A jump cut, as the term implies, is an abrupt change, showing that a piece has been taken out by the editor. The effect is one of a stilted and visible shift to another place on the film or tape. On American programs, when such a shift has taken place, it is done by going behind the person speaking to show the reporter nodding in understanding. This clip of the reporter actually masks the change that has taken place to another part of the film. It isn't visible to the public, because the face of the person interviewed is not on camera at the time of the shift, and there is no dislocating change in that person's speech or face.[58] Occasionally, on a program such as "60 Minutes," for example, the jump cut will be used deliberately to heighten the drama. But on the Soviet news, it is still seen very frequently for no thematic reason; there is little attempt to smooth the editing process.

But there are stories that display far more sophisticated camera and editing techniques. Vladimir Dunaev's story on San Francisco at night is an example of first-rate camera work.[59] Cherkassov, the cameraman, moved with his subjects. With his hand-held camera, he walked around the policemen who accompanied them, thus varying the angle and providing the motion and dynamism that set this story off—quite unlike the fixed position often taken by Soviet television cameraman. Many of the foreign stories use foreign cameramen. A story on Japan seemed to have used Japanese cameramen, whose fondness for interesting angles and original photography makes their pictures distinctive. A story on South Korea was probably borrowed from American-edited film, and one story on the report of the Rogers Commission about the *Challenger* disaster not only used ABC footage, but used it along with some of the narration of the American network's correspondent. The international section of Vremya tends to be more interesting, visually, than the domestic section. It resembles standard Western filming. Some of this is due to the (unattributed) borrowing of Western, often American footage; some of it is due to the use of foreign cameramen in the field. But many of the stories by Soviet correspondents in the field are better than those by their counterparts at home. Standards of filming and editing seem to resemble more those of their foreign counterparts. They tend to use written notes less. The anchors in the studio read from papers in front of them, rather than from a TelePrompTer, and several correspondents do the same. But others, such as the correspondent in West Germany, are skilled speakers and speak into the camera.

In the Ostankino studio in Moscow, where the news originates, the anchors use double desk microphones. In front of each anchor is a set of two rectangular black microphones; one is a back-up in case of a malfunction of the other. They do not use the lavaliere microphones, which are standard in American studios. These are the very small, clip-on microphones the anchors and their guests use. The desk microphones cost about one-third of the more modern, more efficient, and smaller clip-ons. Lavaliere mikes do not turn up in the field, either. Hand-held or directional microphones are used there. It was a directional microphone that was used in the confrontation of the raid story described earlier.[60] In general, the sound quality of news stories is good; natural background noise is used and mixed well. Visually and acoustically (in purely technical, not narrative terms), one of the best news stories was from the 27th Party Congress in February 1986. The Hall of Congresses, where the meetings took place, is well equipped for television transmissions, and the camera work, lighting, and acoustics were excellent. It should be noted that the system of television broadcasting that the Soviets use—a system they imported from the French—provides extremely good pictures. SECAM, as it is called, transmits sequential color information, and the pictures are clear and sharp, with very good, consistently accurate color. For most observers the color performance is superior to the American NTSC system, which, it is often quipped, stands for "never twice the same color."

The Week on Television: The Context of the Soviet News Weekday Programming

For American viewers, the news is part of a larger broadcast day that includes soap operas and sports, game shows and cartoons and a variety of other programs to choose on a number of channels. It is entertainment that surrounds the news and provides the context in which the news is set. In the Soviet Union on a weekday the broadcast day lasts from 12.5 to 13.5 hours.[61] It is very heavily non-entertainment, at least by American standards. Fully 41 *percent* of the entire week we surveyed was devoted to news and public affairs. News and news analysis is firmly fixed at 20 percent of each weekday's television airtime. This includes, on an average day, the morning (a repeat from the night before during the period of this analysis, later repackaged in the live morning program) and evening news, usually two editions of the news analysis program, "Today in the World," and three or four news capsules (each of which runs from 5 to 20 minutes). "Today in the World" is a very highly regarded fifteen-minute program surveying important international news stories and providing interpretation. It is hosted by well-known correspondents, who use lively film footage to accompany their commentary. The audience numbers some 60–90 million people.[62] The public affairs programs fall into two categories: programs on production and the economy and programs on politics and history. The former are usually documentary films or round table discussions. In the week we surveyed, they covered such subjects as: the use of advanced technology in agriculture, the work of an exemplary farmer, oil drilling, a new automobile model, consumer durables, and metallurgical plants in Uzbekistan. The history and politics programs are programs about political/ governmental issues at home and abroad. Some are historical documentaries; some are interpretations or discussions of contemporary processes—for example: journalists discussing preparations for the 27th Party Congress in the Soviet republics; the head of the Military Political Administration of the armed forces warning about the growing military threat of the United States; observations on the history of the K.G.B. and the modern Soviet border guards; a documentary on American Indians.

A somewhat greater share of the weekday schedule, 48 *percent*, is allocated to feature films, culture, and sports. This is the entertainment portion of the weekday. Feature films account for the single largest program category—*over one-quarter* (29 percent) of total airtime.[63] Films may run one evening and be repeated the next morning; they may be broken up into a series of hour-long segments before the evening news over the course of a week or ten days, or they may be bookends on either side of the news. Films may be foreign or domestic, color, or black-and-white. During the week of our sweep we saw the Hungarian movie *Mephisto,* with Klaus Maria Brandauer; a film version of a play about the U.S. Senate's hearings on the Bolshevik Revolution; a movie about Lenin;[64] a movie about former German prisoners-of-war hired by the Americans and the British to fight socialism after World War II in Eastern Europe; the Eisenstein classic, *Battleship Potemkin;* and a film about the Bolshevik Revolution and the Russian Civil War. The audience for movies on television is very large, but certainly not satisfied. They complain that recent films are not shown often and movies that are shown are frequently repeated. Sometimes "movies are shown [on television] that people would be embarrassed to show in theaters," as one irate letter-writer argued.[64] Moreover, a year's study of all films on both national networks found that of 229 films shown, 109 were made in 1970 or earlier.[65] The man in charge of films for national television, Iury Grobovnikov, when asked about these charges, answered that the number of films produced by the Soviet movie industry is too small to permit central television to show films without repeating them. Soviet television shows as many movies in a month as Goskino (the state movie industry) makes in a year and movies will have to be repeated on television every eighteen months to two years. There is a new directive, however, that will move movies more quickly from the movie theater to the television screen. Up to twelve films will go to central television six to nine months after production; another forty-five to fifty will be on television one-and-a-half to two years after completion. The rest will come to television between three and ten years after production. Made-for-television movies will be in the theaters within six months of their television premieres. A television film series, "By Your Request," was started in 1986, and one of the first choices (based on letters from viewers) was *Shield and Sword,* a 1967 black-and-white movie about the heroic exploits of Soviet spies in the Second World War. It is a spectacularly popular movie that in its day sold 70 million tickets. Another requested movie was Nikita Mikhalkov's poignant rendering of *Oblomov.* Still another new film program is devoted to foreign films. It led off with a French movie (a Guy de Maupassant story), followed by movies from East Germany, the People's Republic of China, England (*Jane*

Eyre), and Hungary.[67] Movies are a vital component of Soviet television programming. They attract an immense audience, and the discontents of that audience, even though they emerge only through the very imperfect and unrepresentative channel of letters, are visible. The search for entertainment and escapism makes the Soviet audience not much different from any other, but the choices they have are limited.

The "culture" programs were mostly music. About a third of the total amount of airtime devoted to music was classical music programming (a total during the week of only two and a half hours); while for five hours the television viewer saw folk and pop music and dance programs. There was only one program on art: a four-minute filler on photography, which included some pictures of Afghanistan, and one on literature: a sixty-five-minute documentary on the writers Esenin, Babel, and Mayakovski in the early years after the Revolution—a documentary that detailed the role of writers in the campaign for literacy. The culture programs are not predominantly high culture.[68] Although the line-up varies from week to week, the arts programs are always surprisingly heavy on the kind of escapist entertainment that popular or show music represents.

Weekday programming is also low on sports. We found only two days when sports programs were aired on First Program during our sweep. Major world events alter that: in June 1986, the World Cup soccer competition was broadcast live from Mexico City (when the time zone difference permitted) or on tape. On five weekdays during the second week of the competition (June 8–13), First Program carried it for sixteen hours and forty-eight minutes. But the pattern of rather little sports coverage during the week is much more typical.[69] Surveys tell us that the Soviet television audience has a strong preference for sports programs,[70] but during the week they get relatively little. Early in 1986 a thirty-minute sports program, "Sports for the Week," that had become popular after a year on the Second Program, was moved to the First Program and scheduled for every Monday night, with a repeat on Tuesday morning. A. V. Ivanitsky, head of sports for national television and radio, in announcing this change also referred to other changes in sports programs, but they were all changes relating to increased emphasis on physical fitness and exercise programs. He did not refer to expanded coverage of sports competition.[71] The authorities do not give any indication that they will expand sports coverage on First Program—that channel is too important. Rather, they advise sports enthusiasts to buy themselves a "cheap black-and-white set" and watch their programs on Second Program, while the rest of the family watches First Program.[72]

Eight percent of weekday television airtime is devoted to children's programming. However, *more than half* (56 percent) of this non-news, non-public affairs category is devoted to programs that may be classified as political or career education. The themes of the political and military education programs are nationalism, character building, and the expansionism and threat of international adversaries. One program, "Respond, Buglers," took children on an excursion to Lenin's apartment; another, "The World and Youth," discussed Star Wars, wounded children in Lebanon, unrest in Great Britain, increases in gun sales in South Africa; in another program, tenth-grade children talked to cosmonauts about careers in science. The rest of the children's programming is more nearly entertainment: cartoons and games.

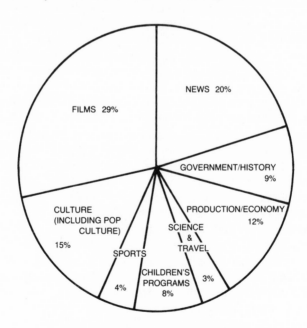

Weekday Programming: Soviet Television

America on Weekday Airtime

The week's programming displays a keen interest in the United States and the West. Certainly, as we have seen, the evening news accords coverage of the United States and its NATO allies considerable time. But outside the boundaries of the evening news (and, of course, its repeat the next morning) there is a great deal more. On Monday of the week we surveyed, eight more programs covered the United States. Three were news capsules, which referred to military tests in Canadian airspace, Libyan concern with American pressure, joint American-South Korean military exercises and other events. Two editions of "Today in the World" covered the tests in Canada, American reaction to Gorbachev's nuclear arms proposals, Libya's denunciation of American economic sanctions, the Martin Luther King, Jr. holiday, and other stories.

Two feature films were about the United States and both were very negative. The first, which ran from 9:10 in the morning to 11:00, was an East German film, dubbed into Russian (with the German sound track still distractingly loud in the background). "Front Without Mercy" is a very long series of films made for television in 1984. The installment broadcast when our week's sweep begins followed the course of two German prisoners-of-war who are released by the United States army, go to a villa in Berlin occupied by the British command, where they are told of British and American plans to break up the Soviet/American alliance and force the Soviet Union into subservience through nuclear blackmail. At all costs, the nascent Soviet atomic research and production effort must be stopped. At the same time, there is much brutal sabotage of the Soviet development of atomic energy for peaceful purposes. The film showed a repellent naturalized British citizen (a German working for the British against his own country's interests) who speaks of America's nuclear monopoly and exults that "socialism will be destroyed one day," and a rather resigned and somewhat pathetic American officer (speaking English) who follows orders. The Russians and their German allies say that "our former allies want to destroy socialism"; that nuclear technology is better used for peaceful purposes than for weapons; and, as they show films of an American nuclear test, that it "took place on an exotic island—sun and palms. After the blast, the island no longer existed. It disappeared."

A second feature film that day, playing at 9:40 p.m., with a five-minute introduction by the director, was the film version of a play about the Intervention and the Senate's hearings in 1919 condemning the Bolshevik Revolution (the film was repeated the next morning)—"The Truth! and Nothing But the Truth!!" by Soviet playwright Daniel Al. This movie inaugurated a monthly series called "Political Theater." Well-known commentator Genrikh Borovik explained that "there is no art and no literature outside politics," but this particular program features movies and plays that explicitly feature sharp political issues, either through the portrayal of an individual's participation in important events or through the clash of political positions.[73] The inaugural movie was filmed in 1969 in black and white. It is a stagey film, with the Senate panel and its witnesses on the stage and an actor in the front row of the audience who stands up from time to time and interjects for the audience his interpretation of what is happening. The senators and their witnesses speak, according to the playwright, the words found in the stenographic record. In addition, there are cuts to the past and the future, to put it in perspective. And, as Borovik said at the outset, there are clear parallels with this event of so many years ago and the present. The title refers to the way each witness begins his testimony to the Senate commission, and the number of "truths" are many. Actors portraying the real historical figures—diplomats and other public figures—assert that the Bolshevik Revolution will not survive. Many of the officials who are called to bear witness to the unfolding of a new order in Russia speak of "shooting people in cold blood in Petrograd"; two caricatures of effete émigré Russians speak of their deprivation, as the luxuries of life have been taken away. But other historical figures appear as friends of the new revolutionary society: John Reed and Louise Bryant, among them. Bryant, a stout blonde, is a firebrand in the old tradition, declaiming and exhorting—perhaps the most decidedly theatrical among the many theatrical actors. At one point, the actor in the audience jumps up and shouts that it is all slander, it is all lies. Actually, the truth was much, much worse, and he goes on to describe the suffering the revolutionaries experienced in the Civil War, the death by hunger of the great poet Alexander Blok, all the tragedies the young Bolshevik republic underwent, and how they were overcome. Clearly, this is a tendentious and deadening way to begin the new monthly series.

Rounding out the attention paid to the United States on that Monday was a Soviet-American competition in pole-vaulting covered from Japan—rather important, considering the little time that the First Program gives sports during an average week.

During the rest of the week the pattern of heavy coverage of the United States on the many news programs and news capsules continued, as did interest in the United States on non-news programs. On Tuesday, the movie about the Senate's opposition to the Bolshevik Revolution was repeated. On Wednesday, there were two programs in addition to the regular news and news analysis programs (one of which called attention to the rising costs of college tuition in the United States) that provided negative coverage of the West. "The World and Youth" presented four "lessons." Two were on domestic matters—a model teacher's techniques and the harmonization (both personal and aesthetic) of a choir—and two were on foreign questions. One was "Lessons of Peace," which showed young workers in a Moscow factory talking to an interviewer about concern over the Strategic Defense Initiative, the hostility of the United States, the need to "struggle for peace." The other was "Bitter Lessons," about the plight of victimized children in Lebanon (shots of infants, wounded children, street fighting), in Great Britain (immigrant children who experience discrimination because of their race—shots of police guarding little children who want to go to school and toughs who threaten them), and of Catholics and Protestants in Northern Ireland (the violence threatening children, and segregation by religion). Immediately following this program was "Program of Our Life," an unadorned lecture by a military officer and professor, Lieutenant-General Dmitri Volkogonov, who is deputy chief of the Military-Political Administration of the armed forces, the unit responsible for the political indoctrination of all of the services. Volkogonov, in uniform, was seated in a red chair behind a glass-topped table. He spoke without notes and had no props or charts, other than a copy of the new Party Program, a page of which the camera showed from time to time. His purpose, he said, was to clarify the role of the armed forces in the new Party document. It was a hard-hitting lesson, referring to the West as "fabricators of death," warning against the alliance of economic wealth and military might that provides the potential for war. But, he countered, there is also the potential for peace, resting on the acts of the Soviet Union and its allies, the developing countries, for whom war would destroy hopes of development, and the anti-war movements. The Soviet armed forces, he repeated over and over again, must be prepared, and their duty to the Socialist homeland is called "sacred." He strongly favors the country's "military-patriotic education" (paramilitary training in the schools, both practical and ideological), and asserts that it does not have a "Platonic character" (by which he means an abstract, theoretical format), but it is an "active patriotism." The lecture ended with a warning about the Strategic Defense Initiative. Throughout Volkogonov had been serious, weighty, but not remote.

On Thursday, although the news and news analysis programs featured the United States prominently and negatively, there were no other programs about the United States—with one exception, and it provides the single instance of positive reference to the United States that week. At 4:55 in the afternoon, the children's show "Chess School" presented some episodes from the history of chess, and among them was a story about an American, Samuel Lloyd, who, in 1867, participated in a memorable international chess championship. The commentator praised Lloyd not only, or even mainly, because of his success, but rather because of the great beauty and grace of his game; one is assigned for the young television audience to work out.

Finally, on Friday from 7:10 to 7:30 in the evening, another non-news program was devoted to the United States: *Free To Be Without Rights* is a documentary film about the repression of native Indians by the United States government. This is a very popular theme on Soviet television, and in particular, the plight of Leonard Peltier has been very heavily covered. Peltier was convicted of killing two federal agents on an Indian reservation in South Dakota in 1975; he has been in prison since 1977 and is considered in the Soviet Union to be the United States' most important American Indian political prisoner. In fact, a committee to raise money for legal battles and draw attention to the state of his health brought its plea to Moscow, along with members of Peltier's family. For Americans, the most vivid demonstration of the salience of Peltier to the Soviet media came in June 1987, when two Soviet ophthalmologists examined Peltier in prison in Kansas.[74]

During the five days of the week, Soviet television viewers saw a great deal of coverage of the United States and its Western allies. The news capsules, news analysis, and news programs—a total of *seven* programs daily—*one-fifth of airtime*—focused heavily, though certainly not entirely, on the West and the coverage was not positive. But, in addition to this consistent fare, four out of five days of the week we surveyed had some non-news programming about the United States, all of it negative. One program, the children's chess show on the remaining day, treated an individual American warmly.

Weekend Programming

Television on the weekend is very different. It is certainly far less focused on serious *news and public affairs* programs. They account for only a *quarter* of all weekend programming—just about half of the weekday share. The drop is not so much a reduction of the news and news analysis programs, which stay fixed at just under 20 percent, but rather of the other kinds of public affairs programs: the ones on economics (industrial and agricultural production), government operations, and history documentaries. The news programs on the weekend are the familiar Vremya and two or three Novosti news capsules. The 45-minute news analysis program, "International Panorama," occupies the 6:00 p.m. Sunday slot. This program is hosted by a leading foreign affairs commentator and journalist (they rotate) and is a combination of film and interpretation. On Saturday of the week we surveyed, we saw another leading news-analysis program, the monthly "Studio 9," an hour-long round-table discussion of world events, with well-known analysts (correspondents and scientific institute personnel, such as the director of a leading international economics institute). There were questions from the audience (this program originated in a factory in Moscow) about American reaction to the Gorbachev arms proposals, the

Strategic Defense Initiative, chemical weapons and Libya, South Africa, and Central America.

Entertainment programming shot up to over *two-thirds* of all airtime on the weekend.[75] The official position, as enunciated by a deputy director of Gosteleradio, V. I. Popov, regards the weekend as leisure hours that must be filled with programs that are "entertaining and substantive."[76] The share of films was 17 percent, less than during the week, and sports rose from 2 percent during the week to 7 percent on the weekend, but a larger increase came with programs on culture taking up almost a quarter of the weekend airtime.[77] Classical music, which was about a third of the weekday cultural programming, was on the weekend a mere 6 percent, while pop and folk music—rock, Soviet-style, pop singers, crooners, folk singers and dancers—were given 78 percent of weekend cultural programming. An interesting cultural program, which, from what we know of audience preferences, would attract few, but highly educated, viewers, was a reading (or rather, as the style dictated, declamation) of the poetry of Valery Briusov, a twenty-minute show about a controversial early twentieth-century modernist poet. This broadcast, as well as some others, such as the one on the poet Anna Akhmatova in July 1986, reflected the reassessment and loosening of the strictures against formalism in particular, and the very narrow interpretation of the Russian literary heritage in general.

In the category of entertainment, there were other kinds of programs, as well, including the travel programs, very popular with viewers (this weekend there were travelogues on India, Australia, Latvia, and the Russian city of Kalinin). Among the most popular staples of this genre is "Travelers' Club," which this weekend focused on the pre-Columbian culture of the Americas—history, art, and myth. For most Soviet citizens, who do not have the opportunity to see the world outside their borders or, perhaps, outside the borders of the socialist bloc, shows about travel and the world outside are surrogates for experience. They are also part of that interest in the outside world that the Soviet media have themselves activated. A new entertainment category was added for the weekend in our survey of a week on the First Program: it is the science program, and the most popular (and one of the most heavily watched shows on Soviet television) is "Incredible But True."

Another new kind of program surfacing on the weekend was the health and family issues program—we have not included it in the entertainment category, since it is very largely instructional. One program on Saturday looked at conflicts within the family and how to treat them. It was a program on parenting, responding to letters raising such issues as conflicts between parents and children over pets, parents' worries about a left-handed child (still very much a live issue in the Soviet Union), and how to curb a child's greed. Another program linked health and environment issues and alerted viewers to the kinds of health services provided in schools and places of work. On Sunday there was rhythmic gymnastics (we would call it aerobics). Later, when the broadcast day was expanded, this would become daily fare on First Program.

Rounding out weekend programming were children's shows. Although there were none on the Saturday of the week we surveyed, on the Sunday broadcast children's programs made up thirteen percent of airtime. But, again, *more than half* of the programs were devoted to political education, and the most notable among them was the hour-long weekly program, "I Serve the Soviet Union," which is designed to inculcate military values in youth and to introduce and attract the boys to their obligation under compulsory conscription. On this Sunday's programs there were interviews with military officers, who talked about the need to train good soldiers and the responsibility of the officer corps. NATO maneuvers in Bavaria were discussed and the Strategic Defense Initiative criticized. A tank commander described his childhood and how he chose his career. Sailors were shown performing their tasks on a ship and a naval chorus sang martial music. Army engineers were shown constructing a pontoon bridge, and photographs of the Afghan war were displayed. Another program interviewed teachers, showed a dance ensemble, covered the work of children (Young Pioneers) who volunteered for civic tasks. But there were also cartoons and an early morning play show, with imitations of animals. On the weekend two of the feature films were designed for children, and if they are added, then the airtime for children's shows on Sunday was 25 percent, quite an increase over the average 8 percent of airtime on a weekday.

America on Weekend Airtime

Over the weekend the focus on America continued. All of the large number of news programs treated aspects of the United States and its foreign policy—relations with Libya, the contras in Nicaragua, support of the Afghan rebel leaders, Star Wars, Secretary of State Shultz's policy declarations on terrorism. Other stories treated opposition to American policies: the statements of the Panamanian Communist Party congress, anti-American demonstrations in Mexico, South Yemen's solidarity with the Soviet Union and warnings to the United States. Most of the references to the United States were negative; some were neutral; none was positive. Among the neutral news items were stories about the flight of *Voyager II* with pictures of Uranus.

Americans figured on other programs on the weekend, as well. The two news analysis programs: "Studio 9" on Saturday and "International Panorama" on Sunday had the United States as a major focus. In fact, "Studio 9" in its entirety (one hour) treated General Secretary Gorbachev's proposals for arms reductions and the reaction in the United States. It included a discussion of SDI, the proposed moratorium on testing, the attenuation of the "spirit of Geneva," the obstinacy of the United States with respect to ending chemical warfare (with references to Hitler), increases in the American military budget, and the American threat to Libya. The entire program was a recital of obstructionist and militarist tendencies aligned against the Soviets. The Sunday program focused on the United States in its first segment; later segments treated Spain, Northern Ireland, and Japan. The American portion accused the United States of starting the arms race and included an interview with former arms control head Paul Warnke about the Gorbachev arms reduction proposals. Warnke, interviewed by Dunaev in Washington, gave a lengthy exposition of his views, saying, among other things, that "the concrete measures proposed by the Soviet Union seem to me to be very, very, constructive." He indicated that he would like to see an end to nuclear tests, but noted that development of the Strategic Defense Initiative would require testing. He stated categorically that such testing relating to SDI is "absolutely prohibited" by treaty and that research should stay in the laboratory.

On entertainment programs, as well, the United States was

still in the center of attention—or very close. For example, a very popular Sunday program on movies, "Movie Poster," featured a piece on the American movie *Missing,* starring Jack Lemmon and Sissy Spacek. *Missing* would appear in Soviet movie theaters the next month, and the program urged viewers to see it. Joining the host to describe the film was a Soviet movie critic who was a judge at the Cannes Film Festival that gave two awards to *Missing.* Three clips of the film are shown (dubbed into Russian). In the second, Lemmon and Spacek are begging the American ambassador to help them find their relative. According to the Soviet critic, the film is not just about "American crimes in South America," but also about how the United States "destroys its own children, the best and the noblest, whenever they stand on the side of struggling peoples." Calling it a "political thriller" with a strong "human element," the host and his guest recall how popular Lemmon's films are in the Soviet Union—*The Apartment* and *The China Syndrome*—and they lavish praise on Lemmon and Spacek for their work in this movie.

A science program on Saturday was devoted to space exploration. Most of the time was devoted to the VEGA-2 mission, an unmanned space flight to Halley's Comet, and there was a brief reference to the American space program. One of the big sports events on television the weekend of our survey was a boxing match between Soviet and American teams. Finally, in children's programming this weekend, the United States was once again featured—in the military education show on Sunday morning—as rehearsing war games with its NATO allies. The NATO powers were referred to as imperialists, and Gorbachev was said to be trying to head off a war with his new proposals. The deleterious effect of the arms race on the developing nations and the threat of SDI ended this segment.

Throughout this week, the United States was a strong and vivid presence on Soviet television on virtually all dimensions of programming—sports, children's shows, films, as well as news and public affairs. With some exceptions, the image is negative. Special events can change that: during the week of the 1987 Washington Summit, America was portrayed in considerably more positive tones (including entertainment shows—a Johnny Cash concert, for example). In general, more varied fare about the United States is being displayed. Billy Joel's concert in Leningrad; the "Capital to Capital" space bridges, the more positive coverage of some American business practices are just some illustrations. Changes take place, but they take place within a context and building on a foundation. The week we surveyed provides a clear picture of the centrality of the United States for the Gorbachev leadership, Soviet television programmers, and the viewing public. It also conveys a flavor of the explanatory framework for understanding the world in which Soviet television (and the other media as well) educate the audience. These lessons, these rationales, and these positions form an essential part of the mechanisms by which change is understood. It is a question to which we shall return in the last chapter.

A Selection of Non-News Programs

Let's Go, Girls

The game shows and the popular music and variety shows are among the most watched and preferred programs on Soviet television. But, surely, the game show is a peculiarly capitalist invention, where greed spurs ordinary people to behave in extraordinary ways—furiously competing with opponents, exposing their private lives for the amusement of the audience, undergoing intense anxiety as they try to tot up the risks of going on or dispiritedly choose to take away their living room furniture and forgo the Cadillac. The American producers of these popular programs would not recognize the Soviet variant. As always, there is a specific rationale for shows on Soviet television. The game show presents an "opportunity for the simultaneous resolution of social-pedagogical and entertainment requirements." And the popularity of these programs is explained by the fact that the audience likes to see how the competition, the result of which is unknown, unfolds. But there is a larger significance, a more generalized meaning to the game show. The theorist speaks: ". . . participants in televised games, receiving the opportunity for public self-expression . . . permit the audience to see themselves typified on the screen."[78] This statement does not simply say that the audience struggles and exults vicariously with the contestants—there's that, of course. But the game show, Soviet style, is intended to instill in the audience the desire to do their jobs better. That becomes clear from looking at one of the most beloved and long-running game shows on Soviet television, "Let's Go, Girls," on the air since 1970.

This quiz program had a contest for bus drivers: a pail of water was placed in a shallow bowl on the dashboard. The object was to drive so smoothly over the city's icy streets, that the least amount of water would spill. Girls took their turn at the wheel, while, in the back of the bus, another contest went on. Construction engineers were given a large piece of cardboard with a section cut out. They had to fill this section with bricks. She who did so in the shortest time with the fewest bricks was the winner. Another broadcast, one that took place in the Soviet East, had young girls prepare a fish dish for a panel of judges. They took a frozen fish, stood it on end, and cut thin slices off the sides. The curled white shavings were put on a plate and given to a judge, who, after dipping them in a sauce and tasting, graded the girl. On the New Year's show, the girls had to compete in gift-wrapping.

As in so much of Soviet life, competing stereotypes co-exist. Here, all the young girls are virtually movie star quality (with healthy and rosy faces); some shows stress the modern Soviet woman, the engineer and bus driver; some relegate women to the same old roles, wrapping gifts and cooking for their menfolk. On a women's show, "Moscow Women," one program showed a heavily made-up hostess introducing crooners at the request of the ladies at home; while another was devoted to the no-nonsense female delegates to the 27th Party Congress.

The Man from Fifth Avenue

In April of 1986 two films on America aired on Soviet television. Each was given a coveted time slot: the first, right after the news on a Wednesday night; and the second, 5:30 on a Saturday afternoon. Each was allocated an article prominently placed in the weekly television guide. The first program was "The Man from Fifth Avenue," broadcast on April 2. This hour-and-a-half documentary was written by two notable figures in Soviet media: Genrikh Borovik and Leonid Zamyatin, ambassador to Great Britain, but at that time head of the International Information Department of the Central Committee and chief international spokesman, whose abrasive manner was on view when he chaired the press conference following the downing of KAL flight 007. In an interview before the broadcast of this film, Borovik told about its production. Unlike virtually all other documentaries, this one relies on footage shot on location in New York. It boasts an "up-to-dateness" that no other program on America had to date. Borovik, together with two cameramen, followed the story of Joseph Mauri, a fifty-four-year-old American who had been evicted from his one-room apartment, when the landlady wanted to use it for a sewing room. Borovik, in his interview, says that Mauri is an able-bodied, intelligent man who is superfluous, out of work, unneeded in this huge city.[79] Guided by Joe Mauri the filmed tour of New York proceeds.[80]

The opening is the Bruce Springsteen video, "Born in the USA," sound track and all. Throughout this documentary, the sound track is loud—with music (folk rock or folk with a very strong beat and electronically enhanced) or natural sound (crowds, sirens). The first shots are of the poor in Washington, D.C. Then the camera enters New York—shots of skyscrapers and the tunnel of Fifth Avenue through the huge buildings. Joseph Mauri is introduced and shows the Soviet filmmakers who accompany him where he lived: the one room, largely empty. He had, he said, begged his landlady to let him stay; he would clean up for her, he pleaded, but she was determined to have a sewing room. There are shots of people on the street; one is on crutches, and Mauri says that after forty it is difficult to get a job and if there are health problems, "First they ask when you go to the hospital, do you have medical insurance. If you don't you won't get in." The film crew and Mauri stop in front of the Plaza Hotel, and Mauri comments: "If I try to go in, they'll kick me out like a dirty dog." The camera cuts to a newspaper box; the newspaper says "Reagan Election Rigged." The next section is about the extreme opulence in this heartless city: Women in luxurious fur coats—and men, too—walk on the Avenue. The camera pans over the windows: Fendi clothes; Charles Jourdan shoes. Then a long series of scenes with an idealistic architect, who is unable to raise the money for his projects to help people, while another American present talks about what a real estate broker does: "buys apartments where old people live and waits and then sells them for many times more." The architect comments that "there is a big difference between profit and profiteering. They don't create anything, don't earn it . . . They get a big profit on someone else's work."

Mauri and the crew introduce the Soviet audience to Fifth Avenue housing. They stop at several condominiums and ask the doormen how much an apartment costs. They hear figures of 2 million dollars, 1,600,000 dollars, or one that is "very small" and the least expensive, 375,000 dollars. The doorman laughs condescendingly at the questions Mauri poses. The life of the rich is shown in many more shots, intercut with shots of the homeless: a man in a fur coat, jewelry in a store window, a homeless person sleeping on the sidewalk, a woman in a fur coat, a homeless person sleeping in a doorway, Trump Tower, a luxuriously dressed woman walking her poodle, and on and on. Mauri walks by looking in windows. The crew enters a store that sells only by appointment and only particularly expensive (and unneeded) items: A huge chinchilla bedspread, an attaché case costing over a thousand dollars, an antique crystal and silver perfume bottle, a designer pistol. Then on to a limousine showroom, where, it is claimed, the most expensive cars in the world are sold. Back with Mauri on the street, he said that he thought he'd be safe in his old age, but there's no place to live.

Opulence gives way to poverty, as the crew goes up to the other end of Fifth Avenue. The audience sees graffiti on the walls and on subway cars and fronts of decaying buildings. Police on horseback seem menacing. An old white man is interviewed by the crew on the street. He is living on social security and can barely make ends meet; all of his family is dead; he's completely alone. This theme of poverty and infirmity mixed with total isolation will be repeated again and again. Mauri searches for rooms and is repeatedly rejected. A shot of a church prompts the narrator to say that Jews are set against Catholics, blacks against whites; everybody is against everybody else in this city. As Mauri says, there are no human rights here. He declares: "My human rights were denied to me. I am being put out on the street." More shots of homeless sleeping on benches and on the street. A young black woman is stopping cars to raise money for a room. A long sequence of breakdancing kids is shown: they are collecting money.

The desperation of the people at this end of town is shown not only by people who beg or perform in the streets, but also by references to the pornography industry and, most insistently, child pornography and prostitution. People on the street tell the cameraman that it's terrible that young kids are exploited, but no solutions are advanced, and, it is asserted, the police are unconcerned. The Soviet crew finds two policemen on the street and asks what they are doing about prostitution. The police refuse to answer. The drug scene is next, beginning with shots of 42nd Street, then sirens, shots of people sniffing cocaine, coke packets. It is shown as a problem out of control, as the "police look the other way."

After a look at professional wrestling, with cheering audiences and no commentary other than the English sound track of the television program, the religion segment begins. Mauri sits on the steps of St. Patrick's Cathedral and remarks that he wrote a letter to the bishop. He asked the bishop to write to his landlady, to plead with her not to turn Mauri out on the street. He did not, he said, receive an answer. A Janis Joplin song is played at great length, and translated: "Lord, won't you buy me a Mercedes Benz, a color TV, a night on the town." The religion part will be tied to the suppression of black people, which begins with the Soviet narrator attempting to interview a black man walking with a woman on the street. The woman goes on ahead, but the man consents to the interview, whereupon the woman comes back, screaming at him, pulling him by the collar, and cursing in expletives that are left untranslated, and the scene shifts to a white man laughing as he sits above a black man shining his shoes. There are more cuts of buildings and church spires and, suddenly, the Ku Klux Klan at a cross burning. A black woman is interviewed, who is an articulate and very angry critic of the American system and its leaders. She says that she has tried to help black people, and the man with her adds that she was railroaded by a court and forced to serve time in prison for it. She was, she says, a political prisoner (shots of jails, corroding metal bars, poverty in prison). The theme of oppression of blacks continues with a shift to lengthy footage of the 1985 burning of the MOVE house in Philadelphia.

The linkage of all of these patterns of misery and oppression on the one hand, and the military threat on the other, is finally made toward the end of the program, as the MOVE segment is followed by a shot of the Statue of Liberty and then young men going into the armed forces. To the sound of highly amplified electronic folk music, we see intercutting of American planes and women in another country sobbing; recruits getting haircuts, Vietnam horrors, flag-draped coffins returning, a Marine recruiting poster, planes taking off from aircraft carriers, bombs falling, Americans looking up in the sky and laughing. Mauri asserts that the money wastefully thrown away on military programs could help people live. But, he says, people are expendable. "It's a terrible crime."

More of Fifth Avenue—Central Park, with people sleeping (Mauri says you have to know how to do it, how to hide). Joggers go by; more skyscrapers. Mauri sadly smiles and says he hopes for a better future. Folk rock is loud in the background, as we see Mauri walking up to the camera, then by it, and then going beyond it. His back is followed out of camera range. A stark epilogue is written on the screen. It says that on November 22, Joseph Mauri was evicted from his apartment.

A few months after this film was shown, Joseph Mauri was invited to the Soviet Union by the trade unions. He was shown on television there and gave talks about the plight of the homeless in America. American newspeople found out from interviews that he was not, in fact, homeless (he lives in a rent-controlled apartment on the West Side—he says the place belongs to his estranged wife, but the neighbors say he has lived there for at least ten years) and that for twenty-five years he has worked part-time as a regular substitute mailroom worker for the *New York Times*, a job he could expand substantially if he wants—he could make as much as $680.00 a week before taxes, but he works so few shifts that in the first seven months of 1986 he made only $3,000.[81]

From Chicago to Philadelphia

The second film that month about America was also a very high profile production, written and narrated by Valentin Zorin, another of the best-known commentators on Soviet television. "From Chicago to Philadelphia," an hour-long documentary, pairs the two cities as examples of the filmmaker's thesis that "many presidents have served their terms in the White House in [the last] hundred years, but not much has changed in America. . . ."[82] It was in Chicago, a hundred years before the making of this documentary, that the Haymarket deaths that began May Day took place. The film goes back to Chicago and considers it then and now. And it is in Philadelphia in May 1985, that the MOVE house was burned, and lengthy footage of this event and its aftermath is shown, along with Zorin's interview of the police commissioner. Zorin asks, at one point, how many were killed. The answer is that we do not use the word killed, because no one killed them; there were twelve deaths. Shots of Independence Hall follow, the words of the Declaration of Independence roll by to a sweet musical sound track. But, the narrator says, the promise of human equality and the commitment to life, liberty, and the pursuit of happiness did not succeed—shots of the MOVE neighborhood and bulldozers bringing down the charred shells of houses.

The film moves to Chicago and with drawings recounts the events of Haymarket Square a hundred years ago. There is a link to modern-day Wall Street and the assertion that rapacious banks determine the fate of American workers. Zorin goes inside the Stock Exchange, which he calls not only a barometer of business, but also a powerful instrument in the hands of banks and big business for their manipulation of workers. Back in Chicago, there is a long piece about a closed United States Steel factory, and then, to a soundtrack of ominous electronic and drum music, the camera roves over a depressed neighborhood, with its abandoned houses, rusting cars, an overturned barbeque grill, empty interiors, broken windows, toys left behind in the yard. Where are the people now?—Zorin asks. Shots of people sleeping on the sidewalks, lining up at soup kitchens, picking things out of trash cans. The main focus of the remainder of the program is on Rudy Lozano, a thirty-one-year-old union leader and political activist, who was closely associated with Mayor Harold Washington. Lozano was killed in June 1983, in his home by an unknown gunman. At Lozano's funeral, thousands marched through Chicago's Mexican community to pay their respects to the popular leader.[83] Zorin takes the film crew to the Mexican neighborhood, and the steps of the crime are enacted, as described by Lozano's widow, Guadalupe. The door is shown opening, a swift cut to the kitchen, a shot of the floor, where Lozano fell. A fighter for human rights has been cut down.

Space Bridge: Moscow-Kabul

On July 26, 1986, there was a first for Soviet television: a "space bridge" (satellite link-up) between Moscow and Kabul. It was to be a "musical space bridge": songs performed in the concert studio of Central Television in Moscow and received in the small television studio in the Afghan capital. It was that, but it was much more. It was a highly emotional tribute to the Soviet forces in Afghanistan and a rousing patriotic show. It opened with the Red Army chorus (in uniform) singing "With You," followed by a female m.c. sending to "you, Afghan friends, and you, dear Soviet troops, words of love, respect and gratitude." The male m.c. adds his gratitude and asks all those in the Moscow studio who fulfilled "their patriotic duty" in the Afghan campaign to stand: a large number of veterans stand up and are applauded. Kabul enters. The studio there is small; no more than fifty people, most of whom are Soviet soldiers. The host is Central Television's Kabul correspondent. The program features performances of songs (or occasionally a comic turn) interspersed with parents in the Moscow studio talking to sons in the Kabul studio. These are, naturally, very emotional, though controlled, scenes. One mother and father wish their son a happy birthday, and he, in turn inquires about their health and says he is coming home soon. The parents all say that everything is fine; they bring up news of the family—grandmother is fine, Dima is doing well, Sasha is fine. A visibly nervous father ends his short statement with a quavering request that his son write. Another father tells his son that he wants him to be conscientious, urges him to develop self-control and patience, because they will help him as a soldier. Many of the performers had entertained the troops in Kabul and remark how unforgettable and significant the experience was. The Russian woman soldier in Kabul who is in charge of the mailroom thanks the home country for its support of the fighting men. A newly composed song is performed in honor of the war dead, those who gave their lives "fulfilling their internationalist duty to the end." Another new song has been composed to honor the service of the airborne troops, and a member

of the unit thanks Moscow. An Afghan composer is introduced
in Kabul: he has written the first revolutionary song, which is
then performed in Moscow, as three Afghan students studying
in Moscow stand and sing along. A father, mother, and sister in
Moscow tell their son and brother in Kabul not to worry. Everything, they say, is fine.

The World and Youth / Twelfth Floor

"The World and Youth" was a popular magazine-format program for teenagers that was split into two different programs in
1987: the live late-night music and information show "Glance"
(Vzglyad) and the weekly public affairs program "Acting Persons" (the title in Russian also means cast of characters in a
play). According to Eduard Sagalaev, the head of the Youth
Programming division at Gosteleradio, the issues treated by
"The World and Youth" required more time and more extensive coverage. Sometimes, as in the edition of "The World and
Youth" cited earlier, the topics include politics in the Middle
East or NATO, or, in other programs, Afghanistan. Interspersed with these are topics about Soviet youth. One of the
most interesting segments was on heavy metal rock music in
the Soviet Union. It began by describing and showing the various ornaments that fans wear: chains, pictures of rock stars,
nail-studded cuffs and dog collars. The program then went
among young people, including "metalisty" (Americans would
call them "metalheads"). A good deal of arguing—at high
pitch—went on. One metalist, dressed in rock star sleeveless t-
shirt, neck chain, muscles bulging, said, "We dress according
to the style of the people whose music we like. Nothing more.
We like rock. They tell us: you don't understand what they are
singing. I don't need it. The combination of voice and good
musical training appeals to me." An angry older man yells in
disgust that "it's cheap to imitate Westerners. This isn't music.
These are kids of 12, 13, 14 . . ." Clips from foreign music
videos are shown, Motley Crue among them. A clean-cut
young boy—not a metalist—says that just because he likes the
music, he's not a fanatic, rushing to put up posters all over
town. A metalist says that people don't understand them, and
don't see them enough. Another metalist is angry that so many

lies are told about them and their music. His metalist friend says very tellingly: "You must explain that we are people like any others. We don't want evil. We don't want anything political behind the scenes and we don't want any put on us. We work and we want to achieve something, but in our free time we're enthusiasts, and that's all." The interviewer raises a question: "I was told today that metalisty are fascists . . ." The metalisty interrupt animatedly and angrily: "No, No. There are 20 million said to have died. I think more died. But such trash grow up here that I would choke them with my own hands. I give you my word of honor."

The question is raised, should we have clubs for metalisty? A long-haired, but not metalist, teen-age boy asks how that's possible, with what funds, since there isn't enough even for clubs already in existence. Another raises the question of a music magazine for youth—it's been talked about for five years, he says, but nothing has happened. Finally, a mother points to her grade-school son, and says that he listens to foreign shows. "What can we offer, instead?" And on that note, the segment ends. What is remarkable about this segment is the openness with which it treats the several points of view it entertains. Further, it takes on, in a sympathetic way, a trend in the youth counterculture that has been roundly condemned by the official press. The program recognizes that co-optation is very much more effective than repression, and that the political resonance of Western rock can be dissociated from its purely musical expression. Again and again, the program presses for measures that should have been taken long ago by the bureaucracy and that have become stalled. How to pre-empt Western influence, how to fill the leisure time vacuum for the young generation is a problem that "The World and Youth" recognizes as critical.

Early in 1986 "The World and Youth" spun off a new show. "Twelfth Floor," one of the most unusual and innovative programs on Soviet television, has an energy and the look of spontaneity. People interrupt each other; voices are raised in anger or excitement; the energy level is higher than for any other program. Editing is rapid; the pace never slackens. It debuted on January 2, 1986. At first it had no name; it was called simply "Supplement to 'The World and Youth.' " According to Sagalaev, the origin of the show began with the question mandated by glasnost: how to bring in the most varied points of view and to have youth of different ages and different social backgrounds present their views as candidly as possible. The director hit upon the idea of satellite link-ups from the Ostankino studio, with young people as close as the Moscow streets and as far away as Novosibirsk. That way they would be on their "own territory," rather than in the unaccustomed surroundings of the television studio. It was, Sagalaev said, to be a kind of "referendum" on the topics most important to teenagers: education, free time, and work. In Moscow, officials and reporters who were involved in these issues responded to and were questioned by the young people outside. Although the interchanges were filmed, they looked lively and unrehearsed. The first program linked Tiumen—site of large oilfields, where Gorbachev had been in a much heralded and covered visit—and Moscow, and additional telephone links were set up. The number of a telephone line to the Moscow studio—283-84-05—was illuminated and calls came in from as far away as Vladivostok and Taskhent. The Tiumen participants questioned A.P. Vasilev, deputy minister of the oil and gas industry, about the tempo of construction of housing, videotape libraries, places for relaxation. "We have nowhere to go, nothing to occupy us. Our only entertainment is a beer bar."

This was to be the theme of the next edition. By February, the "supplement" had a name: "Twelfth Floor," referring to the floor in the Gosteleradio building where youth programs are planned and written. This program was remarkable. During the February show, the Ostankino studio picked up remote locations in other Soviet cities, but also a group of young people sitting in a stairwell of an apartment house in Moscow. Several times, these teenagers rejected what Ostankino was telling them. One girl said she disliked her school; another rejected the statement by an official that "you have the most difficult production; you are producing yourselves, isn't that so?" "No, it's not so," a boy replied. Another said, "We're still kids." After a clip of a cautionary soft rock song entitled "Mannequins," about the superficiality and emptiness of those who run after Western styles, a boy in the stairwell dared Ostankino to show that he was a mannequin. Later in the program, an official in the studio asked that boy if he ever thought about his responsibility—his personal responsibility—for what is happening, for what they were discussing on the program. The boy answered, "I don't feel any." But, he is asked, "Have you ever asked yourself that question?" "No." This program was about leisure time and how few opportunities and places exist for teenagers. It is a problem that has long been recognized and equally long has been mired in the bureaucratic morass. With youth officials (from the ministries and the Komsomol) in the studio and people of all ages, especially youth, interacting from remote pick-ups, discussion—and accusations—went back and forth about what to do. True to the Gorbachev policy, participants were asked to take some initiative, to do something themselves. But the answers were often that they had tried (one boy went as far as the city district government, he said) and failed. The Komsomol came in for some criticism on that score. But if that program was startling in its contentiousness, the edition of May 22 was very much more so.

That day, "Twelfth Floor" took up the question of schools and what should be improved. In the Ostankino studio were the deputy Minister of Education and representatives of the teacher training bureaucracy and the Komsomol, the youth organization. The program again picked up a group of young people in a stairwell in Moscow and another, larger group outside in Tomsk, in Siberia. The program was full of very candid criticism, passion, and anger. It looked spontaneous. The young people in Tomsk complained that "very little happens in school"; "the teacher says one thing and does another"; "they talk only about duties, but you don't hear anything about rights." From the stairwell, a volley of attacks was launched against the deputy Minister of Education: what exactly had he done, what could he say concretely and honestly, did he even understand new methods of teaching? As the official tried to show his command of the situation, he was laughed at and ridiculed by the stairwell, and throughout the long program, he was on the defensive. The talk moved to textbooks, and a girl in Tomsk said: "our textbooks are out of date. We have to know more about what's happening now." A young man asked how they can study Russian literature with the textbooks they have. Many textbooks were called "hopelessly out of date" by the young people. One said her physics teacher had to tell them not to use their books for most problems. A girl said that she liked American and English literature best, but didn't get it in school. A young man said: "I think a textbook on literature is not necessary at all. One should think for oneself and understand the works." From Moscow a hard-line official answered that "There's creativity and the framework for creativity. . . . The textbook perfects creativity." The plea for freedom is answered by the requirement of order, but the plea has been made.

Talking about the activities of the Komsomol, a young man says: "The Komsomol loses its authority among schoolchildren because the majority of its measures are absolutely senseless. . . . Why are things decided on top and not here?" That charge prefigured a large-scale attack on the official youth organization launched by the media. The attack gained additional momentum after the riots that broke out later that year in the capital of the republic of Kazakhstan. There, the Komsomol was taken severely to task by Moscow for losing touch with its constituents, the young people, particularly students, who were among the leaders of the nationalist demonstrations following the removal of the Kazakh leader and his replacement by a Russian. But the problem with the Komsomol went far beyond that locale. The concerns that were broadcast on "Twelfth Floor" were early warning signals that the youth organization had become ossified, remote, and, worst of all, irrelevant. An article in *Pravda* nearly a year after that "Twelfth Floor" program, asserted, in virtually the same words the disgruntled teenager had used on television, that initiative in youth activities could indeed come "from below," that involvement in a host of activities and the pursuit of interests ranging from sports to science fiction to rock music should not have to "depend on who at a given moment was 'on top.' "[84]

These were early signals that organizations, such as the Komsomol, were not to monopolize or stifle initiative. Just over a year later, some forty-seven "informal groups" met in Moscow. This was the culmination of the development of a host of grass-roots initiatives. The groups met under the auspices of the Moscow City Communist Party; they represented areas of interest from the environment to more directly political concerns. Throughout 1987, "informal groups" had begun attracting attention. Some operated loosely tied to larger official organizations, such as the Komsomol-affiliated group of Veterans of the Afghan War, but some went further: the Crimean Tatars, banished from their homeland by Stalin and later "rehabilitated" but not returned to their lands, marched in Moscow. Dissident Sergei Grigoryants, back from prison, openly began publication (using typewriters and carbon paper) of a journal called *Glasnost*. On the darker side of the by-products of glasnost, a Russian nationalist "informal group," called Pamyat (Memory), went beyond its agenda of support for restoration and preservation of the Russian past to march in Moscow with anti-Semitic and anti-Masonic placards. They were received by the Moscow City Party chief, Boris Eltsin. "Twelfth Floor" had told the country that the official organizations could be bypassed—or at the very least supplemented—if the population was to be mobilized and its energies released. Leaders were ridiculed and told their policies were obsolete. Within months the responses outran the plan. Worried about the rise of informal groups outside its domain, the official youth organization drafted a proposal arguing that "the creative quest of young people should be secured above all within the framework of *existing* Komsomol organizations and committees. There is no need for the creation of alternative organizations." This point was made in the context of an articulated need to nurture "healthy principles" and "eliminate ugly phenomena that are alien to the socialist way of life."[85] The ouster in November 1987 of Boris Eltsin, a powerful Politburo figure, was undoubtedly related not only to his radical personnel policies, but also to concern with the way he ran the city. It was he who met with Pamyat demonstrators, according them an official, unscheduled audience, and it was in his city that these events testing the limits of glasnost took place. The Soviet press cited administrative problems in his leadership and published his confession of incompetence.

With its rapid-fire editing and fast, almost frantic, pace, "Twelfth Floor" has been, in my view, the most interesting program on Soviet television. Like its parent show, "The World and Youth," it tackled new currents head-on, and it held the attention as did few other Soviet television programs. The officials had to answer to the grass roots, and the grass roots, in this case the critical generation of adolescents, were brought into the system by being given a sense of authority and importance. Inevitably, their expectations were also raised. One boy in the stairwell on the May program said that they had already talked about these issues on the program two months before and nothing was done, school was still the same and he was angry.

The very success of "Twelfth Floor" gave Gosteleradio pause. Expectations were clearly outrunning results; the reforms had not caught up with the rhetoric. As Sagalaev put it, there is a time to rip shirts and put salt on wounds and a time to heal. Continued exposure of social problems without the concomitant evidence of solutions and changes would only exacerbate the situation. Gosteleradio would have to rethink the premises of "Twelfth Floor," probably the most popular program on television, and, as Sagalaev put it, devise a way to graduate to a higher level, as one moves from the "mathematics of society" to the "algebra of society."

*   *   *   *

These important non-news programs show that new things are happening, as do the changes in the focus of the news since Mikhail Gorbachev came to power. At the technical level and at the political level, substantial rethinking has taken place. Many of the changes are apparent to the viewer. But behind those changes, and preceding them, there has been a reconsideration of the underlying theory of communication: who the audience is or should be and how can Moscow reach that audience. What has to be done if the media are to be politically effective, particularly as the demand for information increases from within and without. It is to these questions that we turn in the next chapter.

CHAPTER FIVE

Television and the Formation of Public Opinion

VIRTUALLY FROM THE BEGINNING of the Gorbachev leadership, the Soviet public and the outside world perceived an elevation of the role of public opinion and a conscious and more knowledgeable utilization of the mechanisms by which public opinion is formed in the modern world. This change is, in my view, to a great extent, a response to the dramatic spread of television in the Soviet Union and the enormous public it has attracted. Under Gorbachev, television has been accorded status as a powerful vehicle for the shaping of public opinion. If the Soviet system is to manage public opinion it must be able to gauge its dimensions, and this, in turn, would require a more rigorous and scientifically grounded understanding of the theory of how messages are assimilated and opinion formed.

The development of television in the Soviet Union, though belated in comparison with the United States, has radically altered the system of communications in the U.S.S.R.: both the orthodoxy of political communications theory and the time-honored practices of the ideology cadres in that country have been powerfully challenged. The Soviets face a rapidly changing communications environment: their policies, formed in the center and applied across the land, have produced many unintended results. Moreover, they have the challenging task of reconciling the new developments to the old doctrine, a doctrine that, though hallowed, as Lenin's words always are, provides scant help in meeting new and far more complex challenges. Because in developing their television industry, the Soviets have been catching up in a characteristically massive way, and because the international communications environment in which the Soviet Union is situated has developed an intrusive technology very rapidly, the Soviet leadership must face widespread results of developments they had not foreseen. One result is the mobilization of attention of the media public to foreign, particularly Western, political systems—a development first seen in newspaper readers and then increasingly in the context of television, the most massive of mass media. This vehicle for the simultaneous and uniform transmission of visual messages stands in contrast to the personalized medium of agitation (the transmission of political information by party members to small groups of co-workers), which had, in the past, according to Soviet theory, channeled and guided information to a largely isolated and uninformed public. It is precisely because of the rapid development of television that the agitator and the shaping of public opinion with which he was charged, are becoming obsolete. To some extent, the new concerns of the Soviet leadership arise because of a faulty understanding of the flow of public opinion and to some extent it occurs because of a radically changed communications environment.

Understanding Public Opinion: Television and Model-Fitting

The Hypodermic Effects Model

Interestingly, in the past Western and Soviet media theorists have held rather similar views about how television—ours and theirs—communicates to and persuades their respective audiences. Essentially, both applied the "hypodermic effects" model to the analysis of media effects. This model asserts the immediate and unaltered reception of all new information carried by the media system, much as a hypodermic needle inserts its dosage into the human organism. In Western research about Western communications systems, this approach has been largely discarded. It was found that it simply could not be proved empirically, and that the audience "could not be viewed as an inert element in the communication process."[1] As McLeod and Becker summarize the rise and fall of this model:

> The hypodermic persuasion model of mass media effects is now well buried under a mound of rhetoric—topped off by a layer of supportive data. Null findings from media campaign studies have testified to the inadequacy of this simple learning model, which predicts that repetitive exposure of media messages is sufficient to change the attitudes and behaviors of large numbers of people in important ways. At its worst, this model makes the tacit assumption that media content equals audience effect.[2]

The theory is not made stronger by application to a society, such as the Soviet, where the media are state controlled: empirical studies there have reached the same conclusion, and the model has been discarded by knowledgeable officials and researchers. Actually, the hypodermic effects theory is a broadcaster's dream: the total actualization of his effort, but like most dreams, wishful thinking. Sometimes, though, the theory lingers on, not as dream, but as nightmare. For example, a Soviet media analyst warned of the powerful effects of capitalist propaganda: "One of the characteristics of anticommunism as 'anti-ideology' is that its existence, its capability of 'extending its own life,' directly depends on regular injections into the consciousness of the masses of new doses of falsifications and slander against the Soviet Union, other socialist countries, [and] against all the sources of the world liberation movement."[3] If this is the challenge, the solution, according to the professional propagandists, is to build up the "ideological immunity" of the Soviet population, especially the young.[4]

When, in the past, the hypodermic effects model held sway among Soviet communications theorists—although it did posit a largely undifferentiated audience—it had, nonetheless, to take into account a basic fact about that audience: its capacity to make sense of communications symbols would vary significantly across the geographic and linguistic regions of the country and up and down the scale of educational attainment. These elements of differentiation are, according to the doctrine, ephemeral, as rising levels of education are expected to wipe out some differences, while the process of *sblizhenie*, or confluence of ethnic and linguistic characteristics, erases the rest. An adequately educated citizenry would no longer have any difficulty understanding (and therefore being persuaded by) media messages. It was simply a matter of time.

However, over seventy years after the Revolution, with an almost totally literate population, and with the saturation of that population by the official media, it was revealed in a reliable survey of an average-sized industrial city in the Russian Republic, that many of the words most often used in foreign affairs reporting were totally meaningless to the citizens. About 25 percent did not understand the word "colonialism." Forty percent did not know what "dictatorship" meant. Almost half could not say what "imperialism" was. Almost 66 percent did not know what "leftist forces" meant and between 66 percent and 75 percent did not understand the terms "reactionary" and "liberal."[5] When a survey studied the television viewing habits of rural Russians, it was found that of the viewers who had not gone beyond the fourth grade 93 percent could not understand programs on social/political topics. It is important to note that about 40 percent of the rural Russian population has no more than a fourth-grade education.[6]

One other transitional and rapidly disappearing element was often said to account for a small degree of variation in the assimilation of communications messages: some people exercise a willful obstructionism, born of a "contamination" with the bourgeois past. This is the well-known "vestiges of the past" argument that now, so long after the 1917 Revolution, has lost much of its force. It still turns up in some official literature, for example, with reference to the acquisitive tendencies of the Caucasian peoples, but its frequency has diminished and it is certainly absent from serious policy and research publications, even those written by Party officials.

It was these passing elements of differentiation in the audience that dictated the policy for whatever minimal differentiation existed in the past among the Soviet media. The hypodermic effects model was, in the past, always standing, simplistically and comfortably, behind these explanations of temporary deviations from the norm. There was no need to question its imputed effects or to doubt its assumed efficacy.

Mass Publics and the Two-Step Flow Model

Television may well be considered the first truly "mass" medium in Soviet history. The term "mass" applied to the audience for media is intended to signal an entirely new configuration, reaching well beyond the traditional family unit or group, or even crowd. The media of modernity, today's channels of communication, and most particularly television, have a new kind of audience: very large and very diverse. This is an audience *created* by the media; the only significant experience they share may, in fact, be media messages. Nothing in the Soviet media system rivals the diversity and size of the television audience, and the same is true in the United States. As George Gerbner noted, "mass production and distribution of message systems transforms selected private perspectives into broad public perspectives and brings mass publics into existence."[7] Furthermore, the messages arrive with heretofore unheard-of rapidity and they are standardized and uniform across this vast public. Both in the West and in the Soviet Union, a patterned system of response to the mass media has been seen in study after study, illustrating the change that has taken place—the mass public has come into being in both kinds of media system.[8] There is, in the mass media, a single sender and many receivers. This permits a simultaneous and immediate response by many different people in the audience. There is no assumption that the impact is uniform; people bring rather different dispositions and histories to the experience. But it is likely that the variability of response will be less in this mass environment than when there is, in Denis McQuail's words, "slow and sequential person-to-person diffusion of information."[9] McQuail here opposes a newer understanding of the media to the older, problematic model of the "two-step flow."

In the West, the two-step flow theory, which was originally formulated in connection with marketing techniques, has lost considerable credibility (as lacking an adequate empirical base and research design).[10] It holds that some people in the public, because of their higher level of education, heightened level of interest, and elite status, are directly exposed to the messages of the media. They then become "opinion leaders," passing the information on to others, who are then only indirectly exposed.[11]

Because of the limitations of the pre-television mass media, this model was applied very seriously and widely to the Soviet Union. The two-step flow was required to stand in for an incomplete and fragmented communications network, a requirement made obsolete when television entered the media system. However, the formalization of the two-step flow resulted in the formation, early in Soviet history, of huge numbers of ideology cadres, whose function became problematic as television saturated the country.

Alex Inkeles, in his pioneering work on Soviet public opinion written before the widespread introduction of television, concluded that the most significant innovation of the Soviet system of communications was the organization of interpersonal communication.[12] Agitation involved the formalization within political structures of the two-step flow of communication. The agitator, described by Lenin in his early work (still the operational code of the media system) *What Is To Be Done?*, is directly exposed to information and then disseminates it, usually in spoken form and much simplified, to those with whom he or she works. Every member of the Communist Party, along with non-Party political activists, has the duty to serve as agitator and communicate with fellow workers on the basis of instructions. These instructions are sometimes conveyed in Party meetings and frequently available in newspapers, where Party policy is spelled out very clearly in special columns—editorials or "Party Life" sections. In the broad sense, instructions may be construed simply as the official version of events as reported in the newspaper and, as they were developed, in the newer electronic media. It is the agitator who is charged with explaining on the spot, on the production line. This theory of the politicization and organization of the two-step flow of communication has certain corollaries. Most important is the setting: those who listen to the opinion leader (the agitator) and who thus derive their information in the second of the steps of the communication flow are fellow workers. The workplace is the setting; the group shares the characteristics associated with the job, or if students, of the student collective. It follows, then, that the message and its subsequent transmission must be related to the characteristics of those in the working collective, to use a Soviet term. The public is seen, under the terms of this approach, as members of a workgroup. It is a multiple set of publics, not really a mass public at all; the media have been personalized and mediated through the agitator and do not really fit the notion of modern mass communications, since it is presupposed that their "reach" is in fact limited, and not mass. While this was certainly true before the era of television, now it is not.

When Inkeles described personal oral agitation, he noted that it performed certain very important functions. First, the agitator extended the often spotty coverage of the media. The vastness of the country, the varieties of ethnic groups, the problem of the shortage of paper—all of these made agitation a valuable and necessary complement to the media. As he wrote: "Many of the workers do not have the initiative (and some are unable) to read the daily newspaper, and access to radios is limited. . . . The agitator, reading aloud from a newspaper, presenting a news digest, or giving a report about Soviet foreign policy, acts as a convenient and effortless source of news for his group."[13]

Both Western and Soviet theories of the Soviet communications system are related to the importance and functionality of agitation, that is, to the primacy of interpersonal communications networks. If we find, as we approach the year 2000, that the functionality of agitation is dubious, that the introduction of television has fundamentally altered how and in what setting communication takes place, then we must reformulate our notions of the media system. There is evidence that this is being done at certain levels of the Party in the Soviet Union. It is a development that would radically redefine the notion of the public, of the media themselves and how they relate to each other, of the appropriate and most useful channels of feedback, and, of course, of the persuasive content of the messages with respect to issues of foreign as well as domestic politics.

To begin, the most obvious fact is the tremendous change in Soviet society since the practice of agitation was first introduced. Whereas in 1920 some 60 percent of the population was classified as illiterate and therefore able to consume only one medium—

radio—by 1979 that proportion was only three-tenths of one percent.[14] This advance in literacy does not preclude the kind of
ignorance of terms used in foreign affairs writing noted above,
but it does represent a significant development.

The vastness of the country and its areas of inaccessible terrain
are simply leapfrogged by the use of communications satellites.
The Soviet Union has a large number of satellites that bring
national network television programming to all eleven time
zones of the country. Although there is still a shortage of paper,
television has developed so rapidly since Inkeles wrote, that it
reaches more than nine-tenths of the population. Television is a
medium that does not depend on reading skills and can, with
the aid of satellites, penetrate the farthest reaches of the country
far more rapidly than the newspaper. An agitator learns of the
news no earlier than the rest of the public.

The workplace has also changed. The workweek has been
shortened, shifting from six days to five in 1967. It is becoming
more and more difficult to arrange the free time needed for
agitation meetings, and there is a real problem of reconciling the
demands of production and agitation at the place of work. As
the imperatives of the economic plan become more pressing,
there is a complementary downgrading of agitation at work,
since it robs the production line of workers during working
hours. In the face of projected declines of rate of entry into the
industrial labor force, the value of each hour of working time is
increased. With the press of family responsibilities, the seemingly limitless forms of evening adult education, and the official
pressure for volunteer civic work—all compressed into afterwork hours—agitators find it difficult to gather an audience after
work. For female workers, some 51 percent of the industrial
labor force in 1981,[15] time spent in agitation meetings during free
time reduces the time they can put into the large number of
tasks, largely unshared, related to household and children. For
them the "double burden" is intensified by the obligation of any
afterwork meetings. As a reaction to the changing work-pattern,
there has been a move to extend agitation to the home—in most
cases, the apartment building—but the degree of organization
seems to be much lower than for the "classical" sessions with a
captive audience at the factory, school, or office. Stephen White
notes that only a small proportion of the population is involved

in agitation at home, and that, in turn, the local Party authorities have accorded it low priority, carrying it out irregularly or not at all. In general, people do not want to be given political lectures and engage in structured political discussion at home.[16] The dispersed population of the countryside is even less likely to be covered by the agitation network.

Inkeles also observed that the agitator represented a link with, or personalization of, the Party, that remote power structure in which the ordinary citizen does not participate. The agitator acted as a kind of safety valve, absorbing demands and dissatisfaction by presenting himself as target, and he in turn would transmit upward the moods and attitudes of the public. The agitator as transmitter of feedback is also a fairly dubious proposition at present. There is no evidence that the agitator is either a preferred or—and more important—a reliable source of representative public opinion. It is a matter of considerable concern to Soviet policymakers that adequate channels of feedback may not exist; they are increasingly aware of the tremendous deficit of feedback their policies and structures have brought about. There is evidence that when citizens wish to express their opinions and demands they prefer, by a wide margin, to address the newspaper rather than any governmental or party representative, or mass or public organization.[17]

Finally, the decline of agitation can be clearly seen in the way it is treated in important statements. When Konstantin Chernenko was the top ideology Secretary, he set the policies and directions of the regime in a long statement on communications and ideology. In it he hardly referred to the process of agitation, and when he did it came in for severe criticism—for *agitpunkty* (agitation rooms) that were mere shells, no longer functioning.[18] The major Soviet survey of public participation in the industrial city of Taganrog did not treat agitation at all, calling it "unsystematic." The implication is that whatever role agitators played in the past, their exclusion from the study may signal, in the researchers' minds, a sharp reduction in the utility of agitation in a more highly developed communications system.[19] Other surveys have found that agitation is the least popular form of political propaganda among factory workers, and that Party officials call it "superficial and lacking in content" and complain that agitation meetings are "held irregularly and attended unwillingly."[20] Further, in a survey it was found that "the proportion of workers who reported that agitational *besedy* (talks) were among their principal sources of information varied between 2 percent and 6 percent."[21] In a Moscow poll, respondents reported overwhelmingly (82 percent) that, in fact, *television* was their most important source of information, whereas agitation provided information to only 3.6 percent.[22] Then, there are many who simply avoid agitation and are effectively outside its net. A survey in Tomsk found that 65 percent of the respondents had not attended any agitation sessions in the previous three months.[23]

The communications environment has changed rather markedly in the Soviet Union since the role of agitation was first conceptualized and related to the two-step flow of communication. Most notably, the new medium of television has reached an audience of a size that no other medium could match. What the two-step flow theory really fails to consider is that the mass media are genuinely mass instruments, creating mass publics. In an earlier time that might have constituted the *potential* of the media, especially in the Soviet Union, which early on recognized the importance of mass media and embarked on a tremendous campaign of development, but still could not saturate the country. It could not be assured that messages from the center would reach the whole country virtually simultaneously. A far greater technological development was necessary for that. At that time, too, it was not at all clear how to fashion messages for a linguistically and educationally diverse population, barely integrated into a national whole. How could the comprehension of such a mass communications system be assumed? As I noted above, this is still a serious question, and one that has not, on the whole, responded as rapidly to the remedy of education as the regime had anticipated. Thus, with little chance of reaching a mass public in a timely fashion and with a sober understanding of the fragmentation of a postrevolutionary population, official implementation of the two-step flow theory made sense, and it was not critical that the sequence of information relay took so much time: there were no viable alternatives.

The theoretical tenuousness of the two-step flow theory has also been raised in the West, though for different reasons. The origins of the model and the subsequent literature, though widely disseminated, were not convincing, and there is, at present, considerable lack of confidence that the way an individual is exposed to information is the product of mediated interpersonal communication. Empirical research has found that there was "no significant difference between leaders' and non-leaders' mode of exposure."[24] The two-step flow was shown not to have occurred: "because of mass media coverage of national political events, interpersonal communication is apparently not very important as a diffusion medium, except perhaps for calamitous events."[25] The two-step flow approach has been called a "flawed, but persistent concept."[26] It is a concept applied to the mass media that fails to comprehend fully the term "mass."

I suggested above that the introduction of television together with the use of communications satellites had significantly changed the communications system in the Soviet Union. It introduced a new opportunity for timeliness of communication and for saturation of the media public. Within such a system the agitator and the agitated receive official communications simultaneously. I do not, however, wish to suggest that the modern Soviet media system has thereby eliminated the need for an interpersonal flow of information or that the official media system has replaced unofficial or even anti-official patterns of communication.[27] The role of the agitator, as previously conceived by the media policymakers, has certainly declined: he or she has little advantage over the viewer of the nightly news on television. But the nightly news may keep both the "front line" of agitators as well as the mass public in the dark if it does not follow the practice of timely transmission of information. Timeliness is the key to information diffusion, and to the degree that the official media fail to communicate in rapid fashion what may become known through foreign media sources or from other people, their efficacy is severely compromised. The capacity to effect persuasive change diminishes when initial impressions have to be altered rather than created.

Although it may well be the case that the "classic" model of agitation has lost its functionality in the television era, it is certainly true that the authorities are more likely to attempt to redefine the function rather than to jettison the institution as obsolete and tell the almost five-million-strong army of volunteer agitators to quit. Their activism and inclusion in Party-sponsored work has always been considered an important element in their own socialization, although their time could well be spent more efficiently. The letters-to-the-editor "industry" is a parallel: although surveys have shown that letters to the editor have little utility as representative public opinion, there has been no move to eliminate the hundreds of full-time positions in Letters Departments at all press, radio, and television editorial offices. These employees continue to collect, code, computerize, summarize, and distribute the material that flows in in huge numbers. I would argue that, similarly—although agitation will have only limited utility to the regime in the television era—it is unlikely that such a revered institution will ever be eliminated.

There is considerable evidence that a reorientation of organized interpersonal communication is taking place. With the introduction of the brigade contract system of labor, the notion of collective responsibility has been extended to the ideological dimension as well.[27] The brigade system is an alternative form of the organization of labor: it is a method of work based on what the Soviets call "economic accountability." A group of workers has a long-range assignment (derived from the economic plan) and shares in a particular job. Pay is at least partially based on the final results of their work and the degree to which it measures up to the contract on which it is based. In this way, the notion of individual interest (maximization of income) is said to coincide with the interest of the collective (fulfillment of the plan). Or to put it more simply, private incentive and the public good coincide to the extent that profit is maximized. We should not too hastily regard the brigade system as revolutionary. It is still constrained by the economic plan and all sorts of red tape and qualifications. What is of interest here, though, is not so much the economic side of brigade, but rather its ideological side—its projected role in the formation of the attitudes of the participants. Boris Eltsin, before going to Moscow to head its party organization, noted that in his home province of Sverdlovsk two-thirds of the people in industrial production were in the brigade system and that the "upbringing [socialization] function" had thereby been enhanced.[29] Others have been more specific. The brigade is theoretically responsible not only for work output, but also, as a collective, for the formation of the opinions and attitudes of its members. At least, that is the stated goal. How it might work is illustrated by the brigade contract system in higher education: At a dental school a contract determined "collective responsibility for the state of instruction, discipline, public activities, everyday life and leisure-time activities in the academic group."[30] In a Ukrainian engineering institute the group took collective responsibility for the failure of one of its members—everyone was to blame for not helping him. A female student who did not fail—who did rather well, in fact—had her stipend taken away by the group, not for academic reasons but because of her individualism. She refused to join in "volunteer" work projects and kept to herself. Another student, an honor student this time, almost had his stipend revoked because he had failed to join the others for a work session on New Year's Eve. Even an instructor had to answer to the rector for marking down the group on an exam. After all, the reasoning went, if the students worked along at a reasonable pace, the instructor was obviously at fault either for making his classes too easy or for grading the exams too harshly. Lest these examples be thought to be the norm, the reader should note that the title of the article does refer to the educational institution as a desirable model to emulate, but not typical at the present time. Another example of the persuasion and social control side of the brigade system may be seen in the construction and management of some new apartment buildings. A group of young workers in Sverdlovsk was given an eleven-month leave from work to build an apartment complex. From the time they moved in, in January 1982, the practice was established that the worker-tenants would spend most of their free time together. They did sports together, celebrated holidays together; they formed clubs for their children. No crime or misdemeanor has been reported.[31] Similar experience was reported in Kazan, where the apartment building is supervised by the Komsomol (Young Communist League), and it is hoped that "every enterprise, not just every city, will be erecting its own young people's housing complex, a unique social and educational laboratory."[32] Is the brigade the Orwellian answer? Probably not. An apartment that was just such an experiment ten years ago is no longer a success story. It lacks adequate funding; the leading activists have risen to more important jobs and spend little time

on residential activities.[33] Combining ideological with economic
tasks may also be too heavy an obligation for the new brigade
system. An official document in _Pravda_ summarizes the distance between expectations and reality:

> When brigades are formed, explanatory work and moral and psy-
> chological factors are often underestimated. The structure, forms
> and methods of the work of party, trade union and Komsomol
> organizations in the conditions of the brigade form of labor are
> being restructured slowly. In some places, close unity among ideo-
> logical, organizational and economic activity is not assured.[34]

The brigade is expected, therefore, not only to perform as a
unit with respect to the labor for which it contracts but also to
forge links internally, assuring the socialization of the group.
Although it is too early to tell how seriously this function will be
promoted and assisted by the Soviet leadership, how many resources will really support it, what real changes in administration and authority will buttress the typically hortatory nature of
the innovation, it does seem to me to be problematic, even if
fully implemented. The reasons why agitation has largely lost its
functionality are the same reasons why this new form of adult
socialization is unlikely to solve the problem. The era of televised communication has eliminated the preconditions for the
traditional two-step flow and created a value for timeliness and
rapid response that cannot logically be transferred to the brigade, no matter how ambitiously the brigade has been defined
on paper. Even if brigade leaders were to be brought to the
required level of political sophistication and knowledge, and
even if the time it takes them to learn about events could be
dramatically shortened (assumptions I think are clearly uto-
pian), there is little likelihood that this group would be the most
important channel of communication for its members. In discussing agitation, I noted that people who worked together formed
the agitation group. There is little evidence that important political and personal communication goes on in those groups. In fact
there _is_ evidence that discussion goes on specifically _outside_ organized groups, and the brigade group would be no exception.
The Komsomol has been taken to task because "real" discussions among young people do not take place under its auspices,

but in "smoking rooms and building entranceways outside the influence and supervision of the Komsomol and in by no means inoffensive groups in which the tone is set not by a political fighter from the Komsomol but by a narrow-minded person, a demagogue. . . . "[35] Even little children, who would be more spontaneous and less cautious, talk about what they see on television mostly with their friends, less often with parents and family members, but hardly ever with teachers or at meetings of the Pioneer and Komsomol organizations.[36] The brigade system will surely join agitation as still another method of attempting to shape public opinion. But things changed with the arrival of television. On theoretical as well as practical grounds it is unlikely that the venerable institution of person-to-person organized persuasion will be able to compete with the newest medium. A noteworthy example is what happened to the Soviet public when television began transmitting more candid battlefield coverage of the war in Afghanistan. A Western study of sources of information in the Soviet Union about the Afghan war found that between 1984 and 1986, the role of agitation declined precipitously as a source of information on that issue.[37]

Tracking the Television Audience:
The Public as Individuals

Loss of confidence in the hypodermic effects theory and the two-step flow concept creates a dilemma for television policymakers. How does one know if the messages are being received—and how persuasive they are. Under the hypodermic effects model, as I noted earlier, some few, largely ephemeral obstacles might hamper effectiveness, but essentially the message was thought to be identical with its assimilation. The two-step flow approach, within the Soviet context, is oriented toward groups, and the crafting of media messages—as well as the activity of agitators—is defined by participation in a work collective. This procedure is intended to enhance and extend the reach of the media. But if a *mass* public has been created, then it is not a group but the individual in direct contact with the medium whose attitudes and behavior must be known. If individuals are directly confronted by a message in private, as they are when they watch television, then the most important characteristics may not have much to do with the workplace. Rather, as individuals, the recipients of mass media communications have a variety of values and predispositions, some of which may relate to the workplace, but many do not. In the past the Soviet leadership had reason to believe it had the capacity to discover popular opinion and thus the ability to gauge the effectiveness of its communications system. In one year alone more than two million letters are sent to Central Television and Radio stations.[38] In 1980 *Pravda* received 581,700 letters. In 1974 the trade union newspaper *Trud* received 647,439 letters. Such voluminous feedback would and did make the communicators confident they knew their audiences. That confidence is, as we have seen, still firm among correspondents. However, it became very clear when reliable surveys were carried out for the first time, that letter-writers as a group diverged rather markedly from the public—they were not representative of that public. This is a conclusion that was well known in the United States, and some of the same patterns turned up. For example, older people, with more time and fewer distractions, contribute letters considerably in excess of their proportion of the readership of newspapers. Among the writers of letters to *Izvestia,* only 7.5 percent are thirty and under, while some 22 percent of the readers are in this group. The occupational spread of the letter-writers does not replicate that of the readership. Engineers, technical and agricultural specialists, the single largest group in the readership of *Izvestia,* account for less than 10 percent of the letters.[39] In contrast, members of the Communist Party, who make up less than 10 percent of the adult population, contribute upwards of one-third of all letters sent to several of the country's most important newspapers.[40]

The letters channel was not the only source of feedback revealed as clearly unrepresentative of the audience. All of the major sources—all those most heavily relied on by the leaders—were shown, not surprisingly, to be dominated by members of the Communist Party, thus severely narrowing the range of subjects and judgments contributed. A major survey under the direction of Soviet academician B. A. Grushin studied several aspects of information flow in the industrial city of Taganrog, a city of a quarter million in the Russian Republic.

The project, from initial planning to the analysis of the findings, took place from 1967 to 1974. The study used random
samples from voting lists, as well as samples of those who
provided feedback in a variety of settings. What this well-
designed and scientifically based survey revealed was that
members of the Communist Party, far in excess of their proportion of the population (Party members are 15 percent of the
city's labor force), are responsible for a very large degree of the
feedback that goes back to the center as the opinion of the
masses.[41] There were five channels of feedback studied: one,
letters to the editor, found that over 45 percent of all the 1,198
letters sent to five national newspapers, the local paper, and
the radio and television studios during the three-month period
surveyed came from members of the Party. The second channel
of feedback normally relied upon by officials is the civic, or
public, organization. These groups, such as trade unions, the
youth league, and factory work-groups, hold public sessions; in
the three months under review the size of the participating
(i.e., making their views public) audience was equal to 40 percent of the city's adult population. However, of that number,
fully 66 percent were members of the Communist Party. The
third channel used for feedback about popular opinions is the
meeting with the local government deputy. Twelve percent of
the adult population met personally with deputies to transmit
information, mostly at open meetings called by the deputies.
Again, Party members accounted for about one-third of those
meeting with deputies more often than once every six months.
The fourth channel—meetings with government and administration officials—included about 15 percent of the adult population of Taganrog. Again, the Party members disproportionately
filled the agenda, making up 40 percent. Finally, the fifth major
channel of feedback is the newspaper story written by the volunteer correspondent. *Taganrog Pravda* is the most widely read
newspaper in the city, drawing about one-third of the entire
newspaper circulation. Over two-thirds of its stories were the
products of volunteer correspondents, people who were not
part of the professional newspaper staff but who contributed
articles on a variety of topics. This is a practice that goes back to
early revolutionary times and has been continued not only at
city newspapers but also at the major national newspapers. It is

through this volunteer "corps" of correspondents that stories are to be uncovered in the city and the countryside. This is populist investigative reporting. The Taganrog study found that 61 percent of the volunteer correspondents were members of the Party.[42]

The Taganrog study, as well as the studies of the letters to the editor of several national newspapers, introduced a new cautionary note: the traditional ways of discovering popular opinion were deficient. They were clogged with members of the Party, whose patterns of media consumption (as well as many other patterns of behavior) differed very substantially from those of most other people in the population.[43]

The surveys also challenged another of the deeply held tenets of official theory and practice. I noted above that the comprehension of media messages was not, as it turned out, a foregone conclusion. The surveys made that clear. But even more serious was the finding that the highly educated were not likely to be more persuaded; quite the contrary, they were more likely to disagree with official communications. In fact, as the surveys revealed, education was found to be inversely related to agreement and satisfaction with media messages. College-educated Russians are the most interested in televison broadcasts of political and news analysis programs, but most critical of them. They are the most avid consumers of newsprint, but most frequently disagree with the editorial point of view. Books by contemporary Soviet authors are received most critically by the college-educated. In the countryside, it is the better educated young workers who complain most about rural conditions and who are most likely to migrate to the cities. Even within the network of political schools run by the Party for its members and for non-Party activists, those with more education are more dissatisfied with the lectures and classes.[44] To the Western observer, the relationship between critical stance and education is a familiar one. If education is understood as providing an awareness of alternatives, then dissatisfaction becomes virtually the emblem of the intellectual. The confidence expressed by official Soviet theory that rising levels of education would be associated with rising levels of persuasive power of the media has been challenged in a fundamental way by the survey findings. Not only was the hypodermic effects model flatly contradicted, but there was now no reliable avenue that the communications analysts could, with confidence, take in order to track their audience and shape their strategies. A Soviet television analyst put it this way:

> At this stage the necessity to know, does the viewer trust the program and to what degree, appears fully justified. What does he want from television and why? It is impossible to answer these questions simply with logical thinking. Of course, to some degree answers are contained in letters of viewers, but it is fully understandable that letters alone, drifting in, are far from satisfactory for the rational construction of programs.[45]

The viewer is seen here as an individual, and this change from group identity to individual—knowable not through the traditional, very skewed channels of feedback, but through reliable surveys—is a distinct, even revolutionary development. Conceiving of the individual as the unit of public opinion is, indeed, revolutionary in terms of traditional Soviet doctrine. To be sure, the studies that do so make sure to pay the usual obeisance to the influence of the work collective and its more populous parent, the social class. But for some time, official publications in the Soviet Union have tacitly discarded the utility of analysis using the traditional class identification. Since only two classes are recognized in the political doctrine— workers and peasants—it is difficult to undertake any refined explanation of variation. The later addition of the intelligentsia as a "stratum" of the working class hardly improved the situation for serious analysts of Soviet society. It has, therefore, become customary to acknowledge the official class structure but further to subdivide it into "social-demographic groups." This permits additional variables, such as age cohorts, urban/ rural residence, gender, education, ethnicity, and some others familiar to Western survey analysts.

A growing body of theory in the Soviet Union is placing the individual at the center of analysis: an individual who has a personal and private history, whose formative influences may include work-related activities, but only among other life events. This individual has passions and predispositions and a family history that is truly individual. If he or she is the target of television messages, what then is the relation of doctrine and theory to the practice of persuasive communication? A major statement by a party communications theorist provides insight into this slippery transition. G. T. Zhuravlev's piece in a collection of articles on the theory and methods of propaganda raises several innovative points. His arguments may be summarized as follows:[46]

1. The political doctrine, or ideology, contained in the historical sources and enunciated by the Party describes very broad patterns of regularities to be expected in Soviet society at some time in the distant future. The political doctrine is correct and predictive, therefore, but only as a descriptor of large social changes—the broadest of brushstrokes—that are to be expected by some period far in the future.

2. The political doctrine provides no concrete elements and predicts or prescribes no single path of development or any details of the picture of the future. That picture is painted with such a broad stroke and in such general terms that the here and now, the contingencies of today, cannot be discerned in the very large picture. A vision of the future, no matter how confidently one expects it, does not prescribe the micro-strategy to get there.

3. Rather, the present may be seen as a number of variants which, together with accidents and unintended consequences, fuse, in time, into the reality of the future. The future is therefore the outcome of many variables, and in the complexity of their large number and unpredictable interaction, it must be much less knowable than the official doctrine had always maintained.

4. The political doctrine and the ideological process it underlies must now be understood to bear a probabilistic character: that is, although the broad picture envisioned by the writings of the historical sources and the interpreters of theory remains authoritative for the far future, in fact, at any given time the political socialization of individuals will (and should) differ markedly. Thus, depending on a number of factors forming individual opinions, official communications will have only a greater or lesser probability of being assimilated, and that assimilation will differ in quality from individual to individual. Zhuravlev is now far from the "hypodermic effects" model. He is talking about *individual* opinion, one that is not fully knowable but only a matter of probabilities. That opinion cannot simply be posited by knowledge of the workplace or by membership in a social class. The key term is differentiation, and it is a characteristic of the individ-

ual qua individual. The process of communication is now a probabilistic enterprise, and that calls for a whole new understanding of the public.

5. In the political communications policy process, it is essential to know, therefore, under which conditions a given result (quality or quantity of assimilation) is probable. In dealing with probabilities instead of the unrealistic certainties the old conception had dictated, Zhuravlev makes the task of the communicator much more difficult. It is not only the correctness (in terms of the official line) of the message that must be assured, but much, much more. The mass media public is far more complex than the old doctrine suggests, and to reach this array of individuals more will have to be known about them.

6. In order to gauge the probability of assimilation, two kinds of information are central: information about the volume and disposition of previously planned communications activity, and information about the interests and values of the audience.

7. Successful communication is achieved only when the communicator has been able to estimate the probability with which a given result is produced under given conditions. In other words, rather sophisticated multivariate analysis is called for, and before it can be done, data will have to be collected that adequately describe the "given conditions" of the entire environment of information as well as the many elements that enter into the formation of an individual attitude.

All of Zhuravlev's points seem almost commonsensical, but in the context of the traditional understanding of the Soviet communications system they are radical. The political doctrine continues to be pre-eminent in this view, but its normative character is now separated from practical strategy or method. Political doctrine is, in fact, considered to be wholly devoid of method and therefore not inherently indicative of whether any given strategy is superior to any other. The assimilation of media and other messages is only probable, not definite, and is accomplished through interaction with an audience and its predispositions. Zhuravlev is no dissident; he is a Party official, a leading Party sociologist in the Central Committee's Academy of Social Sciences, who has written a number of books and articles on communication theory and practice. His works are published in large numbers by Moscow publishers. What we see in the work I described is a movement *within* the Party toward a reconceptualization of both doctrine and practice.

This movement at the level of official pronouncement is related to the effects of a number of changes in the last few years. Public-opinion polling was revived after the long freeze of the Stalin years,[47] and the results of the polls surprised the policymakers. The media public was revealed as far more complex and differentiated than the official doctrine had predicted. Even the newest public, the television public, created on a mass scale relatively late in the Soviet Union, was found to be far from monolithic. A Soviet analyst observes: "Some years ago, when television was just born, there was no urgent necessity to study the public. At that time, viewers were unanimous in their ecstasy before the 'wonder of the twentieth century.' Now that former public has become qualitatively different . . . the process of differentiation of the public is fully evident."[48] Once again, the question posed by the theorist is one of the *probability* of assimilation, rather than of a fixed, knowable reality.

A certain urgency has entered into official Soviet discussions of media policy. Eduard Shevardnadze, an early Gorbachev appointment as Minister of Foreign Affairs, wrote when still head of the Georgian Communist Party: "The entire history of our party, beginning from the first Marxist circles and the first Bolshevik cells, is the history of the struggle for the minds and hearts of people."[49] This is from an article on the importance of understanding the media public. The new urgency is, I believe, related not only to recognition on the part of many that the old doctrine and its policy prescriptions are outmoded and ineffective when television blankets the country, but also to new perceptions of the world environment in which the Soviet Union is embedded. There is an increasingly powerful perception of international tensions and what is in Soviet eyes a hostile and aggressive American policy. This thrust, called "unprecedented" by Chernenko in his June 1983 speech to the Party's Central Committee, constitutes a "real information-propaganda intervention." Media competition with the West for the domestic Soviet audience is seen by the Soviet leadership as more acute because the capitalist countries are ahead of the socialist world in relevant technology. The communications revolution has changed the world and, as the White House TASS correspondent mused,

the airwaves are not constrained by boundaries. "It's much easier to penetrate each others' homes or each others' lives through
radio broadcasts, television broadcasts, whatever. People are
not as uneducated, as unsophisticated as they were twenty
years ago." He referred to this notion of the small world in
connection with his observation that the Soviet media system
was in fact in competition with that of the West and that it ought
to be aware of the nature and effects of that competition. He
found, he said, that "to some extent the United States mass
media were much more effective in some given ways than we
are." There is concern that the official Soviet message be assimilated and that competing messages, since they cannot be eliminated, be resisted by a public already informed or, more graphi-
cally, "immunized" by the Soviet media.

Gauging Media Effects

With the effectiveness of television and the other media becoming such a critical concern of the Soviet leadership, and with the
old hypodermic effects theory revealed as obsolete by their own
researchers, what guideposts are relevant? In the interplay between the power of the monopolist communicator and the diverse and disparate orientations of the receiver, there are certain
regularities or patterns in the role media play in changing the
audience.[50] If we are to begin to assess the impact of television in
the Soviet Union, we shall have to see if certain well-known and
consistent effects, derived from the study of Western media audiences, might apply. First, as to source: the messages coming
from an authoritative and credible source or from a source familiar to and trusted by the receiver will be more effective. This
factor of authoritative credibility is clearly a critical element in
the study of the Soviet media system, and we shall return to it
later. Second, in terms of content: repetition and consistency,
particularly in the absence of competing information sources,
will produce more effective results. On the part of the receiver of
mass media communication, the motivation, interest, and level
of knowledge contribute noticeably to media effect.[51] There are
other variables, the effect of which varies too much to be conclu-
sive, but one other variable has been shown repeatedly to have

an effect on the persuasive power of the media: the distance of the topic from the experience of the receiver. The media very often *stand in* for reality. They mediate, and that is the significance of their name. There are limits to our ability to know from direct experience. Even in the familiar world of our own society there is much that we cannot experience, and far less in the world beyond our immediate surroundings. Our contact with the political leadership of our own country and the world of international relations comes to us from the media. Although the media may not be alone in shaping our notions of the world—domestic and foreign—that we cannot experience, they are for most people the most extensively used alternative.[52] To the extent then that the subject matter of the media communication is remote from the independent knowledge of the receiver, its effect will be greater. This relationship is important in our analysis of the coverage of foreign news by Soviet television. One qualification is obvious: if the issue is not salient to the receiver, then the effect is minimized. To achieve a persuasive effect, the media must raise the salience of the issue. They must set an agenda for the viewer or reader.[53] When there is little information but a generally high interest in public affairs, the potential for persuasion is high. This would be particularly true when new information is transmitted by the news. When there is little information *because* of low salience, or more simply, lack of interest, then it is likely that the audience will not pay attention to the message. In one of their most important roles, then, the media set agendas for their audience and raise to salience issues and judgments that had not been important before.[54] Recent research has pushed the agenda-setting function of the media beyond the formation of issues about which people think. It is likely that the media not only raise the *awareness* of the public but also contribute significantly to the formation of *attitudes* and *opinions* about those issues. That is, the media play a significant role both in directing people to what issues are important and also what positions to take on those issues.[55]

We must always keep in mind that the process is one of interaction between the mass media and their audiences. In this interaction, television is most successful in heightening the salience of an issue or topic when there is little or no opposing information. Once an attitude has formed, counter-persuasion is rendered very difficult. *Changing* predispositions is much less likely to be successful than *activating* latent predispositions or attempting to heighten the salience of a topic about which little information is available. And we return, thus, to the importance of openness and timeliness, the new Soviet initiative, based on the new understanding of the media—an understanding made more acute and necessary by the galloping tempo of the information revolution outside its borders and the discovery of the much more complex audience it has at home.

CHAPTER SIX

The Impact of Television

T ELEVISION HAS BECOME the pre-eminent medium of mass communication in the Soviet Union. It is the medium that has created the first mass public in Soviet history. No other medium has ever transmitted messages to such an enormous number of people. It is a public that embraces the barely literate and the academician, the hero mothers of Central Asia and the engineers of Sverdlovsk. It is a medium whose messages reach over nine-tenths of the entire population of the country. The extension of the new medium has been pushed so far and so fast, that one is reminded of the efforts of the early Stalin years, as huge dams and enormous factories were erected—totems and tools for the new revolution. The massive and sudden introduction of television has also been revolutionary, but its impact has been seriously underanalyzed and underevaluated.

Viewing Patterns

In a major survey of living standards and quality of life in a medium-sized industrial city in the Russian Republic, the noted scholar N.M. Rimashevskaya found that "the necessity for families to acquire a television set today is so great that it is seen as an object of the first necessity. Its presence can be classified as an inelastic type of utility."[1] The amount of time Soviet citizens spend watching television is exceeded only by time spent on the job and sleeping.[2] Not only Russians, but all ethnic groups across the nation, experience the same attraction to the most modern medium of communication. As a large and authoritative survey concluded: "For all nationalities, [there is] one and the same channel in terms of frequency of involvement for the assimilation of culture: television." Further, there is a steadily increasing preference (true of both urban and rural populations) for viewing television over all other forms of leisure time activity.[3] This suggests that the lure of television, far from wearing off, seems to be increasingly powerful. Surveys in the late 1970s found, for example, that factory workers—98 percent of them— watch television daily, far more than they read, go to movies, see friends, or do any of the things they used to do in their leisure time before television entered the home.[4] Surveys done in six cities in the Russian Republic in 1970 and 1976 found that people had *increased* their viewing of cultural events on television, but at the cost of *decreasing* their attendance at live cultural events, all of which registered declines over the six years.[5] In short, the powerful trends that had been observed as television was making its way into the Soviet home are continuing. In some respects television has changed people's lives in the Soviet Union much as it has in the United States: Radio has dramatically decreased in importance; people read less; theaters are now, on the average nationally, about half empty; movie receipts have been adversely affected by television.[6] For every increase in time spent on reading or going to movies and the theater, there has been a fivefold decrease due to television. Among people who live in rural areas, the impact of television is even more marked. With many fewer options (there are not many sources of entertainment and relaxation), difficulties in reaching population centers (roads are often inaccessible much of the year), and a smaller income to spend, rural folk have taken to television even more enthusiastically than their urban counterparts. In fact, although in the beginning it was difficult for them to find the money to buy television sets, their rate of viewing was actually higher than that of people in the cities, who had more sets available. There was more "collective viewing" in the countryside.

Older people are especially avid viewers. They, too, have more limited options and are less mobile. Ill health often keeps them at home, as does the smaller income a pension provides.

People over sixty-one watch more television than any other age group, with the exception of children eleven to fifteen.

Young children are now part of the Soviet "television generation," watching at least as many hours as they spend in school. A school principal in Tbilisi told me that she has been having problems with the children's attention span since the introduction of television. The more children watch television, the less time they spend on homework. In a survey of 1,000 eleven to fifteen-year-old schoolchildren in Perm, it was found that heavy viewers (defined by this study as at least three hours a day, about one third of the time spent outside school) were much less likely to receive good grades in school. It also found that the more television was watched, the less it was controlled or monitored by parents, with teachers having the least influence.[7] A well-known Soviet observer of the effect of television in his country noted that although television had an extraordinary impact and an important role to play, sometimes it was a "direct hindrance to the conscientious completion of school homework." "Children have become less active," he wrote; they watch sports programs more and play with friends less; they help around the house less often; and "less willingly participate in public life."[8]

Housewives watch a great deal of daytime television, though their numbers are quite small.[9] All of these patterns should be familiar to Americans, because they were displayed much earlier in the United States when television began to achieve dominance over other media. It is startling that such similar patterns of behavior result from interaction with television systems of such widely differing content, purpose, and structure.

The most important difference in patterns of viewing is found in the habits of college graduates. In the United States, viewing habits of people with higher education were at first quite different from those with less education. The college educated were skeptical about the new medium and defended the primacy of the written word, and they watched much less. As time went on they continued to be critical, voicing expectations for television that never materialized, but their viewing habits changed slowly and subtly. They still watch less than people who have not gone to college, but only if viewing time is calculated on a base that includes daytime programs. If, however, one compares viewing habits for evening and weekend television programs, level of education accounts for hardly any difference in the total amount of time consumed watching television. Well-educated Americans continue to be dissatisfied and critical of television, but they have succumbed to its lure. In the Soviet Union that has not happened—or perhaps has not happened yet. College graduates watch between one-fourth and one-third less television than the average viewer. At the other end of the spectrum, people who have not gone beyond elementary school have the highest viewing rates.[10] They are true television addicts. It is, I think, likely that the well-educated will eventually resemble their American counterparts more closely, turning increasingly to television. Intellectuals are looking to television to make their mark and to signal changes. The new programming and the new attention to moving films more quickly to the small screen will also attract the well-educated. The audiences for news, news analysis, and films are so enormous that they now embrace literally all segments of the population.

The Mixed Impact of Television

These changes in the way people use their time are really part of a much larger impact that television has produced in the Soviet Union, and this impact, like the metaphorical split signal, has been both anticipated and desirable from the official point of view, as well as unanticipated and worrisome. On the positive side, television can help to saturate free time, which for youth might be otherwise spent in aimless street activity and even delinquency. Saturating otherwise idle time with official and standardized messages pre-empts counter-communications, gossip, and rumor.

But beyond this negative or control aspect of the impact of television, there is, for the regime, a very positive one. Television is a powerful force for integration. It is a national medium attempting to forge a national consciousness and a national culture. The Soviet Union is, as I have noted above, an immense country, with some of the widest linguistic and ethnic differences of any country in the world, and in the early days of the Soviet state, before Stalin's brutal and decisive elimination of the regional political leadership, these differences broke into political divisions. The tensions were also reflected in regional pre-emption of television time before the technology had been developed so that broadcasts from Moscow could be received predictably. It took a reorganization and centralization of the broadcast industry to deny the regions the power to override. The centrifugal pull is still there. The riots in 1986 in Alma Ata, the capital of Kazakhstan, were explosions of pent-up ethnic demands, as were the demonstrations in Armenia and Azerbaidzhan in 1988. The national networks, broadcasting in Russian, have a clear advantage. Their programs are more polished. However, the particular concerns of ethnic life may not be addressed at all by the media. A dual process is at work: the erosion of ethnic differences fostered by an integrative national television system coexists with alienation from the mass media relating to *ethnic* or *local* concerns. In Azerbaidzhan, the protesters sought an Armenian-language television channel; in Moldavia, the Union of Writers wants to convert *all* television broadcasting into Moldavian.[11] The process that glasnost set in motion might well involve the centrifugal force that Moscow found intolerable at an earlier time. But unless the process begins, the national networks will certainly dominate the regions, but at the price of failing to reach the subcultures on questions still of great salience: their ethnic identity.

Without television, rural people and inhabitants of small towns and cities strung across the country would be isolated from the central media. For them, who are out of touch with urban life, television may present the only effective image of a dynamic, modernizing Soviet system. "The television set . . . compensates the countryside, to the extent it is possible, for the absence of the means of culture. . . .[12] It is what keeps some of them on the job in the harsh environment of the far reaches of the country and enables them to consider themselves tuned in to what is happening.

Television communicates with a heretofore unheard-of rapidity. News and information the government wishes to transmit will, because of the technical capability of television and the viewing habits of audiences, almost instantaneously spread across the country in a single approved version. Moreover, the audience considers that version far more credible than any produced by other media. As Soviet television expert E. G. Bagirov noted, " . . . in the credibility of the display of events it [television] has no equal."[13] In the United States, television also surpassed the other media on this dimension,[14] but in the Soviet Union it has happened with impressive rapidity. After all, television saturated the country only recently. The factors that limit or enhance that credibility will be discussed below.

Television also, it seems, helps to guide choices that will sort people out in the job slots they will occupy. A deputy director of Gosteleradio asserted that by far the majority of young people are making their career choices under the influence of television, as he put it. How exactly he isolates the effect of television, measures it, and controls for other variables is not clear, but he probably is on track in saying that television does play a role in the dynamics of social stratification. Certainly there is a great deal of programming that explicitly seeks to guide young people's career choices, and this is especially true for science and the military. Television is also bringing up the lowest classes. People whose level of education is very low, whose cognitive skills are not highly developed (who have trouble reading newspapers), and whose occupational mobility is very limited have in the past been isolated and outside the reach of the written media.[15] Through television, of which they are avid consumers, they have been brought into the modern world. Research on American television has found that it is especially among the less well educated, the "information poor," that television news increases information levels.[16]

But the record is not all positive. There are contradictory results, too. Television may bring the disadvantaged into the modern world, but it consumes so much of their time, Soviet critics say, that they do not seek upward mobility through evening courses or pursue cultural activities. The class lines might, they argue, be hardening, as the poor cut themselves off from outside opportunities to remain indoors with television.[17] Television also portrays a world that makes the hardships of rural life harder to bear. Since the introduction of television, the number of people in the Soviet Union who have become dissatisfied with rural life has doubled.[18] To the extent that Soviet television paints an idealized picture of life, it throws into startling relief the tremendous real disparities between town and country. It thus becomes even more critical for the Soviet leadership to provide salient and timely information to its own population about their own lives.

Television has also, as we saw in Chapter Five, made a huge

and venerated structure of political activities simply obsolete. People now receive news and information, and also entertainment, in their homes. They neither need nor want second-hand instruction from activists who seemingly know no more than any television viewer. There are other effects on private life that the growth of television has ushered in. Time previously spent on sports, hobbies, and tourism has now been given over to television. The television viewer is very much the consumer and not the actor, no longer the *Homo faber* that Marx envisioned— the creative and active contributor, the person who does things; the "new Soviet man" is now in front of the television set, and so is the rest of the family. Socially oriented and organized activities, the collective—so important to Soviet goals in character education—have declined since the introduction of television. This growing privatization of information and cultural consumption without the socialization (and control) benefits of group activity has aroused concern.[19]

Anxiety is particularly sharp about the impact of information that does not come from officially approved sources. Both Mikhail Gorbachev and Konstantin Chernenko before him warned of the West's drive to penetrate the information boundaries of the Soviet Union. Chernenko called it an "information intervention," recalling the early days of the Bolshevik Revolution when the West tried to topple the young republic, Gorbachev called it "information imperialism," suggesting that the newest form of aggressive hostility from the West would be in the projection of its information interests.[20] Gorbachev's charge to the media in his keynote address to the 27th Party Congress in 1986 asserted that a "psychological war" had been let loose by imperialism:

> It is a direct political-psychological preparation for war . . . [having nothing to do with the free exchange of ideas and other matters the West talks about]. Naturally, there is no basis for overestimating the influence of bourgeois propaganda. Soviet people know sufficiently well the true value of various prophets and prophecies; . . . But we do not have the right to forget that "psychological war" is the struggle for the minds of people, their understanding of the world, their life, social and spiritual orientation. . . . He [our adversary] created a gigantic machine of mass propaganda, equipped with contemporary technical means . . . The resourcefulness and lack of principle of bourgeois propagan-

dists must be countered by the high professionalism of our ideological personnel, by the morality of socialist society, its culture, openness to information, bold and creative character of our propaganda. We must be on the offensive—also involving the unmasking of ideological sabotage—and in providing truthful information about the real achievements of socialism and the socialist image of life. . . . The work of the media of mass information will be more fruitful, the more it has thoughtfulness and timeliness, and the less it runs after the random, the sensational.[21]

The profound concern with the porousness of the information boundaries—a concern that has surfaced throughout this study—introduced a note of urgency, even of crisis, and has been perhaps the most powerful explanation for the new reforms in Soviet television and the new interest in finding a reliable and accurate idea of the public. The surveys of the late 1960s and 70s showed the leadership that their notions of the public—its contours and habits, preferences and dislikes—were woefully distorted by reliance on the traditional hallowed, but faulty and skewed, channels of feedback.[22] The Soviet media, and television in particular, had been immensely successful in another area. They had succeeded in setting the agenda for the public insofar as news of the West, especially the United States, was concerned. By dint of constant repetition and allocation of huge amounts of airtime and newspaper space to America and its Western allies, interest in this part of the world had been stimulated to such an extent that it is now the most important category of interest on the part of the Soviet public. As noted earlier, in Chapter Two, at the national meeting of his organization, Komsomol chief Viktor Mironenko expressed his dismay at the fact that Soviet youth knew more about America than about the counties and cities in which they lived. He said, in fact, "it is impossible to accept this." If the unwelcome intrusions of unofficial and unapproved information (whether through the foreign radios or through tourists or the increasing numbers of professional journals, or foreign television in certain parts of the country) are a fact of life, then they must be countered, but effectively—and to be effective, television has to go some part of the way in meeting audience demands. It is a dilemma of control and effectiveness in constant tension.

In his keynote address, General Secretary Gorbachev warned of the new information threat from the West, but he also paid the Soviet people a compliment: he said they were mature enough to handle it, that the effectiveness of the "bourgeois interventionists" should not be overestimated (though he added that the media professionals would still have to counter the hostile thrust). The new theme of the maturity of the Soviet people is linked to changes in the media. It is asserted that these changes, such as glasnost, greater openness and the provision of multiple points of view, in the programs discussed in Chapters Two and Four, are now possible because they will not have the disruptive or dislocating effect they might have had earlier. Certainly this is a recognition of changed demographics—of radical changes in literacy rates, level of education, occupational and geographical shifts—and of a changed world in which information is, in any case, seeping in. It is also a recognition, for the first time, that the country's leadership had been dangerously ignorant of the demands and dissatisfactions of its media public. That public was impatient with a single point of view on what it knew well were complex issues of great import; it was bored and skeptical; alienated from local media and from the coverage it got about local events—events which could be independently verified, which people could observe themselves or could hear about from the well-developed grapevine. There was a crisis of confidence in local reporting. The more educated the public the less confidence it had in the media in general, just the reverse of what the media officials—going on their bureaucratically generated assumptions, but isolated and without much media experience—supposed to be the case. At the same time, the regime had been successful in arousing an interest in information, particularly about the West, that was more intense than it had imagined, or possibly desired. Gorbachev's statement is also an assertion that the political socialization efforts of the system that passed the half-century mark some time ago have had some success. Having seen the public for the first time through the surveys and also from meetings and intelligence passed up through the chain of Party organizations, the Soviet leadership made a determination— during the Chernenko period, but much more vigorously with Gorbachev—that some of the public's information demands could be met without destabilizing the system. The conclusion was drawn that those very complaints and irritations were manifestations of interest and disappointed expectations and could be a source of support if adequately addressed, and a source of instability if ignored. In part, this was a belief in the powers of the media and information technology. Once the media professionals began their counterthrust with adequate technology (since the West's information technology was acknowledged to be far superior, some catching up would have to be done), the messages, it was thought, would become far more persuasive. As we have seen, the look of Soviet television changed suddenly, ranging from the new use of computer graphics to live remote pick-ups from Soviet and foreign sites. Visuals were used much more often and increasingly supplanted the anchor's reading from papers. Live broadcasts, very rarely used in the past, became more frequent. All of this required substantial investment, both at home and in foreign news bureaus.

In part, and related to the modern infatuation with science and technology, the changes in the media, it is thought, will activate, or mobilize, the public. Facing a decline in the economy and the need to increase labor productivity while husbanding scarce foreign currency, particularly in an era of reduced oil revenues, Gorbachev, as did so many Soviet leaders, attempted to attack economic ills first by exhortation and tinkering, rather than by expensive structural reforms. In the past, the modest quests for solutions had always been based on the need to limit capital expenditures and the fear of ceding political control, which a major decentralizing reform would entail. The more ambitious Gorbachev's reform plan became, the more central were the instruments of persuasion. In Lenin's time the newspaper was seen as an organizer. It was the newspaper that would actually organize and direct the revolutionary impulse.[23] Years later, Gorbachev turned to the media to bring about a fundamental reorientation of values and attachment to work, to participation in the workplace and in civic affairs. It is this outcome that the new policies of openness (*glasnost*) and timeliness (*operativnost*) will support. Alienation from the media is being addressed by covering local events more rapidly and more fully, though resistance to change is also greater in the local media. On national television people air their grievances and seek direct action or information by calling in to the new programs on which the government official is forced to respond on air. A range of problems has been exposed, and people are shown grappling with them—and sternly rooting out fraud and corruption, the cancer that had pervaded the country under the permissive (in this respect) leadership of Leonid Brezhnev. According to the new policy, it should now make sense to work and work well and to watch for deviations from the norm. The control dimension of the media here joins the persuasive function, as the story on the "raid" on an inefficient plant shows on a micro scale and the Chernobyl coverage on a macro scale. Chernobyl is the clearest line of demarcation signaling the new policy. It represents a radical departure from the past in its scope, though part of a developing policy, and the first and most serious test of the thinking of the new regime. The Chernobyl coverage illustrates all of these new dimensions of media policy: it was in part a call for an intensified work ethic in the form of contributions to the effort to deal with the disaster (from the volunteers who evacuated local residents to farmers who had to work harder to make up for the produce destroyed). In part it was a monitoring and control effort, as those who did not perform adequately were publicly stripped of their privileges and responsibilities. And, in part, it was an effort to build credibility for the media. After initial, and what is openly acknowledged as damaging, silence, there followed a depth and breadth of coverage unheard of in Soviet media. Once again, split signals are sent: in its efforts to make the media more effective in persuading people to work harder and more honestly and to identify more actively with the goals of the leadership, that tension arises between control and effectiveness, between output of central messages and input of audience demand. While the policy is in the process of developing, there is no clear delimitation between what is permitted and what will bring criticism or worse, as even *Pravda* learned.

As the policy ramifications spin out, both the control function and the boundary issue present increasing problems. While the coverage of malfeasance on television and in the press is intended to mobilize popular participation and reduce alienation, here, too, the lack of clear procedures and limits has resulted in possible miscarriages of justice, uncertainty, and anxiety. A much talked-about new film details the obsessions of a young vigilante, whose devotion to combating evil is excessive. A review in *Izvestia* concludes that "Today, when social justice is being actively affirmed and everything unjust needs to be overcome and put behind us, this film represents a serious attempt to deal with what is by no means a minor part of our troubling social experience. Keenly detecting a social trend that has barely shown up, it warns us: The stance that, in combating evil, gives rise to new evil is frightening."[24] Daily in the Soviet media there are accounts of dismissals for corruption, fraud, or plain incompetence throughout the governmental and Party hierarchy. The numbers are impressive; the procedures, unclear; the tone of the articles, energetically laudatory. Pointedly announcing in its title that although the movie may be about children, its message is for adults, the *Izvestia* article reveals the just-visible and growing nervousness that the absence of political procedures and limits produces.

The definition of glasnost will also be a continuing problem. Clearly it is a central—indeed the central—component of the campaign to render the media more effective. Logic suggests therefore that to limit glasnost is to limit effectiveness and the political impact of the media. The range of untouchable subjects has narrowed beyond the expectations of long-time observers of the system, and the final configuration will be worked out over time. But there do seem to be certain very important built-in limitations to glasnost, and they are best expressed by Gorbachev himself: " . . . I consider it not superfluous to emphasize with all my strength: democracy is by no means anarchy and permissiveness, nor information about personal accounts or the opportunity to defame for profit. . . . It is not allowed to convert a magazine, newspaper, the mass media, [and] public forums into a medium of information about personal accounts. Authentic democracy is indivisible from honesty and decency, responsibility, uprightness in judgments and respect for the opinion of others, [it is also indivisible] from strict adherence to the laws and norms of the socialist community."[25] The requirement for responsibility in news-gathering is a delimiter, because the responsibility involves, as Gorbachev's statement makes quite clear, the needs and values of society as a whole, in contradistinction to the wishes and views of an individual apart from the collective. The process of—or perhaps the struggle for—restructuring does involve rooting out corruption and inefficiency in the interests of society at large. That is where glasnost will operate most powerfully. And that is why, as I noted earlier, in Chapter Two, its impact will be felt most profoundly in the domestic rather than the international sphere. A prominent Soviet journalist has stated that high media officials and reporters were called into a Party meeting in Moscow at which they were told to apply glasnost to international affairs: to exercise their capacity for criticism and judgment with respect to Soviet foreign policy positions. At the end of the meeting, a journalist told his editor that *now* he was going to write an interesting story. The editor immediately replied that he, on the other hand, would not publish it. Glasnost on the international front involves more sensitive issues—the separation of journalists from official positions—and, therefore, much thornier problems of implementation.

Even though the limits of glasnost are being tested in practice and will take time to stabilize, the backlash has begun. An exposé of a youth gang by the magazine *Ogonyok* elicited vociferous complaints against the article precisely about irresponsibility of the press, while others complained that the police were intolerant of the youth.[26] As we saw in Chapter Two, the question of tolerance of opposing views is a very live issue under glasnost. We should not underestimate the magnitude of the change for Soviet television viewers, as a single point of view and a single authoritative explanation give way to debates and arguments. It is not a simple matter to disrupt and dislocate the traditional cognitive patterns within which political information was received and stored. A vivid example of backlash can be seen in a television viewer's fury at what he charged were anti-Soviet emotions whipped up by Phil Donahue with the unpatriotic complicity of Soviet television's own commentator, Vladimir Poznei.[27] As I have emphasized throughout this study, major social and political changes bring in their wake unintended consequences. Expectations can be aroused more easily than problems solved, as the experience of "Twelfth Floor" showed. The television revolution is such a change, and it has occurred with incredible rapidity. There is, as yet, no method in place by which to gauge the strength of the mobilized backlash, the passive middle, or the enthusiastic persuaded.

Assimilating Messages

There is no assurance whatever that a message is assimilated as transmitted. Television certainly has the potential for trust and authority. It is the most credible medium in the United States, as Gorbachev's new propaganda chief Alexander Yakovlev no doubt observed during his stint in North America, and it is also the most credible medium in the Soviet Union. Yakovlev's powerful role, both as a close adviser to Gorbachev and as top media boss, makes him a key figure in the television revolution. He has been quoted as saying " 'The TV image is everything.' "[28] But will this grandiose new plan to harness the media to dramatic but not destabilizing change work? And how will anyone know how the public is reacting to these radical changes? In the spring of 1987, Yakovlev met with members of the Academy of Sciences to discuss the new course of restructuring and reform. At that session the president of the Academy acknowledged that his colleagues were not prepared to analyze and evaluate the changes. There were, he said, no instruments of analysis and not everyone was interested in ensuring an accurate interpretation of results. Further, especially in the provinces, there were those who were reluctant to discover trends—without which input, he concluded, it is impossible to make any reliable and reasoned judgment.[29]

In his day Nikita Khrushchev made radical changes without assessing their impact. Many of these changes, such as those in education, the arts, economic administration, the military, and the role of the Party in society produced contradictory and, in some cases, dysfunctional results. They were called "harebrained." But, as Seweryn Bialer observed, "the reformist zeal and flux of the Khrushchev period was founded on the belief that ideological truths can impress and inspire the masses."[30] The television reforms of the Gorbachev period are derived from the same conviction, packaged, to be sure, in a much more modern way and tied to a seductive new technology.[31] It is perhaps not a coincidence that Central Television's man in Washington, as one of his first stories in the fall of 1985, showed to the Soviet television public the face of Khrushchev for the first time since his fall from power.

To begin to answer questions about the effect of the new

media policies, we must look at how people process information: what they are likely to remember or forget, what catches their attention, what they catalogue as true or untrue. How people process news and information has long interested scholars. Although some of the most important studies are set in the context of American politics and American perceptions, the findings are not really country-specific, but probe how, in Doris Graber's words, human beings function in terms of "biological and psychological determinants that are shared by humans everywhere."[32] In particular, all people order and arrange, select and filter, the vast number of stimuli that reach them from the environment. Information flowing from the mass media likewise must be fit into a cognitive scheme.[33] Sometimes information is discarded—it may not, after all, fit into the mental pictures and patterns that for each of us integrates information and provides the context for sketchy new information. Or because of these mental organizers, called schemas, we may place new information quite readily into our overall understanding and accept it without question. And, of course, there is much in between: we change and shade what we hear and see to meet our expectations; we integrate new information into old; and we do not change easily or willingly what has comfortably and predictably made sense of new information, because, as Graber writes, "rethinking and restructuring one's conceptions is a difficult, often painful task."[34] If change occurs at all, it comes slowly. It is also the case that although the schema process succeeds in reducing information flow to proportions that the human mind can handle, it inevitably pares away the details and facts. Most people simply do not retain large amounts of factual data from the news. Does this mean that they do not understand what they have seen and heard? Apparently not. They do understand the general sense of what the media tell them; they get the point, but often get the names, places, and percentages wrong.

On another level, that of individual news stories, research in the United States and Great Britain has found that television news audiences in those countries often fail to understand or learn from the broadcasts they receive. Stories are often too short and go by too fast; they lack the repetition and redundancy essential for comprehension; they cover people and places, but not causes and effects, and fail to explain the news; the similarity of stories thematically tied in clusters often results in meltdown or blurring of the information.[35] Stories on Soviet newscasts are, on the average, longer, although the TASS bulletins may be very short bites that follow one another rapidly. Soviet news stories are not clustered, except in the general sense of foreign and domestic sections. They do have an explicit, consistent, and repetitive framework for explaining the news, and the pace of news presentation is far slower than that of American broadcasts. A study of the impact of television news in the United States concludes that "events—like statements and actions from foreign countries—seldom speak directly and unambiguously to the public; rather they affect public opinion mostly through the interpretations and reactions of U.S. elites [on the broadcast]."[36] The Soviet news is much more likely to pass events through the explanatory filter of the officially approved understanding.

What does this theory of human information processing tell us about the probable impact of Soviet television? For one thing, we should not necessarily discount the effect of the media if the public does not understand individual words or terms. There is, as the Soviet media officials learned to their surprise and consternation, much of the most frequently used political vocabulary that the public cannot define.[37] But it depends on *how much* of that political discourse is impenetrable and removed from real-life situations. If information comes in abstract scholastic packages unrelated to what matters to people, it will be neither understood nor remembered. Humanizing political discourse has begun on Soviet television, and it will be increasingly dependent on pictures rather than on the dessicated text read by the anchor.

Communications research, from a variety of approaches, methods, and experiments, finds that for messages to be assimilated they must be salient—the public's interest must have been aroused. This is the function of agenda-setting, perhaps the most powerful effect the media produce in any country. As Graber writes, "media agenda setting, to the degree that it does take place, is a powerful force in determining which problems are taken seriously and in providing the context in which policies and individuals will be judged."[38] The Soviet media have, I think, successfully set an agenda focusing on the United States and on the West in general. Issues and events in this area have become intensely relevant to all strata of the Soviet population.

This is a remarkable outcome. In most societies it is normal and expected that on the whole people care most about what is directly around them and have less interest in the world outside. That is certainly the assumption that American television people make about their audience, and they are right. What the Soviets have done is, if anything, becoming more intense with the Gorbachev leadership. The Soviet success in shaping the foreign news and information agenda is due in no small measure to the fact that people have no *direct* knowledge of international news; they have not observed it; rarely do they have friends and relatives who can provide observations and gossip. For Soviet citizens, especially, it is a distant world and they depend therefore much more on the media than they do for events closer to home. Because people cannot engage in reality testing on their own with respect to foreign events, their trust in the official media is relatively high, and studies have confirmed this.[39] Thus, the Soviet media—and most importantly Soviet television because of its greater credibility—can set the nation's agenda with respect to foreign, especially Western information, and they have clearly done so.

Soviet officials, as I have noted above, are increasingly concerned that this advantage in agenda-setting might be undercut by contradictory messages penetrating their information barrier. They understand that the source breaking the story enjoys a significant advantage in persuading the public, and they openly state an intention to transmit the story first—in their approved packaging. The circulation of information generated by the foreign radios (such as the Voice of America, the BBC, Radio Liberty, and Deutsche Welle) is as yet limited, when compared with the massive spread of official television. Moreover, radio lacks the aura of credibility and spontaneity that pictures can provide, if timely. Given the inability to verify foreign events independently and the unwillingness with which most people change their schema for ordering and selecting information, it is not, I think, likely that for most people the impact of television for a given story would be overturned by foreign sources.[40]

Foreign views are increasingly entering through the state-run television system itself. Some information that contradicts official positions has always, in a sense, been provided in Soviet television's own foreign coverage. Viewers see people and products in the background, consumer goods and standards of living at the periphery. For the clever and observant viewer, disparities between these images and official doctrine can clearly undercut the persuasive potential of the medium. The International Life department at Gosteleradio was created by the Gorbachev leadership largely to address this problem. In addition, as part of the plan to pre-empt foreign stories and positions, foreign public figures are permitted to present their (often opposing) views on Soviet television. Audience interest in this development is very high, and audience reaction, though unknown in any systematic way, suggests that on the whole Soviet television has been successful in presenting its own position and rationales and that the opposing points of view have largely been parried. Those foreigners who would address the massive Soviet television public directly should bear in mind that cognitive patterns will not suddenly change, particularly when the context and the explanatory grid remain constant. There is even some important segment of the population that rejects the very process of admitting hostile views to the Soviet airwaves.[41]

Personal experiences are profound shapers of mental pictures and the information-ordering process. When there is the opportunity to check for oneself and to observe an event or a process (whether or not food is plentiful in the store down the block when the television news is boasting of large food supplies), it is highly probable that those impressions override what the media are transmitting. It is for this reason that the issue of domestic reporting—so starkly illustrated by Chernobyl—is most vulnerable. The Gorbachev regime's campaign to breathe life into domestic coverage and to win over the disaffected public has begun, with responsiveness and timeliness the watchwords, but it will have to go a long way to achieve its goal; and whether or not it will rapidly and decisively meet the real demand of the audience to illuminate the most important sides of their lives, no matter what the political risk, is not known yet. The requirement of responsibility in reporting limits the role of the individual. What we are witnessing so far is a dramatic departure in policy based on a revolutionary new medium. Television messages, as we have seen, vary in the degree to which they are likely to be assimilated. Personal experience is a strong factor affecting the impact of the communication: limiting, if it contradicts the message; reinforcing, if it agrees with the message. If the public lacks experience, assimilation is enhanced if the sender is thought to be credible on these issues—and television's pictures help a great deal. Repetition and consistency also affect that impact.

The utility of information is another factor entering into an individual's response to the media message. People are very attentive to information they expect to serve a practical purpose.[42] A Soviet media specialist acknowledged this finding and warned that Radio Liberty had increased its audience in the Soviet Union by beginning its news broadcasts with weather reports.[43] It is the domestic side of Soviet television news that would profit most from increasing the weight of information people can use in their daily lives. Again, Chernobyl stands as a signal example of how much people needed accurate information to protect their health and safety and how little they got from the media. Virtually the same complaints were made after riots in Armenia and Alma Ata. Although, in the latter case, television carried an announcement right away, there was so little follow-up, that rumor took over.[44] The fact that these dissatisfactions were given prominent coverage suggests that changes are on the way, that they are major, and that the impact of the media will be very powerfully enhanced.

The sphere of foreign information is, as I have noted, much less likely to be subject to these pressures of reliability and credibility, but the most crucial exception is information about the fighting in Afghanistan, seeping back through those who have experienced it firsthand and those who have suffered its effects. Numbers are still small in relative terms; the ripples do not go far, but time and numbers will keep extending those ripples and make of this issue a serious liability for Gorbachev's policy of persuasion and mobilization. The very high place on the news agenda that Afghanistan holds is, I think, evidence of concern about just this eventuality, but contradictory actual personal experience will nullify that coverage, no matter how heavy.

When people lack access to information, however, the media stand in for the life that most people cannot experience, and it is for this reason that analyzing what goes out over the media is so important. Or, as an American study put it, "knowing more about the content of media may not prove political effects, but it does give us important clues to understanding them."[45] The information that flows to the Soviet public consistently projects an approved view of the world: events happening all over the globe (and the globe is much larger for Soviets than for Americans) are set into a clear and simple system, in which the United States plays the central role in fomenting disorder and suffering, augmented by a small coterie of a dozen or so countries that mainly act as troublemakers in their regions. Only two genuinely global powers inhabit the earth: the United States and the Soviet Union, and they are inextricably bound by the nuclear threat. Nuclear anxiety and fear of nuclear blackmail hang heavy over the news and over the non-news context in which the news is embedded; and in all of it, the United States is so central and looms so large, that it is not far off the mark to call it an obsession. It is unlikely that Americans have a sufficient understanding of the volume and intensity of the messages of this sort that the first mass public in Soviet history is tuning in to in their information and entertainment programs and how attentive they are to every reported move the United States makes. Their foreign information agenda looks as though it is in large measure shaped by American actions and American interests abroad. We do not see what we might at first have expected: a particular interest in what is most familiar, most similar, and geographically closest (and also least expensive to cover)—the socialist countries of Eastern Europe. These friends and neighbors are of far less interest than the distant adversary.[46]

But the international agenda of Soviet television news is also part of its own strategic design. There are areas of the world in which it takes a special interest. Japan, for example, is treated as a seriously threatening neighbor. The Yemens and Ethiopia are areas of focused Soviet interest. Coverage of China is increasing. India continues to play a major role in news coverage. The South African situation is now said to contain more revolutionary potential, and attention is drawn to the African National Congress as the successor government, warmly supported. Chile is a continuing concern for Soviet news. Although a communist insurgency has for some time existed in the Philippines, the changing dynamics of power that eventually toppled Ferdinand Marcos and installed Corazon Aquino constituted the really big story that Soviet television missed. The potential for influence in that case turned out to be slight. The complete mosaic of international coverage—which under Gorbachev rose to 70 percent of all stories—is discussed earlier. We cannot ascertain or state definitively whether or not this agenda is a mirror of actual foreign policy priorities and if these television messages constitute reflections or signals that should alert us to Soviet intentions. But we do know that the Soviet leadership now has a more realistic notion of how attitudes and beliefs are formed and a more sober appreciation of the reach and potential of its first truly mass medium. The wild swings of policy rationale that characterized the previous regimes are not efficient. The central media may have to build a coherent structure of information, if they are to persuade, if their messages are to enter those schema by which people make sense of what they see and hear. If that is the case we may expect that the signals their population receives do tell us a good deal about the real interests of the government.

There are events that carry a particularly complex and ambiguous message. Summit meetings or the visits of Gorbachev to Western capitals are examples of mixed signals, where positive valuations (greeting the other leader with warmth and apparent friendship, covering the other country as a respected world power) are set in the context of global explanation (i.e., the United States as threatening puppetmaster). These cases are increasing in frequency under Gorbachev, as he solidifies his image as a leader who projects his power and influence on the world outside the Soviet Union, and in particular on the West. The decline in domestic stories, the increased interest in the West, the changes in coverage of the Soviet leader—linking him more and more with international stories—all suggest that projecting the influence of the Soviet Union abroad through the person of Gorbachev increasingly guides information flow. This, it is hoped, is the message of those interactions with adversaries.

Living with Contradictions

What goes out on Soviet television bumps up against reality. Even if the Soviet leadership expands and modernizes information flow to meet the demands of the public and to pre-empt non-official sources—and thus make the media more effective— it is unlikely to go so far as to allow the media agenda to be generated by popular demands. No country's media system is fully attentive to the demands of all the strata of its citizens. The Soviet system will retain significant controls. As Gorbachev carefully noted in his keynote address cited above, no matter what changes are made, the media must be "responsible," they must eschew the "random" and the "sensational." Thus, there will be significant changes, but not upheaval; movement has been initiated but will not be played out to its logical conclusion. Does this mean that the media must lack effectiveness or that partial change cannot make a difference? Must the television public be wholly convinced of everything it sees in order to be convinced of anything? And how does one explain the co-existence of credibility for foreign news with skepticism about local coverage? In fact, people live with contradictory views and perceptions all the time, and it is well known that "cynicism about the accuracy of information sources does not prevent people from accepting the information as long as it fits into prevailing schemas and there is no other credible source for information people want." It is the context that elicits and orders the behavior and attitude, and different contexts may call up quite different views. Thus, contradictions live side by side, and the attitude toward local news may not, in fact, contaminate the credibility of foreign news.[47] I discussed earlier the way that television affects the kind of information people seek (agenda-setting) and the kinds of stories and coverage most likely to be credible.[48] Clearly, coverage of foreign events when transmitted promptly and accompanied by visuals that appear realistic enjoys more credibility. The campaign to create credibility for domestic coverage on the national media and local media begins with many more serious disadvantages, but it is essential to the Gorbachev program of reform.

There is no doubt that in the media, at least, the Gorbachev leadership has embarked on revolutionary change. The media are leading the charge: the policy of restructuring (profound reform and rebuilding) depends for much of its success on the persuasive powers of the media. It is expected that the media, and foremost among them television (because of its reach and integrative capacity), will have the unique ability to bypass the ossified deposits of bureaucratic power and reach in the most direct and emotional way the entire Soviet population. The centrality of the media is spelled out in a Party document in *Pravda:* "There are many facets in the policy of restructuring: economic, social, psychological, moral, [and] cultural. But, perhaps, most comprehensive is the ideological, because without conviction in the necessary course for renewal of all sides of the life of society, qualitative changes cannot be achieved."[49]

Given that role, the question of effectiveness is then absolutely critical. Glasnost is the talisman. Its operation in the media has entered the Soviet human rights lexicon, as an article by a leading legal scholar affirmed: "New legal acts are necessary . . . about guarantees for the implementation of glasnost and the role of the mass media in this work."[50]

The plan to reorient the psyche of a nation is a grandiose one. The method of implementation is daring: radical media changes are to create the environment in which later reforms can take place. The more successful and effective the media are, the less difficult—and expensive—will be the succeeding changes in the political system, the economy, the educational system, the legal system, and all the other dimensions of a society whose leaders acknowledge the need for thorough overhaul and renewal.

The results, both intended and unintended, will not be known perhaps for years. There is certainly no monitoring device in place to send adequate feedback to the leadership on a regular basis. Any policy of this scale produces complex and contradictory changes. And this policy inevitably invites pressures for extension and enlargement beyond the limits thus far defined, even as those rejecting the assault on their traditions argue for tighter and more rigid bounds. The first mass public, the television public, is receiving split signals in the literal, technical sense. Broadcast signals are divided and sent in many directions all over the vast country. But that public is also receiving metaphorically split signals: between credibility and personal experience; between salience and lack of interest; between responsiveness and unmet demands; between mobilization and alienation.

Notes

Chapter One: Television in the Soviet Media System

1. *Narodnoe khozyaistvo SSSR, 1922–1972,* Moscow, 1972, p. 314.

2. L. Fedotova, Ya. Kapeliush, and V. Sazonov, "Televidenie v nebolshom gorode," *Televidenie i zritel,* ed. E.S. Sabashnikova, Moscow, 1985, p. 149.

3. *Sredstva massovoi informatsii i propagandy,* Moscow, 1984, p. 3.

Vladimir Treml notes that the statistic for television saturation is derived not from an actual count or survey of sets in people's homes, but rather from sales of television sets. Official statistics probably overstate the stock of television sets by about 10 percent, since the useful life of the sets is shorter than the estimate, and the frequency of repair, destruction or breakdowns is understated. Communication to the author.

Color television sets have produced the greatest problems; a great many have been produced with defects that cause them to catch fire. A fire at the Hotel Rossia, a large tourist hotel in Moscow, was attributed to just such a defective set.

"Tekhnika televidenia i radioveshchania v 12-i pyatiletke," *Govorit i pokazyvaet Moskva,* May 1, 1986, p. 19. In the United States, 98% of all households own at least one television set.

4. *Narodnoe khozyaistvo v 1985 g.,* Moscow, 1986, p. 447.

5. G. Iushkyavichius, "Televidenie i radioveshchanie v novykh usloviakh," *Radio,* No. 10, 1985, p. 2.

6. "Tekhnika televidenia . . .," p. 19.

7. An installment of the British television documentary "Comrades" follows the life of a fur trapper in remote Siberia. He is out of the reach of all government controls and contact, it appears, *but* he relies on television.

8. For a discussion of these questions, see Chapter Five.

9. For a discussion of the effect of television on political agitation, see Chapter Five.

10. I use the term "move ahead" in order to indicate a process that had started before Gorbachev became General Secretary. See Chapters Two and Five.

11. Numerous personnel changes accompany the changes in media policy. In addition to turnover in Gosteleradio, Novosti, the Union of Writers, the Union of Cinematographers, and a number of newspapers and journals, the Minister of Culture, Petr Demichev, was removed in June 1986.

12. *Sredstva massovoi informatsii i propagandy, op. cit.*, p. 292.

13. V.V. Egorov, *Televidenie i zritel*, Moscow, 1977, p. 51.

14. Local here means the republic level television studios *and* studios at the city or province level as well. This was in the formal announcement of the creation of the Second Program: "Vo vsei strane," *Pravda*, December 24, 1981, p. 6.

15. G.Z. Iushkyavichius, "TV, rezervy tekhniki," *Zhurnalist*, No. 1, 1983, pp. 20–22. I am grateful to Thomas Remington for bringing this source to my attention.

16. V.I. Zadorkin and A.V. Sosnovsky, "Perspektivy kommunikativnykh vozmozhnostei televidenia kak sredstva osveshchenia kulturnogo urovnya," *Issledovanie rosta kulturnogo urovnya trudyashchikhsya*, Moscow, 1977, pp. 90–101. The original body, the State Committee for Radio and Television was formed in 1957.

17. V.V. Egorov, *Televidenie i zritel*, Moscow, 1977, p. 45.

18. Iu. V. Arutiunyan and Iu. V. Bromlei, *Sotsialno-kulturny oblik sovetskikh natsii*, Moscow, 1986, p. 191.

19. A study calculates the linguistic breakdown of programs as announced in republic newspapers in the late 1960s. It found an overwhelming use of Russian. It is difficult to draw firm conclusions from this study because of the changes over time, the problem of determining the language from the program listing (there are some unknowns), and the development of local programming. The citation for the study is: Wasyl Veryha, *Communication Media and Soviet Nationality Policy: Status of National Languages in Soviet TV Broadcasting*, New York, Ukrainian Congress Committee of America, 1972.

20. Tadeusz Swietochowski, "Soviet Azerbaijan Today: The Problems of Group Identity," unpublished paper presented at the Kennan Institute for Advanced Russian Studies, May 6, 1985, pp. 4–5. Cited with permission of the author. It should be noted that rather innovative programming was initiated in the neighboring republic of Georgia, involving call-ins to the studio and that televised press conferences with local officials were broadcast in Estonia before entering the agenda of Central Television.

21. Arutiunyan and Bromlei, *op. cit.*, p. 192.

22. A. Iurovsky, *Televidenie—poiski i reshenia*, Moscow, 1983, p. 48.

23. V. Kichin, "Zhdem novizny: zametki o vtoroi teleprogramme," *Pravda*, January 10, 1984, p. 3. On the second anniversary of the founding of the Second Program, *Pravda* called for new energy and new initiatives and advised that it was local programming that could most fruitfully be expanded. It is true that the Second Program does rebroadcast some news analysis and commentary programs as delayed repeats though not "Today in the World" (which the old Stalinist party official, Vyacheslav Molotov, on his 96th birthday and shortly before his death, announced was one of the only two programs he watched on television—the other is Vremya). Serge Schmemann, "Soviet Paper Depicts a 'Happy' Molotov at 96," *The New York Times*, July 3, 1986, p. 5.

24. N. Vakurova, "Tele-i radioinformatsia v zerkale obshchestvennogo mnenia," *Govorit i pokazyvaet Moskva*, April 10, 1985, p. 19.

25. A. N. Dmitriuk, "Tsentralnoe i mestnoe televidenie, ikh vzaimodeistvie," *Govorit i pokazyvaet Moskva*, No. 12 (March 11, 1987), 19.

26. Vakurova, *op. cit.*, Grigory Shevelev, head of Gosteleradio's information and news department, remarked in an interview with the author that when he removed one of the "Today in the World" programs, Gosteleradio received so many outraged letters and phone calls, that he ordered it back in the schedule.

27. *Ibid.*

28. "Puls 'Vremeni', " *Izvestia*, November 23, 1985, p. 6.

29. S.A. Iosifyan, *Televidenie i zritel*, Moscow, 1975, pp. 57–72.

30. V.V. Egorov, *op. cit.*, p. 53.

31. Iurovsky, *op. cit.*, p. 175.

32. A. Polskaya and E. Yakovich, "Progulka s programmoi i kalkulyatorom," *Literaturnaya Gazeta*, March 21, 1984, p. 8.

33. E. Shafran, "Podchasa premer,' *Izvestia*, January 25, 1986, p. 6.

34. "Kompleksnaya programma razvitia proizvodstva tovarov narodnogo potreblenia i sfery uslug na 1986–2000 gody," *Pravda*, October 9, 1985, p. 1.

35. G.A. Dorokhov, "Zhdet desyat let? Nevozhmozhno!" *Literaturnaya Gazeta*, August 5, 1987, p. 8.

36. K. Abayev, "Pokazhet video," *Izvestia*, June 23, 1985, p. 6.

37. "Video segodnya i zavtra: za chem delo stalo?" *Nedelya*, No. 33, August 12–18, 1985, p. 18.

38. *Ibid.*

39. N. Kishchik and E. Vostrukhov, "Videouroki," *Izvestia*, October 15, 1985, p. 3.

40. B. Pilipenko, "Osoby sluchai: videoformach," *Komsomolskaya Pravda,* September 20, 1985, p. 4.

41. Evgeny Nozhin, "Ni Slova ne vozmut na veru," *Molodoi Kommunist,* No. 8, August 1984, p. 31.

42. "Soviet Moves Against Videos Spreading 'Cult of Violence,' " *New York Times,* September 7, 1986, p. 7.

43. Sergei Sinitsa, "Pechalny detektiv," *Literaturnaya Gazeta,* August 5, 1987, p. 8.

44. "Tekhnika televidenia . . . ," p. 19.

45. Robert W. Campbell, "Satellite Communications in the USSR," *Soviet Economy,* No. 4 (October–December 1985), 313–39.

46. Spartak Beglov, *Vneshnepoliticheskaya propaganda: ocherki teorii i praktiki,* Moscow, 1984, p. 281–82.

47. A great deal has been written about the NWIO and the UNESCO debates. The reader might look at American policy, as described by Wilson P. Dizard, "The U.S. Position: DBS and Free Flow," *Journal of Communication* XXX:2 (Spring 1980), 157–68.

48. *Ibid.,* p. 125.

49. Lawrence W. Lichty, "Americans Still Depend on Newspapers for News," *Atlanta Constitution,* December 26, 1982, p. B-1.

50. Viktor Telpugov, "Rasplachivaemsya zdorovem," *Literaturnaya Gazeta,* August 15, 1979, p. 12.

51. *Formirovania sotsialnoi odnorodnosti sotsialisticheskogo obshchestva,* eds. F.P. Filippov and G.A. Slesarev, Moscow, 1981, p. 122.

52. Iushkyavichius, "Televidenie i radioveshchanie . . . ," p. 3.

53. An 1960 resolution of the Party's Central Committee severely criticized radio: "Radio broadcasts everywhere have a dry and official-sounding character rather than consisting of lively talks on specific subjects. . . . They consist of expressionless readings of articles or artificial reporting with synthetic background music and sounds. Programs based on texts are often long and overloaded with numbers. . . . Radio . . . lacks authoritative commentators capable of delivering simple and popular talks to the millions of listeners on the subjects that concern them." "Ob uluchshenii sovetskogo radioveshchania i dalneishem razvitii televidenia," *Partiinaya zhizn,* No. 4, February, 1960, pp. 26–27.

54. Vakurova, *op. cit.*

55. E.P. Prokhorov, *Sotsiologia zhurnalistiki,* Moscow, 1981, p. 72.

56. *Raionnaya gazeta v sisteme zhurnalistiki,* Moscow, 1977, p. 59.

57. *Ibid.*

58. Prokhorov, *Sostiologia zhurnalistiki,* p. 100; E.P. Mikhailova and N.N. Mikhailov, "Selskaya televisionnaya auditoria," *Televisionnaya auditoria,* Sverdlovsk, 1973, pp. 107–8.

59. L.G. Svitich and A.A. Shiryaeva, *Zhurnalist i ego rabota,* Moscow, 1979, p. 92.

60. *Sredstva massovoi informatsii i propagandy*, pp. 16,36.

61. *Ibid.*, p. 36.

Radio's ability to carry fast-breaking news is relatively recent. In the past, radio broadcasters depended on *Pravda* for their news agendas. TASS releases were to be transmitted simultaneously to newspapers and radios, but the publishing delay would, of course, give radio the advantage. It was only in 1960 that a resolution of the Party's Central Committee directed radio to broadcast news before it appeared in the newspaper.

62. E. Ryigas, "Rol komitetov komsomola v borbe s natsionalisti-cheskimi predrassudkami i perezhitkami," *Internatsionalnoe vospitanie molodezhi: aktualnye problemy natsionalnogo i internatsionalnogo v dukhov-nom mire sovetskogo cheloveka*, vyp. 2, Baku, 1985, pp. 39, 47.

63. K. Vaino, "S Tochnym znaniem obstanovki," *Kommunist . . .*, No. 4, March 1983, p. 54.

64. Tom Kneitel, "Jamming: The Electronic Iron Curtain," *Popular Communications*, January 1983, cited in Harry Caul, "Inside Soviet Jam-ming Stations," *Popular Communications*, December 1983, p. 36. I am indebted to Kurt Oppenheimer for bringing this source to my attention.

65. Research on the audience for the Western radios concludes that in the years between 1977 and 1980, about a third of the Soviet adult population was exposed to Western radio broadcasting in the course of a year, and about one-fifth during a week. The Western radios are: BBC (Great Britain), Deutsche Welle (Federal Republic of Germany), Voice of America (United States), and Radio Liberty (United States). Much of the attention to these radios focuses on music, particularly popular music. The research was done by informal surveys of Soviet travelers (not émigrés) mainly in Western Europe. The findings are most reliable with respect to urban Russian males in the European part of the Soviet Union. They are least secure in providing generalizations about Central Asians and rural populations as a whole. For an account of the meth-ods, see R. Eugene Parta, John C. Klensin, and Ithiel De Sola Pool, "The Shortwave Audience in the USSR: Methods for Improving the Esti-mates," *Communication Research*, IX:4 (October 1982), 581–86. For fur-ther analysis of the foreign radios and their audiences, see Chapter Six and Ellen Propper Mickiewicz, *Media and the Russian Public*, New York: Praeger, 1981.

66. This highly controversial episode has been variously reported as having resulted in a premature and damaging agreement on the part of the United States Information Agency (later disavowed) (for this view, see William Safire, "You've Got a Deal!," *New York Times*, November 10, 1986, p. 21) and as "having involved no agreement of any kind to end Soviet jamming of the Voice of America at the expense of Radio Free Europe and Radio Liberty." (For this position, see the letter to the *New*

York Times, November 20, 1986, p. 28, by Charles Horner and John Korder of the United States Information Agency.) In any case, late in the spring of 1987, when VOA jamming ceased, Radio Moscow did begin broadcasting on AM to Florida through Cuba

67. When jamming of Voice of America ceased, at least some of the freed jammers were turned to Radio Liberty.

68. Korobeinikov, *op. cit.,* p. 104.

69. Lilita Dzirkals, Thane Gustafson, and A. Ross Johnson, *The Media and Intra-Elite Communication in the USSR,* RAND report R-2869, Santa Monica, September 1982, p. 13.

70. V.G. Afanasyev, in "Na Pulse perestroike," *Pravda,* March 15, 1987, p. 3.

71. For a discussion of this body, see Thomas F. Remington, "Politics and Professionalism in Soviet Journalism," *Slavic Review* 44:3 (Fall 1985), 498–99.

72. For a discussion of this process, see Michael Voslensky, *Nomenklatura: The Soviet Ruling Class,* New York: Doubleday, 1984.

73. *Ibid.,* p. 111.

74. Khelemendik, *op. cit.,* p. 300.

75. S. V. Tsukasov, *Nauchnye osnovy organizatsii raboty redaktsii gazety,* Moscow, 1977, pp. 11–14.

76. *Ibid.,* pp. 287–92.

77. V. V. Egorov, *op. cit.,* pp. 39–42.

78. H. Kent Geiger, *The Family in Soviet Russia,* Cambridge: Harvard University Press, 1968.

79. See Donald D. Barry and Carol Barner-Barry, *Contemporary Soviet Politics,* 2nd edition, Englewood Cliffs, N.J.: Prentice-Hall, 1982, pp. 150–53.

80. At present, the Soviet Union is not yet a communist country. By its own doctrine, it is still in the process of building communism, having achieved the first step, socialism.

81. By using the term "socially necessary," Marx meant that scarcities of some goods that now cause societal conflict would persist: diamonds and gold, for example. But these things are hardly socially necessary— they are not basic needs for human survival and development—but rather are valued, he argued, only because of the very skewed and irrational system that pre-communist economies impose.

82. E.V. Kruglov, "Zashchishchaya revoliutsionnye zavoevanie," *Vestnik Moskovskogo Universiteta,* seria 10, Zhurnalistika, No. 5, 1982, p. 58.

83. The denial of this understanding of pluralism, whether in media policy or in electoral processes, is often referred to outside the Soviet Union as the crushing of alternatives by a group of leaders who wish to maintain their power. Maximization and maintenance of power by the leadership may well be a factor, even the overriding factor, in media policy. However, it is also the case that the doctrine which legitimates that power does reject pluralism on philosophical grounds, which also explain media doctrine. It would be a mistake to ignore the ideological foundations of the state and attribute policy solely to power maximization considerations. Ideology may have its limits, but it also provides limits.

84. On this point, see Chapters Two and Six.

85. Robert G. Kaiser, *Russia: The People and the Power*, New York: Pocket Books, 1976, p. 236.

Chapter Two: Looking Outward

1. G. Iushkyavichius, "Televidenie i radioveshchanie v novykh uslo-viakh," *Radio*, No. 10, 1985, p. 1.

2. "Aksenov, director dé la televisión soviética: 'Queremos impulsar el processo espiritual del hombre,' " *El Pais,* March 26, 1987, p. 32.

3. Eric Chivian, John E. Mack, Jeremy P. Waletzky, Cynthia Lazaroff, Ronald Doctor, and John M. Goldenring, "Soviet Children and the Threat of Nuclear War: A Preliminary Study," *American Journal of Orthopsychiatry* LV:4 (October 1985), 491. These preliminary findings are from a survey conducted of 50 children in two summer camps in the Soviet Union. The mean age for the children was thirteen years. The authors conducted the survey. I am grateful to Dr. Chivian for providing me with this article.

4. William Zimmerman, "Mobilized Participation and the Nature of the Soviet Dictatorship," *Politics, Work, and Daily Life in the USSR: A Survey of Former Soviet Citizens,* Cambridge: Cambridge University Press, 1987, p. 340. There are two main reasons why his interview analysis is wide of the mark. The first reason relates to interpretation: the question asked of the respondents related to medium preference for (1) news and (2) "variety" (defined for television as "variety and musical shows" and for newspapers, presumably articles about the shows and musicals). Naturally, it was found that respondents, in turning to the newspaper, looked more for news than for "variety." Television, of course, is much better (and better than radio, too) at satisfying the demand for "variety." However, it is not necessarily the case that because a medium is unique or nearly so for some preferences, it does not also satisfy others along the way. American television, too, presents entertainment better than do the newspaper and radio, but the American viewing audience, though it values television most for entertainment, *also* finds television the most credible source for news and information. To extrapolate from the Soviet data that because television is nearly unique in its ability to provide entertainment—as the public recognizes—the increasing attention to television will result in decreasing attention to political news and information is simply mistaken.

A second reason why the analysis founders is related to events beyond the control of the researchers. The sample of their respondents left the Soviet Union before the Gorbachev media revolution and the reorientation of television: before the contentious programs aired, before the live call-in shows, before the space bridges, before the appearances of Westerners arguing their positions with their Soviet hosts, before the programs on long-suppressed Russian literary figures. The extraordinary mobilization of attention that television has been able to effect is due to some significant degree to the new understanding of media in the Gorbachev years.

5. James F. Larson, *Television's Window on the World: International Affairs Coverage on the U.S. Networks*, Norwood, N.J.: Ablex, 1984, p. 7.

6. V.E. Shlapentokh, "K voprosu ob izuchenii esteticheskikh vkusov chitatelya gazety," *Problemy sotsiologii pechati*, vol. 2, Novosibirsk, 1970, p. 61, and V.E.Shlapentokh, *Sotsiologia dlya vsekh*, Moscow, 1970, p. 172.

7. *"Literaturnaya Gazeta" i ee auditoria*, Moscow, 1978, p. 56.

8. *Raionnaya gazeta v sisteme zhurnalistiki*, Moscow, 1977, p. 91.

9. These figures are based on a survey of news coverage in Gayle Durham Hollander, *Soviet Political Indoctrination*, New York: Praeger, 1972, p. 43.

10. V. Kelnik, "Bolshoi mir i malenkaya gazeta (O vystupleniyakh na mezhdunarodnye temy v raionnoi i gorodskoi pechati)," *Gazeta i zhizn*, Sverdlovsk, 1975, p. 137.

11. V.S. Mironenko, "Otchet Tsentralnogo Komiteta VLKSM i zadachi komsomola po dalneishemu usileniu kommunisticheskogo vospitania molodezhi v svete ustanovok XXVII sezda KPSS," *Pravda*, April 16, 1987, p. 3.

12. E.P. Prokhorov, ed., *Sotsiologia zhurnalistiki*, Moscow, 1981, p. 87.

13. *Literaturnaya Gazeta . . .* , p. 127.

14. Three months later, Petrovsky was promoted to Deputy Foreign Minister. He continued to be a prominent figure on Soviet television, active in press conferences, including those that combined international nuclear issues and the Chernobyl nuclear reactor accident.

15. "Byl pervy opyt," *Izvestia*, January 18, 1986, p. 6.

16. The "space bridge" is an important innovation for Soviet television. There have been a number of such programs. Each involves a satellite-linked studio audience in the United States and in the Soviet Union. In each studio there is a screen large enough to give the impres-

sion of immediacy and genuine interaction, and the studio audience is relatively large—at least one hundred, often more. In the Soviet Union, the space bridges have been taped, edited, and then shown in prominent time slots. A great deal of publicity has attended these showings and the television audience has been extremely large. The subjects for space bridges have varied: from music festivals (two US festivals in California) to children's stories and film, Soviet-American collaboration in and views of the Second World War, women's issues, and others. These space bridges are not simply teleconferences or round-table discussions (which the Soviets also do with increasing frequency) but larger scale, more unfettered interaction with the studio audiences. In the United States, the fate of space bridges has been spotty. They have not normally been shown on the networks, but packaged either for public television or sold, as was the case with the Donahue/Pozner program from Seattle and Leningrad, to affiliates or independent stations. A notable exception were the "Congressbridges," a discussion between members of the United States Congress and the Supreme Soviet. These aired live in both countries. In the United States, they occupied ABC's "Nightline" slot. The audience in the United States has been a very small fraction of the Soviet audience, and this bothers the Soviets. Some of the space bridges were not picked up at all by any American station. The commitment of the Soviets, notwithstanding the rather extreme asymmetry in numbers between the American and Soviet television audiences, has been strong, but knowledgeable officials at Gosteleradio argue that viewer interest may have peaked, particularly because of the proliferation of spacebridges (for example, with Sofia, Helsinki, and Warsaw) that lack the dramatic political significance of the Soviet-American programs. The space bridge will undoubtedly continue to be problematic for American television stations. It is a genuine attempt to communicate, to elicit spontaneous reactions to common stimuli. The production values can be improved—because of the need for translation and the time lag involved, the interchanges tend to be stilted. Then, too, the problem of credibility arises. Soviets in the studio audience generally do not disagree with government positions.

17. There was also a two-hour version.

18. Vladimir Pozner, "Za kulisami telemosta 'Leningrad-Sietl,' " *Sovetskaya kultura,* December 20, 1986, p. 8.

19. Observations by Vladimir Pozner at annual meetings of International Communications Association in Chicago, May 23, 1986.

20. Rose E. Gottemoeller, "Soviet Arms Control Decisionmaking After Brezhnev," *The Soviet Calculus of Nuclear War,* ed. Roman Kolkowicz and Ellen Propper Mickiewicz. Lexington, Mass.: D.C. Heath, 1986.

21. Seth Mydans, "For the First Time on the Moscow Beat: News with a Human Face," *New York Times*, October 1, 1984, p. 8. Gorbachev replaced Lomeiko with Gennady Gerasimov, an experienced, less contentious, and smooth journalist, who speaks English fluently.

22. Seth Mydans, "In Helsinki, Russians Court Press," *New York Times*, August 2, 1985, p. A-3.

23. See footnote 14 above.

24. "Chto eto: direktiva?" *Pravda*, May 31, 1986, p. 5. The editors of *Pravda* provided a reply at least as long as the letter and castigated Combs for presuming to "censor" newspapers and asked if he would do the same with the *Washington Post*.

25. Bernard Gwertzman, "A Pre-Summit Parley Yields No Progress," *New York Times*, August 29, 1986, p. 4.

26. As noted above, under Gorbachev's policies, the pages of the press increasingly opened to the views of Westerners, often with commentary. An April issue of *Pravda* presented two articles side by side: one, a lengthy (though somewhat edited) piece by Edward Teller, reprinted from the *New York Times Magazine*, strongly supporting SDI; and the other, by *Pravda* political observer Vsevolod Ovchinnikov, critical of the American space defense program. Edward Teller, "Luchshe shchit, chem mech," and Vsevolod Ovchinnikov, "Ne Budet mecha—ne ponadobitsya shchit," *Pravda*, April 16, 1987, p. 5.

27. As we shall see in the next chapter, a major American television network was roundly criticized for failing to set the context, intervene, and debate a Soviet spokesman who was allowed to speak at considerable length.

28. *Perestroika: New Thinking for Our Country and the World*, New York: Harper and Row, 1987, p. 13.

29. *New York Times* Moscow correspondent Bill Keller noted in March 1987 that the increased candor and criticism in the press was resulting in some degree of confusion and skepticism about all of the proposed changes, as well as a sense of personal threat among those whose privilege or status might be undermined by the broom of reform. "A Steady Diet of Criticism Frazzles Nerves in Russia," *New York Times*, March 8, 1987, p. E3.

30. G.N. Bochevarov, "Uchit nenavisti?"; and A. Bovin, "Net, Uchit vzaimoponimaniu!" *Izvestia*, March 14, 1987, p. 7.

31. A.V. Zhavoronkov, "Potreblenie materialov gorodskoi gazety," *Sotsiologicheskie problemy obshchestvennogo mnenia i deyatelnosti sredstv massovoi informatsii*, Moscow, 1976, p. 60.

32. I.D. Fomicheva, *Zhurnalistika i auditoria*, Moscow, 1976, pp. 110–15, 132.

33. Valery Kondakov, "Osvedomlennost: razmyshlenia publitsista," *Sovetskaya Rossia*, Nov. 24, 1985, p. 1.

34. G. Stepanov, "Oskorblenie nedomolvkami. Govorya konkretno," *Sovetskaya Rossia*, December 15, 1985, p. 3.

35. E.A. Blazhenov, "Zhurnalistika i kommunisticheskoe stroitel-stvo," *Vestnik Moskovskogo Universiteta*, Seria 10, Zhurnalistika, No. 3, 1981, p. 8.

36. A space bridge bringing American and Soviet journalists together in May 1987 was particularly instructive on this point. Stuart Loory, former CNN bureau chief in Moscow, asked the Soviet journalists how they would handle the hypothetical problem of corruption at the level of the Politburo. The responses ranged from refusing to answer the question to assertions that such a hypothesis is unimaginable.

37. E. Chekalova, "Dialog u teleekrana," *Pravda*, April 1, 1983, p. 3.

38. A. Mostovoi, "Kogda zatsvetaet mak," *Komsomolskaya Pravda*, June 8, 1986, p. 2.

39. T. Samolis, "Oshishchenie," *Pravda*, February 13, 1986, p. 3.

40. "Rech tovarishcha Ligacheva E.K.," *Pravda*, February 28, 1986, p. 4.

41. "Pochta stranitsy," *Izvestia*, February 1, 1986, p. 6.

42. A November 1986 issue of *Zhurnalist* notes that Polish and Hungarian press laws serve as models. Iury Borin and Mikhail Fedotov, "Pravo na informatsiu," *Zhurnalist*, No. 11, November 1986, pp. 24–25. I thank Thomas Remington for bringing this source to my attention.

43. M. Odinets and M. Poltarinin, "Za poslednei chertoi," *Pravda*, January 4, 1987, p. 3.

44. For a summary of American news coverage on Chernobyl, one that faults US media and even goes as far as calling its coverage a "propaganda campaign," see Tom Gervasi, "Charting the Double Standard in the Coverage of Chernobyl," *Deadline* I:3 (July–August 1986), 1–5. It is certainly true that the American coverage was wrong on a number of issues and that the corrections, coming later, probably did little to efface initial impressions. But there were corrections, and the amount of information provided by the Soviets was very little during the first few days of the accident. A very large fire that broke out in No. 4 reactor nearly a month after the original accident was not reported for almost three months.

45. Vremya, on May 5, announced that a Brazilian newspaper revealed that the CIA was responsible for fabricating the exaggerated death toll.

46. Philip Taubman, "At Moscow News Session: Brief and Not to Point," *New York Times*, May 7, 1986, p. 9. Taubman does note, however, that other Soviet press conferences for foreign and Soviet correspondents have been relatively open and allowed clearly contentious questions to be posed. The press conference in which Marshal Ogarkov addressed questions on the downing of the KAL plane did have this kind of give-and-take and lasted more than two hours.

47. "Reportazh iz Chernobylya," *Govorit i pokazyvaet Moskva*, June 1, 1986, pp. 3, 19.

48. Seminar at Emory University, February 28, 1986.

49. Press conference, Chicago, May 23, 1986.

50. "There Aren't Poor Questions, Only Poor Answers," *Deadline* I:3 (July–August 1986), p. 8.

51. For example, contrast to the careful and slow series of moves in the aftermath of Chernobyl the rapid, decisive action taken when a young West German citizen landed his small aircraft in Red Square in the spring of 1987. The latter incident was immediately followed by the firing of those who had jurisdiction over air defenses, including the Minister of Defense.

52. Vladimir Gubarev and Mikhail Odinets, "Trudnye dni Cherno-bylya," *Ogonyok*, No. 20 (May 1986), 4.

53. B. Dubrovin, " 'Khochu rabotat na stantsii,' " *Pravda*, June 15, 1986, pp. 1, 6.

54. A. Pokrovsky, "Zona povyshennogo vnimania," *Pravda*, June 5, 1986, p. 3.

55. Paul Lewis, "Soviet Aides Offer First Nuclear Fallout Estimates," *New York Times*, June 12, 1986, p. 7.

56. "Liubosvetov, *op. cit.*

57. Fedor Burlatsky, a prominent media figure in the Gorbachev mold went further in a newspaper article. He argued that the demon-stration effect of this more positive coverage was needed because Soviet media had not been candid with their public about economic problems. He went on to say that the Soviet media's understanding of the West should also be more complex and more nuanced, because a time of "genuine dialogue" was beginning. "Dva vzglyada na mezhdunarod-nuiu zhurnalistiku," *Sovetskaya kultura*, May 21, 1987, p. 6.

58. I. Ya. Matiukha, *Statistika zhiznennogo urovnya naselenia*, Moscow, 1973, p. 116.

59. A.G. Kharchev and S.I. Golod, *Professionalnaya rabota zhenshchin i semya*, Leningrad, 1971, p. 3.

60. Interview on C-SPAN, July 10, 1986.

61. Remarks on C-SPAN, July 10, 1986.

62. *Newswatch*, New York: Simon and Schuster, 1982, p. 62.

63. Edward Jay Epstein criticizes this "professional analogy," point-ing out the differences between superficial similarities and underlying dissimilarities, but he confirms the sense that journalists have that they are autonomous professionals interested in peer evaluation. *News from Nowhere*, New York: Random House, 1973, pp. 25–37.

64. See Herbert Gans, *Deciding What's News*, New York: Pantheon, 1979.

65. Bernice Kanner, "Now, People Meters," *New York*, May 19, 1986, p. 16.

66. For a discussion of the characteristics of letter-writers and the problems encountered in relying on them for an accurate picture of the readership, see Chapter Five.

67. In 1983, *Pravda* had a full-time staff of seventy. Only three years later, it had increased to eighty. See V.S. Korobeinikov, *Redaktsia i auditoria*, Moscow, 1983, p. 233.

68. *Sotsiologia zhurnalistiki*, pp. 157–62.

69. "Televidenie v 1986 godu," *Govorit i pokazyvaet Moskva*, January 8, 1986, p. 19.

Chapter Three: The Worlds of Soviet and American Television News

1. It is not the purpose of this study to compare the entire media systems of the United States and the Soviet Union. I do look closely at the role television plays in Soviet society and the values it purveys. However, in the comparative part I am looking at the content of the news in these two systems, and the kinds of attitudes that contribute to the working journalist's or producer's understanding of issues that surface as important to this content—for example, the place of international news in general and coverage of the Soviet Union specifically; or the use of certain formats; or images of the public in shaping news stories. There are numerous studies on the television industry in America as embedded in larger value sets and constraints. A short illustrative list would include: Edward Jay Epstein, *News from Nowhere*, New York: Random House, 1973; Herbert J. Gans, *Deciding What's News*, New York: Pantheon, 1979; Herbert I. Schiller, *The Mind Managers*, Boston: Beacon, 1973; Gaye Tuchman, *Making News: A Study in the Construction of Reality*, New York: Free Press, 1978; and Edwin Diamond, *Sign Off: The Last Days of Television*, Cambridge: MIT Press, 1982. The memoirs of television managers and correspondents also shed some light on this larger question of institutional and professional autonomy and the values that create certain points of view about what is news and how to play it.

2. A. Iurovsky, *Televidenie—poiski i reshenia*, Moscow, 1983, p. 118.

3. See, for example, Michael J. Robinson and Margaret A. Sheehan, *Over the Wire and On TV*, New York: Russell Sage, 1983, p. 24.

4. Elapsed time is coded in units of fifteen seconds. A story is defined by a change in field correspondent or a change in subject, if read by the anchor. The anchor's lead-in or introduction to a story by a correspondent is coded with that correspondent's story. In American network news bureaus, people tend to talk of an average story as a minute and a half; our finding is, indeed, very close to that.

5. Wilbur Schramm has called attention to the pattern of the flow of news as one of stable patterns over the long term, with spikes of attention to single events, such as disasters, wars, or political crises. *Mass Media and National Development,* Stanford: Stanford University Press, 1964.

6. The facilities for viewing First Program are located at Emory University. Recording and coding the news programs were done by the author and a team of graduate and undergraduate students. Certain data are missing from the set. On November 7, 1984, the Soviet Union celebrated the anniversary of the Bolshevik Revolution. Parades replaced the news that day. Three days each are missing from ABC and Vremya because of technical difficulties: for ABC: October 16, 1984, September 18 and 19, 1985; for Vremya, October 16 and December 5, 1984, and September 11, 1985.

To establish an inter-coder reliability rate, 2,145 data points were independently coded by two pairs of coders: one for ABC and one for Vremya. There was 86 percent agreement.

7. Every story was coded for 24 variables, as appropriate: up to three countries, up to three subjects (from a choice of 75 listed), and up to four newsmakers (from a list of 53 categories). In addition, elapsed time, sequence, and format of story were coded. A number of other variables were used for affect of broadcaster and the assignment of responsibility. Variables treating media coverage of oneself and other countries were also used.

8. James F. Larson, *Television's Window on the World: International Coverage on the U.S. Networks,* Norwood, N.J.: Ablex, 1984, p. 40.

9. Westin, *Newswatch,* p. 67.

10. "Rabotat tvorcheski, preodelevat nedostatki," *Pravda,* November 21, 1986, p. 2.

11. Our coding scheme recognized that many stories are not just about one country, that countries are often shown or cited in a relationship with one another. Therefore, we coded stories for up to three countries. Coverage could include showing a country or referring to it. We included all the countries listed in the standardized codebooks. In addition, however, to capture important information, we accorded identity to certain territories under dispute (Northern Ireland and Namibia) or not included in the usual codes (the Vatican). We also included aggregate bodies, when none of the members is identified separately: NATO, COMECON, the Warsaw Pact, OPEC, and the United Nations.

Finally, we added the Palestine Liberation Organization as a separate entity. Israel, in our coding scheme, includes Jerusalem, but Jordan includes the West Bank. This adds up to 156 countries or specially identified world actors. We give "primary country" status to the country on which the story is primarily focused—not necessarily the first mentioned—but because we have left room to code two more countries, we are assured of capturing virtually all of the references to additional countries in a given story. The residual category of "other" accounts for a total of 0.4% of the primary countries, 0.6% of the secondary countries, and 0.4% of the third countries in the entire data set.

12. Virtually the same relationship obtains if one looks at the coverage of the other superpower as primary and secondary country in a story. According to this measure, the Soviet Union is covered in 7% of the stories on ABC, and the United States, 10% of the stories on Vremya. This percentage is calculated on a base of total stories plus stories in which a second country is included.

13. For the United States, the country with the second largest volume of coverage is Great Britain; for the Soviet Union, it is the United Nations at 4%, followed by India at 3%.

14. If one looks at one country per story—as the most important subject of the story—this agenda is virtually the same. There are two differences: on the American side, the United Nations is not as often the primary country of coverage as it is on the Soviet side, but rather the second subject of a story. We shall see later the highly asymmetrical role the United Nations plays for the Soviet Union and the United States. The other difference relates to Israel: again, as will be discussed later, Israel is not a principal topic of coverage for Vremya, but rather a state actor that is implicated in rather than generating international behavior.

15. If one looks at only one country per story—the primary subject of the story—the difference in news agendas comes only from Vremya, which would include among its news leaders Poland, Austria, and Chile. As noted elsewhere, anti-Pinochet demonstrations are heavily covered by Vremya.

16. "The Soviet Public and the War in Afghanistan: A Trend Toward Polarization," *Soviet Area Audience and Opinion Research,* AR 1-87, Radio Liberty, Radio Free Europe, March 1987, p. 12.

17. To remedy this situation, Congress approved a plan in 1985 to create an Afghan news service, staffed by Afghan refugees. The next year the contract for training the future journalists was awarded by the USIA to Boston University, although Bernard Redmont, dean of the College of Communications, resigned over the agency's insistence that the training program take place in Pakistan. Alex S. Jones, "Boston U.

and Federal Agency To Help To Train Afghan Reporters," *New York Times*, August 18, 1986, p. 11. By the end of 1986, the Hearst Corporation, which was to help set up distribution, had terminated its association with the project. "Alex S. Jones, "Hearst To Bow Out of Role in Project for Afghan News Service," *New York Times*. November 3, 1986, p. 11.

18. Observations made on the "MacNeil/Lehrer Newshour," July 10, 1986.

19 Alex Jones, "Pretoria's Press Curbs Limiting Coverage of Strife," *New York Times*, March 1, 1987, p. 12.

20. "Svobodu nelzya rasstrelyat," *Izvestia*, January 26, 1985, p. 2.

21. Kurt Campbell, *Soviet Policy Towards South Africa*, New York: St. Martin's, 1986, p. 157.

22. Since 1983, when these reports were first issued, member countries on the average voted with the United States just over 20% of the time. For a breakdown of the figures, see: Elaine Sciolino, "Report Shows U.S. Was Outvoted in the U.N. Through Most of 1985," *New York Times*, July 4, 1986, p. 4. Although there were reports from the American delegation that its position was markedly improving, a year later, the figure for member countries voting with the United States had increased only one percentage point. "Report Sees Little Rise in U.S. Power at U.N.," *New York Times*, July 15, 1987, p. 9.

23. This is measured by the presence of Cuba as first or second country in a story. Calculating only one country per story—the most important—Cuba still accounts for less than 1% of the total number of stories.

24. If one looks at first and second country in a story, the picture does not change much. The rank-order of importance remains the same for Vremya, where the main difference in this method of measurement is that the US/NATO figure is 21% and the USSR/Warsaw Pact figure is 48%. The rest of the figures differ by less than a single percentage point. The same kind of difference can be seen for ABC: the US/NATO figure is 68% and the USSR/Warsaw Pact figure is 8%. The Middle East figure is increased by 3%. The rest differ by less than a percentage point. The rank-order changes to put the Middle East in third place, instead of tied for fourth. For discussion of regions, as opposed to individual countries, the United Nations is not included.

25. The figures for stories about the United States and the Soviet Union as secondary country are: 5% for the Soviet Union on ABC (or 2 hours) and 7% for the United States on Vremya (or 4 hours and 48 minutes). The figures for third country are: 2% for the Soviet Union on ABC (or 40 minutes) and 10% for the United States on Vremya (or 6 hours and 27 minutes).

26. As secondary country, the figures are: near 0% for Warsaw Pact on ABC and 6% for NATO on Vremya. Eighty percent of the elapsed time on both newscasts lacks coverage of a third country in a story.

27. Primary country is used.

28. Primary country is used. There is only one story on Libya as secondary country.

29. Larson, *op. cit.*, pp. 113–28.

30. The region with the lowest proportion of its coverage in pictures is South America, which was the primary subject of only 12 stories, 4 of which were read by the anchor. The region with the highest proportion of its coverage in pictures is Asia, with 86%. Primary country is used. Nonstate actors, such as the United Nations, and the European Economic Community are excluded.

31. This is true when first, second, and third country in a story are analyzed.

32. Counting all stories on the countries of Asia as primary, secondary, and third country in a story, there were a total of 164 during the coded period.

33. As before, significant means at least 1% of all stories. This is figured using both primary and secondary country in a story. If one uses primary country only, the coverage is heavy enough for inclusion. Thus, it is the linkage or tie with China as secondary country in a story that moves it up to the list of very salient countries.

34. We coded for 75 different subjects. They fit into larger clusters. The most important are: *national politics*, which refers to *formal* political processes, such as national ceremonies and celebrations, local and national elections, appointment and resignation of officials, governmental decrees or announcements; *international politics*, the *formal* aspects of international relations, such as intergovernmental meetings, official visits, and formal diplomatic procedures; *political protest*, nonviolent demonstrations against one's own or other governments; *political violence*, a spectrum of events of increasingly disruptive force, ranging from demonstrations that turn violent to terrorism, guerrilla warfare, and civil war; *citizenship*, which includes civil rights/civil liberties stories and stories about emigration (or defection) and repatriation (or redefection). *Disasters* and *accidents* form another cluster. All stories relating to arms control, the arms race, and nuclear issues are coded for the *arms control* variable. As in the coding of countries, we recognize that more than one subject may be contained in a single story, and we have, accordingly, coded for primary, secondary, and third subjects.

35. The figure for secondary subject is 16% and for third subject, 13%.

36. For secondary subject, the figure is 11% and for third subject, 7%.

37. These figures are based on the official visit as the primary subject. When a visit occurs it is always coded as primary subject.

38. Michael Massing, "CBS: Sauterizing the News," *Columbia Journalism Review*, March/April 1986, pp. 28, 30.

39. Peter J. Boyer, "CBS News in Search of Itself," *New York Times Magazine*, December 28, 1986, p. 17.

40. "Making News in 1985," *Baltimore Sun*, January 5, 1986, pp. 1–3.

41. For an example of such a news story, see, later in this chapter, "Subjects and Stories: The Weight of Time."

42. As secondary and third subjects, less than one-half of one percentage point separates the proportion of stories devoted to political violence on the two news programs.

43. See Chapter Two.

44. As secondary subject, the figures are 3% for ABC and 0.2% for Vremya and as third subject, 3% and 0.3%, respectively.

45. Primary subject is used.

46. Primary subject is used.

47. For examination of this difference during a week of heightened Soviet-American interaction, see Ellen Mickiewicz and Gregory Haley, "Soviet and American News: Week of Intensive Interaction," *Slavic Review* XL:2 (Summer 1987), 214–28.

48. Third subjects take up 30% of the newstime on Vremya and 33% on ABC.

49. Dmitri Liubosvetov, "Vremya na ekrane," *Pravda*, May 19, 1986, p. 3.

50. In this section we have used only the primary subject and primary country of a story.

51. For these country/subject linkages, we have used primary country and primary subject.

52. These subjects account for roughly three-quarters of the total number of stories on ABC about the Soviet Union and its allies and 79% of Vremya's stories about the United States and its allies.

53. This includes both primary and secondary subjects in a story.

54. Primary subject is used here. For three of the five, virtually the same percentage is also found when secondary story is used. The rank order is the same between primary and secondary story.

55. Thomas Whiteside, "Onward and Upward with the Arts: Stand-ups," *The New Yorker*, December 2, 1985, p. 110.

56. The showcasing of anchors is gaining momentum on the American network news in another way, as well. Live interviews and "crosstalk" are becoming increasingly popular. This practice, where the anchor conducts a live, unedited interview with a major figure or questions field correspondents (crosstalk), clearly promotes the figure of the anchor and, it is hoped, the popularity of the news program. In addition, the increasing competition from local news programs is creating pressure on the national networks to be distinctive. In my talks with news producers, this was one issue that concerned them all. With the increasing availability of communications satellites and the introduction of lightweight portable equipment, local stations have the same capability to transmit pictures and to cover news outside their regions. For example, when *Challenger* exploded, many local stations could dispatch their correspondents to Cape Canaveral to bring the story back by putting it up on a satellite and beaming it down at home. The networks will have to be increasingly distinctive to assure their popularity in a more competitive market, and building attachment to the network anchor is one way of achieving that distinctiveness. On the other hand, network executives say that the anchors are skilled interviewers and help the public to understand important events. Detractors say that with newstime so limited, unedited interviews can result in material dominated by the public figure interviewed and unenlightening for the public. For a discussion of these issues, see Peter J. Boyer, "NBC News May Adopt 90-Minute 'Newswheel,' " *New York Times*, February 12, 1986, p. C-22; and Peter J. Boyer, "Live Interviews and 'Cross-Talk' Put Spotlight on Anchors," *New York Times*, April 28, 1986, p. 16. These arguments cannot be separated from the new austerity imposed on the major networks by financial troubles. As cutbacks and downsizing continue, and as bureaus are closed, there is an even greater attention being paid to the role of the anchor, using satellites to bring in footage from location much more cheaply than do the bureaus and their correspondents. The anchor would then be the chief interpreter of an increasing proportion of the news, assisted by a small core of star correspondents. For discussion of this aspect of the changes in American network news, see Peter J. Boyer, "Mood of Austerity Prompting Change in TV News," *New York Times*, February 23, 1987, p. 14; and Peter Boyer, "A Clash Between Two ABC News Executives," *New York Times*, February 26, 1987, p. 20.

57. The Soviet model, though, is much closer to the European. On the Italian news, for example, "a good deal of the . . . news report is simply read by the announcer, without any accompanying visual images." Daniel C. Hallin and Paolo Mancini,"Speaking of the President," *Theory and Society* XIII (1984), p. 838.

58. Interviews, mainly in the studio, take up 3% of ABC's newstime and 1% of Vremya's. Radio hook-ups, where the correspondent reports from location without pictures—often to cover fast-breaking news from an area where pictures cannot be put up on the satellite—is rare on both programs, accounting for less than a single percentage point. The commentary, the remaining talking head format, is used 3% of the time by Vremya and 2% by ABC.

Chapter Four: Dimensions of News and Their Settings

1. The classic study of the difference between the pattern of selection made by television broadcasters and patterns of events as observed on the spot was done by Kurt Lang and Gladys Engel Lang. "The Unique Perspective of Television and Its Effect: A Pilot Study," in Wilbur Schramm and Donald F. Roberts, eds., *The Process and Effects of Mass Communication*, Urbana: University of Illinois Press, 1971, pp. 169–88.

2. "Ideological Perspectives and Political Tendencies in News Reporting," *Journalism Quarterly* XLI:3 (1964), 495–508. See also the sources listed in Chapter Three, note 1.

3. For an examination of this question, see Benjamin I. Page, Robert Y. Shapiro, and Glenn R. Dempsey, "What Moves Public Opinion?" *American Political Science Review* LXXXI:1 (March 1987), 23–43.

4. The use of clustering and the imposition of narrative unity are by no means universal. The Italian media system, for example, makes little attempt to impose this kind of coherence. Daniel C. Hallin and Paolo Mancini, "Speaking of the President," *Theory and Society* XIII (1984), 829–50.

5. Barrie Gunter, "Forgetting the News," *Mass Communications Review Yearbook*, Vol. 4, Beverly Hills: Sage, 1983, p. 168.

6. W. Gill Woodall, Dennis K. Davis, and Haluk Sahin, "From the Boob Tube to the Black Box: TV News Comprehension from an Information Processing Perspective," *Mass Communications Review Yearbook*, Vol. 4, Beverly Hills: Sage, 1983, p. 193. Emphasis in the original.

7. *Ibid.*

8. We have coded for "responsibility." This variable is used where there is a *clear* reference to one country's responsibility for an event beyond its borders without its direct interference. We have also coded for "secondary responsibility," which is found when one country is said to be behind the activities of a second country influencing the events in a third country. When one country directly performs an act that is criticized, this is not judged as responsibility—examples during our coding period such as the unauthorized Soviet overflight of Japanese airspace or the shipment of what was initially thought to be MIG fighter planes to Nicaragua, were not coded for responsibility, since they are direct acts by a country in pursuit of its foreign objectives. However, when an action or situation is not directly tied to the responsible country, and occurs without its specific intervention at a given moment, it is coded for responsibility. On the Soviet news this could mean the hidden American bolstering of the South African regime's policy of apartheid or a more general case of American culpability in creating a situation in which the nuclear sword of Damocles hangs over the world—in this case, the policies of individual NATO countries are said to be directed by the United States.

9. This figure is based on primary subject and primary responsibility.

10. It is only after our coding period that direct American involvement in Afghanistan becomes important. Early in 1986 it was not unusual to sees stories about bombs concealed in toys for Afghan children as part of an *American* plot.

11. "World News Tonight," December 28, 1984.

12. We did not include emotionally colored stories about oneself—in the Soviet case these tend to be positive judgments about the operation of the economy—on the Soviet and American news broadcasts. This variable applies only to evaluation of foreign countries.

13. This material is drawn from Aldo Vacs, "From Hostility to Partnership: The New Character of Argentine-Soviet Relations," *Soviet-Latin American Relations in the 1980s,* ed. Augusto Varas, Boulder, Colo.: Westview Press, 1987.

14. For a discussion of Soviet-North Yemen relations, see: Mark N. Katz, *Russia and Arabia: Soviet Foreign Policy Toward the Arabian Peninsula,* Baltimore: Johns Hopkins University Press, 1986, chap. 1.

For an analysis of the flare-up in the Yemens during the Carter administration and the American response, see Raymond L. Garthoff, *Detente and Confrontation: American-Soviet Relations from Nixon to Reagan,* Washington: Brookings Institution, 1985, pp. 653–60.

15. A good summary is provided by Susan Lesley Clark, "The Soviets and Japan's Defense Efforts," *Soviet Union,* Vol. 13, No. 2, 1986.

16. The negative emotional loading for Italy is the result of two stories, one which blames Italy for the Antonov trial and the other, a story on the Mafia, that asserts that "the fact that the Mafia . . . has ties and enjoys the support of Rome has long been known." The rest of the story pursues this line.

17. Chapter Two discusses these points, largely in the words of the Soviet media people themselves.

18. Primary country is used. When both primary and secondary country are used—two subjects for a story—and the base is figured as the total number of stories plus stories in which a second country is covered, the direction is the same: 18.6% to 23.5%

19. As primary country. The weight of South Africa is even higher when a second country is considered: 61% of all the stories on South and East Africa as second country and 54% as third country.

20. When two countries are included as subjects of stories, then the coverage diminishes much less: just about half a percentage point, suggesting that the region is very often tied to stories principally about others, when not the principal actor.

21. The subcontinent declines even more when two countries are used: from 5% to 2%.

22. The rank-order of regions in the two periods is:

1984	1985
USSR/WARSAW PACT	USSR/WARSAW PACT
US/NATO	US/NATO
INDIAN SUBCONTINENT	SO. AND EAST AFRICA
ASIA	NON-NATO W. EUROPE
MIDDLE EAST	ASIA
CENTRAL AMERICA	CENTRAL AMERICA
SO. AND EAST AFRICA	MIDDLE EAST
NON-NATO W. EUROPE	INDIAN SUBCONTINENT
SOUTH AMERICA	SOUTH AMERICA
CARIBBEAN ⎫ same	CARIBBEAN
CENT. AND W. AFRICA ⎭ percentage	NORTH AFRICA
NON-WARSAW PACT ⎫ same	NON-WTO E. EUROPE
E. EUROPE ⎬ percentage	CENT. & W. AFRICA ⎫
NORTH AFRICA ⎭	⎬ same
COMECON (as collective)	SO. PACIFIC ⎭ perc.
EUR. ECON.	EUR. ECON. COMM.(col.)
COMMUNITY (as col.)	
SO. PACIFIC	

When one looks at the secondary country in a story, there are far fewer shifts. South African coverage still shows a very strong increase over the two periods, and India, a decrease, but the other changes are less sharp. When the third country is examined, there is actually an increase in coverage of the Indian subcontinent, and South Africa still registers a notable gain over the period. The proportion of stories about the Soviet Union and its East European allies declines sharply, and coverage of the United States and its allies increases, but not by much. A country appearing as third country in a story is not at all the main focus of the story. It may be only mentioned, sometimes as part of a longer list of participants in an international meeting or noted as the site of some negotiation between other parties. It tells us something about the linkage that is made among countries in a story. On Vremya, third countries are part of stories in under 20% of all stories. Second countries are part of stories in just under 50% of all stories. Combining first and second country in a story and calculating on the base of all stories with first and second country in a story, the rank-order does not change at all for the Chernenko period (except that ties are eliminated by small differences), but it does for the Gorbachev period, in which Asia and the Middle East are placed ahead of Central America.

23. As in the previous chapter, leading newsmaker is defined by at least 1% of the total number of stories. Using primary country or primary and secondary country produces the same pattern for these countries.

24. For a discussion of changes in coverage of the PRC, see the previous chapter.

25. This occurs when primary and secondary country are used. If only the principal country in a story is used, Israel is not a subject for significant coverage in either the Chernenko or Gorbachev period, but India is in the earlier period. Israel does, as discussed later in this chapter, figure importantly under Gorbachev in the share of *newstime* it receives.

26. This is true whether figured as the principal country in a story or in the larger pool of primary and secondary countries.

27. This is for the primary country in a story.

28. Primary subject has been used.

29. See Chapter Two.

30. Examination of the second and third subjects of stories shows the same trend, with even more emphasis on the arms race under Gorbachev, taking up 20% of the third subjects of stories.

31. The rank-order of primary subjects (% stories over 1%): Vremya

1984	1984
Economic issues	International politics
National politics	National politics
International politics	Economic issues
Political violence	Political violence
Media	Media
Political Protest	Space/Science
Arts	Disaster/Accident
Space/Science	Pol. protest, arms control
Arms control	Military issues
Legis. Process	Arts
Military issues	Crime
Crime	
Spying & Intelligence	

32. Primary country is used. An even more dramatic decline takes place if one uses both primary and secondary country: the share declines from 4.2% to 0.1%.

33. Using both primary and secondary country, there is a similar increase in stories, from 2.5% to 4.3%.

34. There is a much slighter increase if both primary and secondary countries are used—only one third of a percentage point. But Vremya's coverage of the region declines using this measurement from 3.6% to 2.9% of the total number of stories.

35. Coverage doubles whether only one country or both primary and secondary countries are used.

36. Using both primary and secondary countries in a story, coverage of the United States and NATO declines from 71% to 64%, an identical percentage decline. Coverage of the Soviet Union rises from 5% to slightly over 9.5%, virtually the same as the primary country difference.

37. Using both primary and secondary countries in a story, coverage of the United States on Vremya increases from 9.6% to 10.2%, a percentage increase difference of only half a percentage point from the measure using primary country only.

38. As a kind of limiting case, we also looked at a week of unusually intense Soviet-American interaction on the newsfront. During the week of September 14–20, 1986, there were five major news stories involving Soviet-American relations: the visit of Foreign Minister Shevardnadze to New York and Washington; the expulsion of 25 Soviet employees from the United Nations Mission in New York; the drama of Nicholas Daniloff and Gennadi Zakharov under arrest in the custody of their respective ambassadors; the settling of a Summit date; and the visit of more than 250 Americans to the Soviet resort of Jurmala for a "Town Meeting" sponsored by the Chautauqua Society. In fact, during this unusually active period of superpower news, the American news overtook the Soviet news in the percentage of the number of stories about the other. However, the Soviet news still devoted more time—both as a proportion of the whole and in the aggregate—to the United States than did the American news to the Soviet Union. In this week of saturation reporting, many of the most important asymmetries were still in effect. Ellen Mickiewicz and Gregory Haley, "Soviet and American News: Week of Intensive Interaction," *Slavic Review* XL:2 (Summer 1987), 214–28.

39. Analysis of secondary subject in a story shows rather little change in ABC over this period. The only sharp changes were an increase in crime stories from 6% to 10% and a decrease in a category that combines religion, ethics, and social fabric stories (e.g., family issues) from 11% to 7%. There is little notable change in third subjects in stories between the two periods.

40. As Robinson and Sheehan point out, campaign coverage was much lighter twenty years ago, *Over the Wire and on TV*, New York: Russell Sage, 1983.

41. Primary country is used, excluding the United States and the Soviet Union.

42. In terms of elapsed time for coverage as second country, ABC gives heavy coverage to two additional countries: Vietnam and West Germany, in each of the two periods. On Vremya, only East Germany receives heavy coverage across the two time periods. Yugoslavia and Israel, heavily covered as secondary country during the Chernenko period, virtually disappear under Gorbachev—Israel is moved up to primary country—Israel also shows up with heavy coverage under Gorbachev, as third country in a story.

43. Alexander Bovin was quoted in Chapter Two as favoring more frequent live broadcasts, a position that Vladimir Pozner has also supported and that is a new official position. That this is a departure from the past is clear. Previously, the very limited use of live coverage was justified not only by technical constraints (which were more serious in the past than at present, though certainly still a factor to contend with), but also by a substantive rationale. The argument went as follows: Since there is so much information in a society, and to broadcast all of it is impossible, it is necessary to edit and reduce what one selects for broadcast. This leads to efficiency and coherence. The live transmission should be an "extraordinary phenomenon." The events that should be seen when they occur are: important state visits, openings of Party congresses, festive processions in Red Square, and important sports competitions. "Only in these cases does the showing of the event take up as much airtime as the event itself." What is left out of this rationale is live coverage of newsmakers, accidents or other unforeseen non-ceremonial events (like Chernobyl), and many other events. Bovin favors the sense of immediacy and authenticity that live coverage provides: the old understanding, quoted here, favors a "safe" and contained (and extremely limited) live coverage of state occasions. For elaboration of the older view (now being replaced), see G. Kuznetsov, "Pravo na efir," *TV-Reporter*, ed. E.G. Bagirov, Moscow, 1976, p. 22.

44. Dmitri Liubosvetov, "Vremya na ekrane," *Pravda*, May 19, 1986, p. 3.

45. For this variable, we coded for 53 different types of people . They include categories of government officials, Party officials, scientists and educators, economic leaders, lawyers, physicians, the military (officers and rank-and-file), people in the arts and sports, religious leaders, astronauts/cosmonauts, and many others (including ordinary, unidentified people). We coded for up to four newsmakers shown or cited in a story. Some stories have no reference to people; some others will have more than four. The first three persons in a story provide 94% of the total number of people covered by ABC and 89% of the total covered by Vremya.

46. We have used here any reference to the given leader as first, second, third, or fourth person, when his country is the first, second, or third in a story. Thus, we include references when the leader's country is not the main subject of a story, but the leader's name or image appears in the story. There are a total of 2,365 cases of persons covered or cited on ABC and 3,313 on Vremya. Given the much larger number of stories on Vremya, it is apparent that the degree of personalization or "humanization" of the news is very much less in that country: individuals are featured less often.

47. Again, to some extent this is a European model. On the Italian news, the role of the "common man" is far smaller than on the American. Hallin and Mancini, *op. cit.*, pp. 838–39.

48. These percentages are arrived at using the following procedure: up to four people covered on the news have been coded for each country's news program. "Official" includes a country's leader, other officials at the national and subnational levels, diplomats, Party officials at the national and subnational levels, and official spokesmen, such as Larry Speakes. The officials may be from any country covered in a news story. The figures are for the combined 1984–85 period.

49. This is the percentage for the combined 1984–85 period. It should be borne in mind that the people covered may be shown in a story about any country.

50. This table uses the total five months of broadcasts.

51. This category includes scientists, scholars, university administrators, and experts in a field.

52 Used only if the doctor shown or cited is covered as a medical specialist. Physicians in their role as political activists would not be included.

53. Includes both officers and rank-and-file and includes those military personnel who are shown or cited in peacekeeping activities, such as confronting rioters and protesters. The largest number of military as newsmakers relates to the U.S.S.R., Afghanistan, Lebanon, Nicaragua, Poland, South Africa, Jordan, and Chile.

54. Religious leaders, such as Bishop Desmond Tutu, who speak out on political issues are included.

55. Ordinary people are people who are not identified in a specific category or who are not identified at all. They include industrial workers below the managerial or specialist level, children, and massed individuals. They are coded only if they are actually part of the story, active in making news, not just as background to news. Thus, if a presidential candidate in the United States addressed a number of people, they would not be included. However, if a number of people were creating riots or demonstrations, they would be included as a single entry.

56. See Chapter Two.

57. Alexander Bovin brings up this point, too, in the important article cited earlier (Chapter Two), "Byl pervy opyt," *Izvestia*, January 18, 1986, p. 6.

58. In her examination of the *Westmoreland v. CBS et al.* libel suit, Renata Adler refers to this practice as part of a "code," which should alert the viewer to an illusion of authenticity that is not, in fact, there. The picture of the nodding interviewer should, she argues, be treated skeptically, since it may well be editing, not the unrolling of the dialogue that has created the agreement. "Just because the camera cuts . . . to someone nodding while someone else is speaking, the nodding person need not . . . have agreed with what the speaking person is saying; he may not even have heard it; he may not even have been present; there was just some footage of somebody speaking and some footage of somebody nodding, and the producer wanted, in this way, to make a point. . . ." *Reckless Disregard*, New York: Knopf, 1986, p. 205. Adler is quite right that cuts splicing in the interviewer can be used to alter very significantly what might in fact have occurred. However, such cuts are very widely used simply to maintain smooth transitions when short fragments are taken out of longer interviews. Some editing must be done, and this preserves the effect of continuity. The room for distortion is naturally quite considerable, though responsible journalists are certainly aware of the problem. Av Westin, vice president for program development at ABC News, regards the use of the "reverse question" (the interviewer is shot asking the questions again at the end of the interview for the camera alone, and these are spliced into the interview later) to be a valid tool, but one where "the potential for error is great if extreme care is not taken to use precisely the same words and inflection," *Newswatch*, New York: Simon and Schuster, 1982, p. 244.

59. See Chapter Two.

60. See Chapter Three.

61. The length of the broadcast day during the week varies. The findings that follow are drawn from a full week's sweep of programming on First Program from January 20–26, 1986. The broadcast time, naturally, excludes the late morning/early afternoon break, during which programming ceases. The percentages may not equal 100 because of rounding.

62. See Chapter One.

63. This includes the program about movies, "Kinopanorama," a 90-minute program on Friday, January 24.

64. The anniversary of Lenin's death was observed during the week of our sweep and the programming for that day reflected the event. It should be borne in mind, though, that hardly a week goes by without some official day: the Day of the Rocket Forces, International Women's Day, Lenin's birthday, Cosmonauts' Day, the anniversary of the founding of the Young Pioneers, Geologists' Day, Chemists' Day, Medical Workers' Day, to name only a few. The number of these special days is extremely large, and some of the programs are chosen for thematic reasons. Thus, it is the rule, rather than the exception, to have at least one thematically arranged day of programming to honor a nationally designated observance.

65. "Filmy na 'malom' ekrane," *Govorit i pokazyvaet Moskva.* February 5, 1986, p. 19.

66. A. Polskaya and E. Yakovich, "Progulka s programmoi i kalkulyatorom," *Literaturnaya Gazeta,* March 21, 1984, p. 8.

67. *Ibid.* See also: A Shlienkov, "Ostankino-86," *Izvestia,* January 4, 1986, p. 6.

68. The prestigious Tchaikovsky competition, held in June 1986, was covered on weekday broadcasts four times during the week of June 16: twice for twenty minutes and twice for fifteen minutes after the news. During its last week, the week of July 1, some 4 hours and 10 minutes were devoted to the competition.

69. Between one and three hours for total sports coverage over five weekdays is much more common. Sometimes, as during the week of February 10, 1986, two 30-minute "sports roundup" programs constitute the entire week's offering in sports.

70. See Ellen Propper Mickiewicz, *Media and the Russian Public,* New York: Praeger, 1981, chap. 2, "Watching Television in Russia."

71. "Sportivny teleekran: glavnaya tema—zdorovy obraz zhizni," *Govorit i pokazyvaet Moskva,* February 19, 1986, p. 19.

72. Shlienkov, *op. cit.*

73. Genrikh Borovik is one of the "stars" of Soviet public affairs programs. As a well-known commentator, he often narrates programs, comments in news analysis programs, and provides interpretation of news stories on Vremya. His English is excellent, and he has worked in the United States. He was one of those who interviewed President Reagan. He was also the one who was chosen by Vremya to do the commentary on the story of President Reagan's joking remarks about bombing the Soviet Union. Borovik's commentary was extremely biting, acerbic, and militant.

74. The visit raised the story to the status of a media event in the United States as well. Representative Steny Hoyer, head of the committee charged with monitoring progress under the Helsinki accords, indicated that he had been instrumental in arranging the visit to counteract the Soviets' use of the Peltier story.

75. This includes all non-news and public affairs programming: feature films, sports, children's programming, travel, popular science and culture. It does not include health and family programs.

76. "Televidenie v 1986 godu," *Govorit i pokazyvaet Moskva*, January 8, 1986, p. 19.

77. During the week, culture programs accounted for only 14% of airtime.

78. A. Iurovsky, *Televidenie—poiski i reshenia*, Moscow, 1983, p. 132.

79. " 'Chelovek s pyatoi aveniu,' " *Govorit i pokazyvaet Moskva*, March 26, 1986, p. 3.

80. A week after this movie aired in Moscow, *New York Times* reporter Robert O. Boorstin interviewed Mauri in New York. Mauri defended his role in the film, stating that none of the scenes was staged, that he wasn't paid, and that he willingly showed the Soviet crew examples of the economic inequality that had caused his own housing problems. Although he left his background and current financial status vague, he did reveal that he had visited the Soviet Union in the 60s and had considerable sympathy for their collective welfare system, which, he thought, compensated for "certain restrictions" they might experience. "Man Defends His Role in Soviet Film," *New York Times*, April 9, 1986, p. 13.

81. Felicity Barranger, " 'Homeless' New Yorker's Story: A Postscript in Soviet Union," *New York Times*, August 11, 1986, p. 4; and "The Great Pretender," *Time*, August 25, 1986, p. 23.

82. T. Nikitina, " 'Ot Chikago do Filadelfii,' " *Govorit i pokazyvaet Moskva*, April 16, 1986, p. 3.

83. For an account of the event, see Joanna Brown, "Thousands Mourn for Chicago's Leader," *Los Angeles Times*, June 14, 1983, p. 13.

84. S. Kushnerev, " 'A Vy kto takie?' " *Pravda*, March 30, 1987, p. 4.

85. Quoted in Bill Keller, "Soviet Youth Arm Seeks To Rein in Political Groups," *New York Times*, November 8, 1987, p. 1. Emphasis added.

Chapter Five: Television and the Formation of Public Opinion

1. Cliff Zakin, "Mass Communication and Public Opinion," in *Handbook of Political Communication*, ed. Dan D. Nimmo and Keith R. Sanders, Beverly Hills: Sage, 1981, p. 371.

2. Jack M. McLeod and Lee B. Becker, "Testing the Validity of Gratification Measures Through Political Effects Analysis," in *The Uses of Mass Communications: Current Perspectives on Gratifications Research,* ed. Jay G. Blumler and Elihu Katz, Beverly Hills: Sage, 1974, p. 137.

3. Spartak Beglov, *Vneshnepoliticheskaya propaganda: Ocherk teorii i praktiki,* Moscow, 1984, p. 230.

4. Evgeny Nozhin, "Ni Slova ne vozmut na veru," *Molodoi Kommunist,* August 1984, p. 29.

5. B.A. Grushin and L.A. Onikov, *Massovaya informatsia v sovetskom promyshlennom gorode,* Moscow, 1980, p. 245.

6. S.A. Iosifyan, *Televidenie i zritel,* Moscow, 1975.

7. Cited in Garth Jowett and James M. Linton, *Movies as Mass Communication,* Beverly Hills: Sage, 1980, p. 75.

8. The history of Soviet opinion surveys is now well known. It developed with the early pioneering studies of Pitirim Sorokin and others and then was cut off by Stalin. When Khrushchev came to power some methodologically weak polls were begun, such as newspaper write-in surveys, where coupons could be clipped and opinions registered. Very soon, however, more serious, rigorous, and reliable polling was undertaken by such well-known Soviet sociologists as Vladimir Shlapentokh, Boris Firsov, A.G. Kharchev, T.I. Zaslavskaya, B.A. Grushin, Iu. V. Arutiunyan, and others. The early developments in Soviet opinion research have been chronicled by Elizabeth Ann Weinberg, *The Development of Sociology in the Soviet Union,* London: Routledge and Kegan Paul, 1974; and Gayle Durham Hollander, *Soviet Political Indoctrination,* New York: Praeger, 1972.

Analysis of the surveys of media behavior does show a patterned response. The patterns hold across the various locales where the surveys were taken and are repeated results of different surveys undertaken by different research teams. Real questions may be raised concerning methods, reliability, and replicability in Soviet surveys. It is essential to separate those that are conducted with accepted scholarly research methods from those that are not. For a discussion of this problem, see Ellen Propper Mickiewicz, *Media and the Russian Public,* New York: Praeger, 1981, chap. 1.

9. *Mass Communication Theory,* Beverly Hills: Sage, 1983, pp. 34–35.

10. For a critical appraisal of the reliance on what he considers to be outmoded theory, see Robert L. Savage, "The Diffusion of Information Approach," in *Handbook of Political Communication,* pp. 101–19.

11. Doris A. Graber, in her seminal work on processing the news, did not find any evidence of this indirect flow of information. Rather, the panelists in her study, "with few exceptions, received their mass media information directly. When they engaged in conversations with others, or listened to others, they learned little new." *Processing the News: How People Tame the Information Tide,* New York: Longman, 1984, p. 101.

12. *Public Opinion in Soviet Russia,* Cambridge: Harvard University Press, 1962.

13. *Ibid.,* p. 127.

14. *Narodnoe khozyaistvo SSSR 1922–1982,* Moscow, 1982, p. 41.

15. *Ibid.,* p. 403.

16. Stephen White, "The Effectiveness of Political Propaganda in the USSR," *Soviet Studies* XXXII:3 (July 1980), 339.

17. E.O. Dobolova and S.G. Komissarova, "Raionnaya gazeta v otsenke svoikh chitatelei," *Iz opyta konkretno-sotsiologicheskikh issledovanii,* Ulan-Ude, 1972, p. 90.

18. Konstantin U. Chernenko, "Aktualnye voprosy ideologicheskoi, massovo-politicheskoi raboty partii," *Pravda,* June 15, 1983, pp. 1–3.

19. Grushin and Onikov, *op. cit.*

20. *Pravda,* May 23, 1977, quoted in Stephen White, *op. cit.,* p. 327.

21. White, *op. cit.,* p. 333.

22. Stephen White, "Propagating Communist Values in the USSR," *Problems of Communism* XXXIV:6 (November–December 1985), 5.

23. *Ibid.,* p. 6.

24. Lyman E. Ostlund, "Interpersonal Communication Following McGovern's Eagleton Decision," *Public Opinion Quarterly* XXXVII:4 (1973), 607.

25. *Ibid.,* p. 609.

26. Savage, *op. cit.* Maxwell E. McCombs, "The Agenda-Setting Approach," in *Handbook of Political Communication,* p. 129.

27. Another source of oral propaganda, one that is addressed to large numbers rather than very small groups, are public lectures, an "oral mass medium." Lectures cover a variety of subjects, but the majority deal with economics, international relations, and Party history. It is the question period that is most satisfactory for the audiences, and in the absence of mass media communications on the subjects, provides needed information about the micro- and macroworlds of the listener. Here, too, though, to the degree that television, with its visual images, can provide timely and credible coverage, the importance of the lecture may well decline. For a discussion of this channel of information, see: Mickiewicz, *Media and the Russian Public,* chap. 8; and Vladimir Shlapentokh, *Soviet Public Opinion and Ideology: Mythology and Pragmatism in Interaction,* New York: Praeger, 1986, pp. 99–112.

28. I am grateful to Alexander Pravda and David Lane for their observations on the issues of the brigade system and ideological issues.

Lane, who has done extensive research on labor in the Soviet Union, finds the brigade system to be fundamentally and virtually totally concerned with economic, rather than ideological or socialization, tasks. The problem of the "multiplicity of goals" has also been noted by Darrell Slider in his article, "The Brigade System in Soviet Industry: An Effort to Restructure the Labour Force," *Soviet Studies* XXXIX:3 (July 1987), 388–405. The small size of the brigade, its intensive economic functions, and the pressure for productivity all militate against the absorption of still other, unrelated, ideological obligations.

29. "Sovershenstvovanie razvitogo sotsializma i ideologicheskaya rabota partii v svete reshenii iunskogo (1982 g.) Plenuma TsK KPSS," *Pravda*, December 11, 1984, p. 3.

30. L. Maslennikova, "Pochemu ne zhalko Fediu," *Komsomolskaya Pravda*, May 4, 1985, p.2.

31. Sergei Vlasov, "Dom i kollektiv," *Ogonyok*, No. 38 (September 1984), 9–11.

32. A. Pankratov, "Dom nadezhdy nashei," *Pravda*, March 17, 1985, p. 2.

33. Vlasov, *op. cit.*

34. "V TsK KPSS, Sovete Ministrov SSSR, i VTsSPS," *Pravda*, December 3, 1983, p. 1.

35. V. Mishin, "Po-Leninski uchitsya kommunizmu," *Pravda*, June 12, 1984, p. 2. That entrance way, where so many real conversations take place among young people, became one of the remote locations for the television program "Twelfth Floor" (see Chapter Four).

36. These are findings from a survey of 1,000 Moscow area schoolchildren, aged 11 to 17. G. Galochkina, "Kogda sprosili u detei," *Teleekran priglashaet detei*, Moscow, 1976, p. 173. 0.9% of the children said they talked with teachers or at youth group meetings, while about 36% talked with parents and 52% talked with their friends.

37. "The Soviet Public and the War in Afghanistan: A Trend Toward Polarization," *Soviet Area Audience and Opinion Research*, AR 1-87, Radio Liberty, Radio Free Europe, March 1987, p. 12. Because this study averages years before and after the change in the policy of television coverage of the war, it is likely that the rapid rise of television as a source of information would be even clearer with a narrower time frame.

38. V.S. Korobeinikov, *Redaktsia i auditoria*, Moscow, 1983, pp. 176, 233. A. Vasilenko, "Ot nashego glavnogo korrespondenta," *Gazeta, avtor i chitatel*, Moscow, 1975, p. 30.

39. V.T. Davydchenkov, "Organizatsia sotsiologicheskogo obsledovania i vnedrenie poluchennykh rezultatov v tsentralnoi gazete," *Problemy sotsiologii pechati*, Vol. 2, Novosibirsk, 1970, p. 148.

40. I.D. Fomicheva, *Zhurnalist i auditoria,* Moscow, 1976. G.D. Tokarovsky, "Pisma trudyashchikhsya kak kanal vyrazhenia obshchestvennogo mnenia," *Sotsiologicheskie problemy obshchestvennogo mnenia i deyatelnosti sredstv massovoi informatsii,* Moscow, 1976, pp. 113–26.

41. Grushin and Onikov, *op. cit.*

42. A more detailed analysis of this study and related issues may be found in Mickiewicz, "Feedback, Surveys, and Soviet Communication Theory," *Journal of Communication* XXXIII:2 (Spring 1983), 97–110.

43. For an analysis of the differences between the communications behavior of Party members and others in the media audience, see Mickiewicz, *Media and the Russian Public.*

44. *Ibid.*

45. E.V. Vasilevskaya, *Ocherki istorii razvitia televidenia v zapadnoi sibiri,* Novosibirsk, 1978, p. 60.

46. The following is part of a discussion of Soviet theory in Mickiewicz, "Feedback, Surveys, and Soviet Communication Theory," pp. 104–5.

47. See note 10. A formal specialization in sociology has also been established: first, for institutions of higher education in Moscow, Leningrad, Kiev, and Kharkov; with later additions planned.

48. Vasilevskaya, *op. cit.,* p. 60.

49. E.A. Shevardnadze, "Izuchenie obshchestvennogo mnenia— vazhny faktor razvertyvania initsiativy i tvorchestva mass," *Sotsiologicheskie issledovania,* No. 3, 1984, p. 9.

50. In Western media theory, the hypodermic effects theory overlooked the individual and was concerned only with the mass. It posited near total efficacy for the communicator. Its successor, the "limited effects" model did the opposite. As McLeod and Becker summarize: "The 'limited effects' model, by making the audience member so active and selective that any effect can be obtained from any message, comes close to substituting the fable of the omnificent audience for . . . the 'myth of the omnipotent media.' . . . In rejecting the hypodermic effects model, we should avoid developing an unwarranted disregard for the effects of communication." McLeod and Becker, *op. cit.,* p. 137.

51. McQuail, *op. cit.,* pp. 183–84.

52. *Ibid.,* p. 52.

53. For a classic exposition, see Maxwell McCombs and D.L. Shaw, "The Agenda-setting Function of the Press," *Public Opinion Quarterly* XXXVI:1972, pp. 176–87.

54. Zukin, *op. cit.,* pp. 371–78.

55. David Weaver, "Media Agenda-setting and Public Opinion: Is There a Link," *Communication Yearbook 8,* ed. Robert N. Boestrom, Beverly Hills: Sage, 1984, pp. 689–90.

Chapter Six: The Impact of Television

1. *Semya i blagosostoyanie v razvitom sotsialisticheskom obshchestve*, eds., N.M. Rimashevskaya and S.A. Karapetyan, Moscow, 1985, pp. 204–5. The survey was conducted between 1978 and 1980.

2. B. Sapunov, "Televidenie v sisteme sotsialisticheskoi kultury," *Televidenie vchera, segodnya, zaftra: '86,* Moscow, 1986, p. 17.

3. Iu. V. Arutiunyan and Iu. V. Bromlei, *Sotsialno-kulturny oblik sovetskikh natsii,* Moscow, 1986, p. 221.

4. Less than two-fifths do "some reading" once a week; a quarter go to the movies once a week; 16% see friends daily. *Kulturnaya deyatelnost: Opyt sotsiologicheskogo issledovania,* ed. L.N.Kogan, Moscow, 1981, p. 177. The survey included 1,700 people.

5. *Ibid.,* p. 200. The survey included 2,494 respondents.

6. A study of leisure-time use in the city of Pskov, a city midway between Leningrad and Riga, found that between 1965 and 1987, time spent watching television was rapidly approaching the number of hours the residents of Jackson, Michigan, watched. But the amount of time spent reading had decreased. These findings come from a collaborative survey conducted by the Survey Research Center of the University of Maryland and the Soviet Academy of Sciences. These results were reported in the *New York Times,* October 26, 1987, p. 20. Elem Klimov, Gorbachev's head of the Cinematographers' Union, appointed a sociologist to survey audience demand soon after he took office in 1986. In addition, Klimov began an aggressive campaign on television to call attention to new movie releases.

7. S. Feiginov, "Mesto i pedagogicheskie funktsii televidenia v strukture vneshkolnogo vremeni podrostkov," *Televidenie vchera, segodnya, zavtra,* vyp. 2, ed. E.S. Sabashnikova, Moscow, 1982, pp. 149–69.

8. V.S. Korobeinikov, *Goluboi charodei: televidenie i sotsialnaya sistema,* Moscow, 1975, p. 125.

9. Only about 15% of the Soviet adult female population neither works nor studies, and this proportion includes women who are unable to work because of ill health and those at home with exceptionally large families.

10. The patterns of viewing described here are analyzed at length in Mickiewicz, *Media and the Russian Public,* chaps. 2 and 3.

11. "Natsionalnye protsessy v SSSR: itogi, tendentsii, problemy," *Istoria SSSR,* No. 6 (1987), 117.

12. Arutiunyan and Bromlei, *op. cit.,* p. 223.

13. "Televidenie kak sotsialny institut politicheskoi struktury obshchestva," *Zhurnalistika v politicheskoi strukture obshchestva,* Moscow, 1975, pp. 102–3.

14. See, for example, as noted in Chapter One, James F. Larson, *Television's Window on the World,* Norwood, N.J.: Ablex, 1984, pp. 7–10.

15. The audience for newspapers is highly skewed in terms of education. The intelligentsia (defined as those with higher education in jobs requiring higher education) make up three-fourths of the readers of *Literaturnaya Gazeta;* two-fifths of *Pravda,* half of *Izvestia,* and a quarter of *Trud.* Under 10% of the Soviet population over 20 has had some college education.

16. John P. Robinson and Mark R. Levy, *The Main Source: Learning from Television News,* Beverly Hills: Sage, 1986.

17. E.P.Mikhailova and N.N.Mikhailov, "Selskaya televisionnaya auditoria," *Televisionnaya auditoria: struktura, orientatsii, kulturnaya aktivnost,* Sverdlovsk, 1973, p. 110.

18. I.D. Fomicheva, *Zhurnalistika i auditoria,* Moscow, 1976, p. 91.

19. For a discussion of these effects of television, see *Media and the Russian Public,* chap. 3.

20. The close similarity in these two formulations may well be an indication of the influence Gorbachev had during the tenure of the weakened leader, Chernenko. The kinds of moves in the arena of media and information that started before Gorbachev took power may have been the results of his influence before Chernenko's death. Describing another example of Gorbachev's influence before becoming General Secretary, Seweryn Bialer writes of a semi-secret speech about the social and economic ills besetting Soviet society. *The Soviet Paradox: External Expansion, Internal Decline,* New York: Knopf, 1986, pp. 122–23.

21. *Pravda,* February 26, 1986, p. 10.

22. For an analysis of the reliability of these surveys, see *Media and the Russian Public,* chap. 1. For a discussion of the feedback problem, see Chapter Five of this book.

23. See his *What Is To Be Done?,* New York: International Publishers, 1969.

24. M. Murzina, "About Children, for Grownups," *Izvestia,* February 23, 1987, p. 3. Reprinted in *Current Digest of the Soviet Press,* XXXIX:9 (April 1, 1987), 6.

25. "Molodezh—tvorcheskaya sila revoliutsionnogo obnovlenia: vystuplenie M.S. Gorbacheva na XX sezde VLKSM," *Pravda,* April 17, 1987, p. 1.

26. For a collection of press articles about the case of the "Lyubery" youth gang, see *Current Digest of the Soviet Press* XXXIX:10 (April 8, 1987).

27. See Chapter Two.

28. Harrison Salisbury, "Gorbachev's Dilemma," *New York Times Magazine,* July 27, 1986, p. 33.

29. "Poznat dialektiku perestroiki," *Pravda*, April 18, 1987, p. 2.

30. Bialer, *The Soviet Paradox . . .* , p. 52.

31. Reminiscent also of Khrushchev's reforms is the decision, by Elem Klimov, the head of the Soviet Cinematographers' Union, to review about 25 feature films that had been put on the shelf because of censorship problems. Klimov was named in 1986 after an overhaul of the entire leadership. The Union of Writers was similarly set for renovation, and here too a review of previously censored works was undertaken.

32. Doris A. Graber, "A Cross-Cultural Perspective on Opinion Formation: Clues to 'the Riddle Wrapped in a Mystery Inside an Enigma,' " unpublished paper. I am grateful to Professor Graber for her permission to cite this work. See also Graber, *Processing the News: How People Tame the Information Tide*, New York: Longman, 1984.

33. Schema theory clearly does not answer all questions about information organizing and retrieving. A good summary of criticism may be found in W.Gill Woodall, "Information Processing Theory and Television News," in *The Main Source, op. cit.*

34. Graber, *Processing the News . . .* , p. 76. Change tends to occur rather slowly and only if the new, discordant, information is (a) high in volume, (b) often repeated, and (c) "does not clash with basic cultural norms." Graber, "A Cross-Cultural Perspective . . . ," p. 7.

35. Robinson and Levy, *op. cit.*

36. Benjamin I. Page, Robert Y. Shapiro, Glenn R. Dempsey, "What Moves Public Opinion," *American Political Science Review* LXXXI:1 (March 1987), 38.

37. See Chapter Five.

38. *Processing the News . . .* , p. 112.

39. See *Media and the Russian Public*, and Vladimir Shlapentokh, "Two Levels of Public Opinion: The Soviet Case," *Public Opinion Quarterly* XLIX:1 (Winter 1985), 443–59.

40. Discordant information—information that diverges from media images—will probably be discarded by most people if it is not based on personal experience or if it does not come from highly credible sources. What we know about the Soviet public in general suggests that in the realm of foreign affairs at least, the foreign sources of information lack the power it would take to alter dramatically a whole cognitive structure. It is also the case that the size of the public highly attuned and attentive to foreign news broadcasts—the heavy consumers—is limited. But those heavy listeners are more apt to be well educated and located in the Western urban parts of the Soviet Union. The reader is directed to the audience research reports prepared by Radio Liberty's research staff. They examine the audiences for this and the three other major Western broadcasters.

41. See Chapter Two.

42. David O. Sears and Jonathan L. Freedman, "Selective Exposure to Information: A Critical Review," *Public Opinion Quarterly* XXXI:2 (1967), 194–213.

43. Spartak Beglov, *Vneshnepoliticheskaya propaganda*, Moscow, 1984, pp. 241–42. Beglov writes that "although the 'criterion of utility' appears secondary [and] peripheral in the thinking of the communicator, it often plays a decisive role in securing the attention of the audience."

44. A. Maryamov, "Vmeste u televizora: pryamaya rech," *Izvestia*, January 17, 1987, p. 7.

45. Michael J. Robinson and Margaret A. Sheehan, *Over the Wire and on TV*, New York: Russell Sage, 1983, p. 12.

46. The fact that these kinds of messages reinforce the messages produced in early childhood socialization and resonate with the messages of the educational system, adult education, and the other media—and that they are all consistent and repetitious—tends to enhance the likelihood of being processed in schemas.

47. Graber, "A Cross-Cultural Perspective . . . ," p. 19.

48. It is also the case, as many scholars have concluded, that attitudes may diverge from behavior. They do not consider this difference between beliefs and behavior as evidence of deception or self-deception, because thinking and behavior depend on context, and, as Graber observed in summarizing these findings, "Beliefs that are accurately expressed in a general context may seem inappropriate in behavioral or attitudinal settings which are quite different from those routinely imagined. . . . Conflicting schemas can live side-by-side quite comfortably in the human brain." *Ibid.*, p. 24. A different approach to this question is that of the "mythological" and "pragmatic" strata of belief systems. See Vladimir Shlapentokh, *Soviet Public Opinion and Ideology: Mythology and Pragmatism in Interaction*, New York: Praeger, 1986. The author notes that during periods of mobilization, the differences between the two contract. Another way to look at the issue, following Graber, is to note that mobilization provides a much wider, more explicit, and more consistent setting or context for both thinking and behavior.

49. O. Latifi and N. Lyaporov, "Glavnoe v perestroike—prakticheskie dela," *Pravda*, April 8, 1987, p. 2.

50. V. Kudryavtsev, "Demokratia i prava cheloveka," *Pravda*, April 3, 1987, p. 3.

Index

ABC [American Broadcasting Corporation], 79, 101, 122. *See also* "World News Tonight"; *name of specific person*

Academy of Sciences [Soviet], 217

Academy of Social Sciences [Soviet], 199

Achille Lauro [Italian cruise ship], 87

"Acting Persons" [Soviet program], 172

Adler, Renata, 253n58

Advertising, 29

Afghanistan: American criticisms of Soviet policy in, 52, 129, 130; Chernenko/Gorbachev regimes' coverage of, 135; and the credibility of the Soviet media, 222; and the Donahue/Pozner space bridge, 45, 46; and the geography of news, 91, 92, 113, 135, 141; and "Moscow-Kabul" [space bridge], 171–72; news service for, 241–42n17; newsmakers in, 252n53; and opinionated newswriting, 130, 131; and public opinion, 193; and reform of the media system, 28; and responsibility for events, 129, 247n10; and Soviet youth, 160; U.S. role in, 162; and weekend programming, 160

Africa. *See name of specific region of Africa or country*

African National Congress, 94, 95, 139, 223

Agenda setting: national, 219–20. *See also* News agenda

Agitation, 4, 180, 184–90, 192, 193, 210

Akhmatova, Anna, 160

Al, Daniel, 156–57

Al-Ahram [Egyptian newspaper], 77

Alcohol in the USSR, 59, 115

Algeria, 91, 131

Allilueva, Svetlana, 86

Alma Ata, 222

Americans. *See* United States; *name of specific person or program*

"Amerika" [ABC mini-series], 88, 107

Anchors: American, 120–23, 244–45n56; and Chinese news, 103; and correspondents, 122, 239–40n4, 244–45n56; and disaster/accident stories, 137; and emotional coloration/opinionated writing, 126, 130–33; as interpreters of the news, 244–45n56; personality of, 123; and pictures, 120–21, 213, 219, 243n30; role of, 120–21; Soviet, on Vremya, 88; and technology, 149–50; time taken up by, 123; and voice-overs, 118, 120–23

Angola, 52, 73, 129, 131

Antonov trial [Italy], 247n16

Apartment, The [American film], 163
Argentina, 130, 131
Arledge, Roone, 116
Armenia, 208, 222
Arms control: American role in, 162;
   Chernenko/Gorbachev regimes'
   coverage of, 136; and the
   Chernobyl disaster, 62, 67; definition of, 243n34; Gorbachev's proposal about, 155, 159–60, 162,
   163; and multiple points of view,
   44, 49; and pictures, 118; and responsibility for events, 127, 128,
   129; and Soviet news conferences,
   49; television as main source of information about, 32; time devoted
   to stories about, 108, 110, 114,
   136, 249n31; and weekday/
   weekend programming, 155, 162;
   and weekend programming, 162
Asia, 96, 102, 113, 243n30, 243n32,
   248–49n22. *See also name of specific
   country*
Assimilation of messages, 182, 198–
   200, 217–24
Atlanta, Georgia, 78–79
Attitudes, 202–3, 224, 225, 262n48
Audiences: alienation/skepticism of,
   60–61, 147, 224–25; American, 79,
   80–81, 218, 234–35n16; British,
   218; characteristics of, 54, 81–83;
   and coherence, 125–26; and communication symbols, 181–82; complaints of, 152; differentiation/
   diversity of, 79, 180–83; and domestic news, 60–61; and education, 261n15; and familiarity with
   news, 220; feedback from, 67–68,
   79, 81–83, 194–96; and the hypodermic effects model, 180–83; impact on programming of, 82,
   229n26; impact of television on,
   69; as individuals, 193–201; and information processing, 217–24; maturity of, 211–12; and the media
   as a change agent, 201; and multiple points of view, 54–55, 221;

and oral propaganda, 257n27; radio, 231n65; and space bridges,
   234–35n16; and the two-step flow
   model, 183–93; and weekday programming, 152, 153. *See also* Public opinion; *name of specific medium, network, or type of program*
Australia, 103, 160
Austria, 135, 141, 241n14
Azerbaidzhan, 7, 208

Bagirov, E. G., 208
Baltimore Sun [American newspa-
   per], 48, 84
Bangladesh, 91
Barry, Marion, 78
BBC [British Broadcasting Corpora-
   tion], 20, 22, 220, 231n65
Becker, Lee B., 181
Beglov, Spartak, 15, 263n43
Belorussia, 137
Benin, 90
Bhopal disaster, 86, 93, 135, 136, 138
Bialer, Seweryn, 217, 261n20
Blix, Hans, 62–63
Boorstin, Robert O., 255n80
Bochevarov, G. N., 55
Borovik, Genrikh, 53, 156, 165–66,
   254n73
Boston, Massachusetts, 70–71
Boston University, 241–42n17
Botswana, 95
Bovin, Alexander, 39, 50, 55, 94,
   251n43
Brazil, 237n45
Brezhnev, Leonid, 214
Brigade system, 190–93, 257–58n28
Brighton Beach [Brooklyn, N.Y.],
   53
Britain. *See* Great Britain
Briusov, Valery, 160
Broadcast day, 10, 18, 22, 140, 160,
   253n61
Broadcast language, 5, 6–7, 208,
   228n19

Broadcasters. *See* Anchors; Correspondents; *name of specific person*
Brokaw, Tom, 122
Bryant, Louise, 156
Buchanan, Patrick, 88
Bulgaria, 21, 91–92, 99, 100, 130, 135, 141
Burlatsky, Fedor, 238n57
Burma, 91
Burmistenko, Alexei, 25–26, 76, 81, 115
Business news, 106
"By Your Request" [Soviet program], 152

Cable News Network, 84
Cameramen, 149
Campbell, Robert, 14
Canada, 128–29, 155
"Capital-to-Capital" [space bridge], 49, 163–64
Caribbean region, 98, 113, 248–49n22
Carter, Jimmy, 77, 78
CBS [Columbia Broadcasting System], 79–80, 90, 101, 104, 105, 121. *See also name of specific person*
Censorship, 10, 12–13, 23, 93–94, 262n31. *See also* Jamming
Central Africa, 102, 113, 248–49n22. *See also name of specific country*
Central America, 96, 98, 100, 112–13, 114, 139, 159–60, 248–49n22. *See also name of specific country*
Central Committee. *See* Communist Party
Central Television, 25, 82, 171–72, 194, 217, 228–29n20. *See also* National networks; *name of specific person*
Chad, 90, 129
Challenger disaster, 37, 149, 244–45n56
Channels, allocation of, 16
Chautauqua Society, 52, 250n38

Chernenko, Konstantin, 143, 144, 186, 200, 210
Chernenko [Konstantin] regime, 86, 134–42, 212–13, 248–49n22, 261n20
Chernobyl, 29, 50, 60–68, 107–8, 130, 147, 214, 221, 222, 234n14, 237n44, 237n45, 237–38n46
Chervov, Nikolai, 35–39
"Chess School" [Soviet program], 158, 159
Chicago, Illinois, 169–71
Chief Administration for the Affairs of Literature and Publishing Houses. *See* GLAVLIT
Children. *See* Youth
Chile, 86, 99, 130, 132, 133, 223, 241n14, 252n53
China. *See* People's Republic of China
China Syndrome, The [American film], 163
Christian Science Monitor [American newspaper], 84
CIA [Central Intelligence Agency], 237n45
"Cinema Panorama" [Soviet program], 10
Cinematographers, Union of, 23, 228n11, 260n6
"Citizens' Summit" [space bridge], 43–48, 55
Citizenship issues: and civil rights/liberties, 110, 114, 118, 127, 140, 243n34; definition of, 243n34; and emigration, 44–45, 47, 52, 53, 114, 118, 127, 140, 243n34; and pictures, 118
Civil defense, Soviet, 22
Civil rights/liberties, 110, 114, 118, 127, 140, 243n34
Class/social stratification, 197, 198, 209
Clifford, Clark, 51
Coherence, 125–26, 129, 246n4, 251n43
Collective responsibility, 190–93

Combs, Richard, 50

COMECON, 96–97, 135, 240–41n11, 248–49n22

Communication theory. *See* Public opinion

Communist Party: and agitation, 4, 184–90; American, 84; American coverage of the, 115; in Argentina, 131; and the brigade system, 192; coordination of the media by the, 6, 9, 22, 23–24, 25; and corruption, 59, 136, 215; criticism of Soviet foreign policy by the, 216; and disaster/accident stories, 137; and education, 196; and feedback, 194, 195; and glasnost, 59, 216; and letters from Soviet citizens, 194; and local broadcasting, 6, 24, 25; and media policy, 200; members in the Union of Journalists, 23–24; and multiple points of view, 28–29; in Panama, 162; personalization of the, 187; and political doctrine/lectures, 186–87, 196, 198–200, 257n27; and public opinion, 184–90, 192, 194–96, 257n27; and radio, 230n53, 231n61; role of the, 136, 217; and socialization, 189–90; and South Africa, 94; and vestiges of the past theory, 182; and volunteer correspondents, 196; and youth, 175–77, 192. *See also* Communist Party Congress; Communist Party, directives/ policies; Politboro; Young Communist League; Young Pioneers

Communist Party, directives/ policies, 28, 88, 104, 109, 110, 136, 157–58, 184. *See also* official stories

Communist Party Congress, 5–6, 111–12, 117, 136, 150, 151, 165, 210–11, 251n43

"Comrades" [British documentary], 227n7

Congo, 90

"Congressbridges" [space bridge], 234–35n16

Content, 104–20. *See also name of specific subject or country*

Coordination of the media, 4–5, 6, 10, 22–26, 62, 65, 67, 69, 214–16, 224–25

Cordtz, Dan, 118

Correspondents: and access to officials, 76–77; American, 69, 122; and anchors, 122, 239–40n4, 244–45n56; attitudes/approaches in the West of Soviet, 68–84; differences between Soviet and American correspondents, 69; and elapsed time, 239–40n4; and emotional coloration/opinionated writing, 126, 130–33; and pictures, 245–46n58; star, 244–45n56; and technology, 72–73, 121–22, 146, 149–50; volunteer, 195–96. *See also* Journalists; *name of specific correspondent*

Corruption, 59, 60, 106, 136, 214–16, 237n36

Council of Ministers, 61–62

Coverage: in-depth/breadth, 101–2, 214. *See also* News: geography of the; *name of specific story, subject, or country*

Credibility: of the American media, 217; and discordant information, 262n40; of domestic news, 57, 225; of local media, 57, 212, 213, 225; and mixing, 147; of Polish media, 63–64; of radio, 220, 230n53; of the Soviet media, 57, 60, 189, 201, 208–9, 212, 214, 217, 220, 222, 225, 233–34n4; of space bridges, 234–35n16; of the two-step flow model, 183–84

Crime, 30, 107–8, 110, 111–12, 114, 118, 127, 249n31, 250n39

Criticism: audience attitudes about response to, 45; and educational level, 196, 206–7; and glasnost/ timeliness, 213–14; increase in USSR of, 236n29; of news and public affairs programs, 196; of newsmakers, 244–45n56; of Soviet foreign policy, 216; in the United States/West, 196, 207, 236n27; and viewing patterns of television, 206–7; of youth, 216

Cross-talk, 244–45n56

Cuba, 96–97, 99, 130, 231–32n66, 241–42n17

Culture/arts: coverage of Soviet, 115, 138; and Fourth Program, 9; importance in Soviet Union of, 120; and the news agenda, 108, 119; pictures of the, 120; and radio, 231n65; time devoted to stories about, 108, 112, 138, 140, 249n31; and weekday/weekend programming, 151, 153, 160, 254n68, 255n77; and youth, 172–73

Cuts splicing, 253n58

Cyprus, 87

Czechoslovakia, 21, 100

Daily World, The [American newspaper], 84

Daniloff, Nicholas, 52, 250n38

Daytime television, 206

Demonstrations. *See* Protests/demonstrations

Denmark, 90

Depth/breadth coverage, 101–2, 214

Deutsche Welle, 20, 220, 231n65

Deviance in the USSR, 27, 57, 214

Diplomatic relations and the geography of the news, 92–93, 94–95, 103

Direct-broadcast satellites. *See* Satellites

Disasters/accidents: Chernenko/Gorbachev regimes' coverage of, 64, 136–38; definition of, 243n34; live broadcasting of, 251n43; and news agendas, 96, 119; newsworthiness of, 102, 107–8; and pictures, 119; and responsibility for events, 127; time devoted to stories about, 109, 110, 112–14, 136–38, 140, 249n31; in the USSR, 136–37; and the work ethic, 214. *See also name of specific disaster or accident*

Discordant information, 218, 262n40

Discrimination: in the U.S., 168; in the USSR, 46, 50, 177

Dissident movements, 115

Distinctive features in news stories, 126, 244–45n56

Djerijian, Edward, 77

Documentaries, 9, 151, 159. *See also name of specific documentary*

Domestic leaders as newsmakers, 142–43

Domestic news: American, 90, 104–5, 112, 113–14, 139–41; and the assimilation of messages, 221–22; audience alienation concerning Soviet, 60–61; Chernenko/Gorbachev regimes' coverage of, 134–35, 138, 139–40, 221, 224; and the content of news, 104–5; credibility of, 57, 225; and investigative reporting, 58–59, 60; and the local media, 56–57; and the news agenda, 88, 90, 104, 106; and pictures, 142; and responsibility for events, 128–29; time devoted to stories about, 112, 113–14, 139–41; and timeliness, 56–57, 60–68; and unreality of news reports, 57; unreported, 57. *See also name of specific country or type of news, e.g. Economic issues*

Dominican Republic, 90

Donahue, Phil, 43–49, 53, 55, 216, 234–35n16

Donaldson, Sam, 51

Drug abuse, 59

Duarte, Jose Napoleon, 87

Dukakis, Michael, 70–71

Dunaev, Vladimir: access to American officials of, 77; audience of, 81–82; background of, 70; and coordination of the media, 26;

Dunaev, Vladimir (*continued*)
    coverage of U.S./West by, 69–75,
    84, 146; equipment/crew needs of,
    72–73, 121–22, 146; letters to, 81–
    82; and mixing, 147; and pictures
    for stories, 121–22; sources of
    American news for, 84. *See also*
    Dunaev, Vladimir, comments
    about; Dunaev, Vladimir, stories
    about
Dunaev, Vladimir, comments about:
    American coverage of the Soviet
    Union, 115; future of Soviet televi-
    sion, 83; surveys of audiences,
    82–83
Dunaev, Vladimir, stories about:
    American farmers, 73–74; At-
    lanta, 78–79; Boston, 70–71; dem-
    onstration in Washington, 73;
    Great Britain, 121–22; Iowa, 75;
    McDonald's, 74–75; Northern Ire-
    land, 121–22; Pushkin sympo-
    sium, 73; San Francisco, 70, 149;
    [Paul] Warnke, 162

Earthquakes, 87, 113, 135, 141
East Africa, 96, 102–3, 112–13, 134,
    247–48n19
East Germany, 91–92, 130, 135, 152–
    53, 155–56
Eastern Europe, 100, 113, 223, 248–
    49n22. *See also name of specific
    country*
Economic accountability, 190–93
Economic issues: American cover-
    age of, 88, 106; and the brigade
    system, 192, 257–58n28;
    Chernenko/Gorbachev regimes'
    coverage of, 106, 136, 138; criti-
    cism of coverage of Soviet,
    238n57; and emotional coloration,
    247n12; Gorbachev's views about,
    213; and the impact of television,
    213; and investigative reporting,
    111–12; and managerial practices,
    65–66; and the news agenda, 88,

106, 119; and pictures, 118, 119–
    20; and political ideology, 257–
    58n28; and public lectures,
    257n27; and responsibility for
    events, 127; television's influence
    on, 28, 31–32; time devoted to sto-
    ries about, 109, 110–11, 113,
    249n31; and weekday/weekend
    programming, 151, 159
Editing, 43–48, 148–50, 253n58
Editors, 24
Education/educational level: and au-
    diences, 261n15; and the brigade
    system, 191; career, 154; and the
    Communist Party, 196; and criti-
    cism, 196, 206–7; and discordant
    information, 262n40; diversity of,
    188; and foreign broadcasts,
    262n40; as a function of the Soviet
    media, 164; and the hypodermic
    effects model, 181–82; and the im-
    pact of television, 207, 209, 212;
    and information processing,
    263n43; Lenin's views about, 27;
    and models to emulate, 191; and
    newspapers, 196, 261n15; and offi-
    cial stories, 196; and opinion lead-
    ers, 184; and persuasion, 196; po-
    litical, 26–30, 27, 56, 154, 160, 188;
    and public opinion, 181–82, 184,
    188, 191, 196; in the rural areas,
    182; and the two-step flow model,
    184; and viewing patterns, 206–7;
    and weekday/weekend program-
    ming, 154, 160; and youth, 160,
    175–76
Educational television. *See* Third
    Program
Egypt, 91, 141
Ekran satellites, 14
El Salvador, 87, 91–92, 132, 141
Elapsed time, 89–90, 98–103, 120–
    23, 135, 140, 141–42, 239–40n4,
    243n26, 251n42
Elections: and political officials as
    newsmakers, 145; presidential,
    86, 89–90, 104, 140, 143; time de-

voted to stories about, 105, 108, 110, 113, 140, 143

Eltsin, Boris, 177, 190

Emigration, 44–45, 47, 52, 53, 114, 118, 127, 140, 243n34

Emotional coloration/opinionated writing, 114, 126, 130–34, 247n12, 247n16

Entertainment, 117, 151, 153, 154, 160, 162–63, 164–78, 233–34n4

Epstein, Edward Jay, 238n63

Equatorial Guinea, 90

Equipment, 72–73, 146, 244–45n56

Espionage/intelligence stories, 87, 127, 249n31

Estonia, 20–21, 22, 228–29n20

Ethical/moral values, 27–28, 33, 55, 110, 250n39

Ethiopia, 86, 99, 103, 113, 119, 131, 136, 141, 223

Ethnic groups, 204–5, 208

European Community, 243n30, 248–49n22

Evaluation of change, 217. *See also* Feedback

Evening television, 206–7

Fairness, 42–43, 124

Falkland Islands [Malvinas], 131

Familiarity/personal experience, 219–20, 221–22

Family issues, 160

Fast-breaking news, 18, 20, 29–30, 116, 231n61, 245–46n58

Fast food in USSR, 74–75

Features/soft news, 26, 33, 34, 69–76

Feedback, 187, 194–96, 211, 217, 226

Films: audiences for, 207; and censorship, 12–13, 23, 262n31; for children, 160; foreign, 152–53; on television, 152, 207, 260n6; underground, 12–13; and VCRs, 11–13; and weekday/weekend programming, 151–52, 155, 160, 163

Finland, 15, 20–21, 90, 99, 131

First Program, 5–10, 43–48, 153–54,

157, 160, 253n61. *See also name of specific program*

Foreign broadcasts. *See* Foreign sources of information; *name of specific system, e.g. Radio Liberty*

Foreign officials, 50–51, 221, 236n24, 236n26

Foreign policy, 49, 224

Foreign sources of information, 20–21, 107, 147, 189, 211–12, 220, 222, 225, 262n40

Format, news, 117–23, 245–46n58. *See also* Pictures/graphics

Fourth Program, 9

France: Chernenko/Gorbachev regimes' coverage of, 135; films shown in USSR from, 152–53; and the geography of news, 91, 135, 141; Gorbachev visit to, 49–50, 93, 99, 108–9; and opinionated writing, 132; and responsibility for events, 128–29

"Free to Be Without Rights" [Soviet documentary], 158–59

Freedom of speech, 45, 47, 53

"From Chicago to Philadelphia" [Soviet documentary], 169–71

Front Without Mercy [East German film], 155–56

"Frontline" [American program], 53

Gale, Robert, 62–63

Game shows, 164–65

Gandhi, Indira, 86, 93, 112, 135, 138

Gandhi, Rajiv, 86, 112–13, 135, 138

General Staff, Soviet. *See name of specific person*

Geneva Summit [1985], 50, 86, 140

Geography of news, 89–103, 112–17, 134–42. *See also name of specific country*

Georgia [Soviet], 59, 228–29n20

Geostationary satellites, 14

Gerasimov, Gennady, 235–36n21

Gerbner, George, 124, 183

Ghorizont satellites, 14

"Glance" [Soviet program], 172

Glasnost: backlash against, 7; and Chernobyl, 29, 60–68; and the Communist Party, 59, 216; and corruption, 214–16; and criticism of issues in the USSR, 58–59; definition of, 215–16; and diversity, 208; Gorbachev regime emphasis on, 56, 65; and the impact of television, 211–12, 214–16, 226; importance of, 203, 213; in international news, 34–51, 60–68; and investigative reporting, 58–59; and journalists, 216; and the legal system, 58, 60, 215, 226; limits of, 58–59, 69; and local officials, 58; and the maturity of audiences, 211–12; and multiple points of view, 29, 216; and newsworthiness, 30; and responsibility, 215; and Soviet self-criticism, 58–59; and Soviet social problems, 59; and youth, 173–74

Glasnost [journal], 177

GLAVLIT [Chief Administration for the Affairs of Literature and Publishing Houses], 23

Gorbachev, Mikhail: and the airing of foreign programs on Soviet television, 53–54; and alcohol restrictions, 59; American coverage of, 114, 117; arms control proposal of, 159–60, 162, 163; book by, 53; and Chernobyl, 62, 65; and economic issues, 213; family of, 44; and glasnost, 215; image of, 224; and the image of the U.S., 128; influence in Chernenko regime of, 261n20; and Japanese relations, 132; as a newsmaker, 143–44; political strategy of, 65–66; press conference of, 49–50; and responsibility for events, 128; and space bridges, 53–54; speeches of, 62, 210–11, 225; visits to foreign countries by, 49–50, 86, 92–93, 99, 108–9, 224; and Western influ-

ence on the Soviet media, 210–12. *See also* Gorbachev [Mikhail] regime

Gorbachev [Mikhail] regime: Chernenko regime compared with, 134–42. *See also name of specific country or topic, e.g. Glasnost*

Goskino, 23, 152

Gosteleradio: Communist Party interactions with, 25; coordination of the media by, 22, 25; International Life Department of, 34, 221; and international news, 34; local organizations of, 25; and multiple points of view, 47–48; news bureaus, 92, 103; personnel changes at, 228n11; and space bridges, 47–48, 234–35n16; and the "Twelfth Floor" program, 178; and weekend programming, 160

Gosteleradio, comments about: the expansion of the broadcast day, 10; the influence of television, 32; radio, 17; television's influence on career choices, 209

Government. *See name of specific ministry, agency, or person*

Graber, Doris A., 218, 219, 256–57n11, 262n48

Graphics/pictures, 93, 117–20, 142, 147–48, 213, 219, 243n30, 245–46n58

Great Britain: audiences in, 217; Chernenko/Gorbachev regimes' coverage of, 135; Dunaev's stories about, 121–22; films shown in USSR from, 152–53, 227n7; and the geography of news, 91, 92–93, 99, 135, 141, 241n13; Gorbachev visit to, 86, 92–93; Mitterand visit to, 86; "Open Question" program of, 39–41; and opinionated writing, 131, 132; perceptions of the Soviet Union in, 41–43; protests/strikes in, 86, 92–93; and responsibility for events, 128–29; Soviet perceptions of,

155; terrorism in, 86; youth in, 39–41. *See also* BBC

Greece, 97

Grigoryants, Sergei, 177

Grobovnikov, Iury, 152

Grushin, B. A., 194–96

Guatemala, 90

Guinea, 90

Guinea-Bissau, 90–91

Haiti, 90

Hard news, 26, 71–72

Healy, Brian, 101, 117

Health issues, 47, 160, 222

Hearst Corporation, 241–42n17

Heckler, Margaret, 122

"Hello, We're Looking for Talent" [Soviet program], 10

Hess, Stephen, 106

Holland, John, 90

Homeless, 47, 71–72

Hoyer, Steny, 255n74

Human interest stories, 108, 114, 117

Human rights, 52, 131, 167

Hungary, 90, 91–92, 100, 135, 141, 152–53, 237n42

Hunger, 47

Hypodermic effects model, 180–83, 193, 196–97, 198, 259n50

"I Serve the Soviet Union" [Soviet program], 160

Iceland, 51, 90

Ideology. *See* Political doctrine

Image of the public, 79–83

Image of the world, 222–24

"Incredible But True" [Soviet program], 160

India: crises in, 86; and the geography of news, 91, 99, 112, 135, 138, 139, 141, 223, 241n13, 248–49n22; and opinionated writing, 131, 133; and responsibility for events, 129; travelogues about, 160. *See also*

Bhopal disaster; Gandhi, Indira; Gandhi, Rajiv

Indian subcontinent, 112–13, 135, 248–49n22. *See also name of specific country*

Indonesia, 91

Information intervention/ imperialism, 210

Information processing, 217–24, 256–57n11, 262n40, 263n43

Inkeles, Alex, 184, 185, 187

Intelsat, 14–15, 73

International Atomic Energy Agency, 62, 66–67

International Court of Justice, 86

International Life Department, [Gostelradio], 34, 221

International news. *See name of specific subject or event, e.g. Chernobyl*

International Organization for Radio and Television [OIRT], 15

"International Panorama" [Soviet program], 8–9, 74–75, 78, 159, 162

International politics, 106, 112, 114, 119, 127, 128–29, 136, 138, 140, 243n34, 249n31

International security, 32

Interpersonal communications, 184–85, 189

Interviews, 76–77, 244–45n56, 245–46n58, 253n58

Intervision, 15

Investigative reporting, 58–59, 60, 63, 111–12, 195–96

Iowa, 75

Iran, 127

Iraq, 131

Israel: Chernenko/Gorbachev regimes' coverage of, 135, 141–42, 251n42; definition of, 240–41n11; and the geography of news, 87, 91, 92, 93, 135, 141–42, 241n14, 251n42; and opinionated writing, 130, 132, 133; and responsibility for events, 127, 128–29, 141–42, 241n14; Soviet perceptions of, 130, 132, 133, 141–42; and terrorism, 87

Italy, 75, 87, 91, 99, 132, 135, 141, 246n4, 247n16, 252n47
Iushkyavichius, G. Z., 6
Ivanitsky, A. V., 153
Izvestia, 50, 55, 59–60, 62, 82, 194, 215, 261n15

Jackson, James, 51
Jackson, Michigan, 260n6
Jamming, 16, 21–22, 231–32n66, 232n67
Japan: and the geography of news, 86–87, 91, 92, 135, 141; and opinionated writing, 131, 132; and responsibility for events, 127, 128–29, 132; Soviet perception of, 223; and weekday/weekend programming, 157, 162
Jennings, Peter. *See* "World News Tonight" [ABC]
Jews. *See* Discrimination; Emigration
Jones, David, 51
Jordan, 129, 240–41n11, 252n53
Journalists: access to Soviet officials by American, 116–17; American, 41–43, 79–81, 116–17; codifying the rights of Soviet, 60; Communist Party coordination of Soviet, 24, 25–26, 69; differences between American and Soviet, 238n63; and glasnost, 60, 216; image of the public of, 79–83; and media planning, 25–26; and peer evaluation, 238n63; role in presenting controversial views of, 48–49, 221; Soviet, 24, 25–26, 41–43, 52–53, 60, 69, 81–83, 146, 216, 221, 238n63; and space bridges, 48, 52–53, 146, 237n36; Union of, 23; values of, 41–43. *See also* Correspondents; *name of specific journalist*
Jump cuts, 149
Jurmala, Latvia, 52, 53, 250n38

K.G.B., 60
Kalinin, 160

Kalyagin, Boris, 35–39
Kampuchea, 131
Kazakhstan, 176, 208
Kazan, 191
Keller, Bill, 236n29
Kendall, Donald, 75
Kennedy, Edward, 77
Kennedy, Joseph P., 2nd, 71, 78
Khrushchev, Nikita, 67, 217, 262n31
Kiev, 62
King, Martin Luther, Jr., 78, 155
King, Melvin, 71
Klimov, Elem, 23, 260n6, 262n31
Kohl, Helmut, 86
Komsomol. *See* Young Communist League
Korean Airlines story, 46, 49, 165–66, 237–38n46
Kravchenko, Leonid, 64–65
Krutov, Alexander, 63

Lane, David, 257–58n28
Language issues, 5, 6–7, 181–82, 188, 208, 228n19
Laos, 91, 129
LaRocque, Gene, 77
Late-night shows, 54, 172
Latvia, 52, 53, 160, 250n38
Lebanon, 91, 93, 127, 128–29, 133, 135, 141, 252n53
Legal system, 13, 58, 60, 111–12, 127, 215, 226, 237n42
Legislative issues, 110, 127, 136, 138, 249n31. *See also* Official stories
Legitimacy: foreign sources as factors for, 147; and official visits, 136; and pluralism, 232–33n83; of Soviet media policies, 67; for Vremya, 114
Lemmon, Jack, 163
Lenin, Vladimir Ilich, 27, 180, 184, 213, 254n64
Leningrad, 9
Lesotho, 95
"Let's Go, Girls" [Soviet program], 164–65

Letters from Soviet citizens: as a channel of feedback, 195; and Chernobyl, 66; compared to the public generally, 194; and glasnost, 58–60; impact of, 67–68, 81–83; and the local media, 66; and multiple points of view, 50, 55; and public opinion, 190, 194, 195; quantity of, 81–82; and responsiveness, 66; and sociodemographic characteristics, 194; and timeliness, 59–60; and VCRs, 11; and weekday programming, 152, 153. *See also name of specific newspaper or journal*

Libya, 99–100, 129, 155, 159–60, 162, 243n28

Ligachev, Egor, 59, 90

Limited effects model, 259n50

Literacy, 182, 185–86

Literaturnaya Gazeta, 10, 11, 35, 54, 261n15

Live broadcasting, 9–10, 39, 50, 54, 84, 120–21, 213, 234–35n16, 251n43

Loaded words. *See* Opinionated writing

Local broadcasting: authority of, 6; broadcast language of, 6, 7; Communist Party coordination of, 6, 24, 25; content of, 7; coordination of, 2, 24, 25; and domestic news, 57; and language, 228n19; and the national networks, 5, 25, 244–45n56; and planning, 25; programming of, 5, 6; quality of, 6, 7; and Second Program, 6, 8. *See also name of specific region*

Local media: American, 244–45n56; and Chernobyl, 66; credibility of, 57, 212, 213, 225; definition of, 228n11; and letters of Soviet citizens, 66; resistance to reform by, 213; and responsiveness, 66

Local newspapers, 33–34, 57, 195–96

Local officials, 58, 228–29n20

Lockshin, Arnold, 53

Lomeiko, Vladimir, 49

Loory, Stuart, 237n36

Lown, Bernard, 70

Lozano, Rudy, 170–71

Lukonin, Nikolai, 66

McDonald's [fast food], 74–75

MacFarlane, Robert, 84

McLeod, Jack M., 181

McQuail, Denis, 183

Madagascar, 91

Mafia, 247n16

Mali, 90

Malta, 90

Malvinas [Falkland Islands], 131

"Man from Fifth Avenue, The" [Soviet documentary], 165–69, 255n80

Man-in-the-street stories, 76

Marx, Karl, 27, 28, 125, 210, 232n81

Mass publics and the two-step flow model, 183–93

Matlock, Jack, 51, 52

Mauri, Joseph, 166–69, 255n80

Mauritania, 90

"Mayak" [radio program], 18, 21

Media: differences between American and Soviet, 85, 87; stories about the, 114, 127, 249n31. *See also* Media, American; Media, Soviet; *name of specific type of medium or subject*

Media, American: changes in coverage patterns of the, 138–42; choices among the, 87; content of the, 104–8; credibility of the, 217; criticism of the, 236n27; cutbacks/downsizing of the, 121, 244–45n56; domestic/international news priorities of the, 89, 115–17; and entertainment, 233–34n4; impact/influence of the, 85, 202; and the local media, 244–45n56; mission/role of the, 90, 124; similarity of news on the, 87, 126,

Media, American (*continued*)
217–18. *See also name of specific subject or type of medium*
Media, Soviet: access to the, 18–19; ambiguity of policies concerning the, 67; bi-polarism of the, 128; centrality of the, 225–26; as a change agent, 26–30, 201; and changes in Soviet leadership, 134–42; Chernobyl as a watershed for the, 64; content of the, 104–8; coordination of the, 4–5, 6, 10, 22–26, 62, 65, 67, 214–16; credibility of the, 57, 60, 189, 201, 212, 214, 217, 220, 222, 225, 233–34n4; education as a function of the, 56; effectiveness of the, 201–3; and the image of the world, 222–24; international/Western influence on the, 200–201, 210–12; and interpretation of the news, 125; Marxist base for the, 27–29; mission of the, 26–30; and planning, 24–26; and reality, 202; responsibility of the, 221, 225; socialization as a function of the, 27–28, 57; Western influence on the, 210–12. *See also* Public opinion; *name of specific media or topic*
Media professionals. *See name of specific type of professional, e.g. Journalists*
Mexico, 87, 91–92, 99, 113, 135, 136, 153, 162
Middle East: and the geography of news, 93, 96, 100, 112, 113, 139, 242n24, 248–49n22; political violence in the, 112, 113; terrorism in the, 87. *See also name of specific country*
Mikhail Somov [Russian ship], 137
Military issues, 114, 127, 136, 151, 158, 160, 162, 163, 249n31
Miller, FBI agent, 86
Ministry of Defense, Soviet, 238n51
Ministry of Education, Soviet, 12, 175

Ministry of Foreign Affairs, Soviet. *See name of specific person*
Ministry of Nuclear Power, Soviet, 66
Ministry of Trade, Soviet, 75
Minorities, Soviet, 6–7, 120
Mironenko, Viktor, 34, 211
Missing [American film], 163
Mitterand, François, 49–50, 86
Mixing, 147
Models. *See name of specific model*
Moldavia, 208
Molniya satellites, 13–14
Molotov, Vyacheslav, 229n23
Mongolia, 91, 99, 131
Morocco, 91
Moscow, 9, 11, 12, 174, 175, 176, 188, 207–8
"Moscow Women" [Soviet program], 165
"Moscow-Kabul" [space bridge], 92, 171–72
Mother Jones [American magazine], 84
"Movie Poster" [Soviet program], 163
Movies. *See* Films
Mozambique, 91, 95, 131
Multiple points of view: and the airing of foreign programs on Soviet television, 43–48, 54; and the assimilation of messages, 220–21; and audiences, 54–55, 211–12, 221; and the "Citizens' Summit" program, 43–48; and Communist doctrine, 28–29; concerns about, 54–55; demand for, 34–51, 67–68; foreign officials' voicing of, 50–51, 221, 236n24, 236n26; hostility toward, 221; and international news, 34–51; and newsworthiness, 28–29; and objectivity, 55, 124; Soviet surveys about, 34–35; and youth, 39–43, 45, 173. *See also name of specific program or event, e.g. Afghanistan*
Music. *See* Culture/arts

Namibia, 240n11

National Catholic Reporter [American media], 84

National holidays. *See* Official stories

National liberation movements, 52

National networks, 5–10, 208. *See also name of specific network*

National politics: definition of, 243n34; and responsibility for events, 127; time devoted to stories about, 140, 249n31. *See also* Domestic news; Elections

Nationalism, 207–8

NATO countries: Chernenko/ Gorbachev regimes' coverage of, 134, 139–40; disasters/accidents in the, 112–13, 114; domestic news stories of, 113–14; and the geography of news, 96, 97–98, 99, 102, 113–14, 134, 139–40, 240–41n11, 242n24, 243n26, 248–49n22, 250n36; political violence in the, 112, 113; and weekday/weekend programming, 155, 163; and weekend programming, 163. *See also name of specific country*

NBC [National Broadcasting Corporation], 50–51, 90, 101, 105, 122. *See also name of specific person or program*

New World Information Order, 15

New York City, 166–69

New York Times, 41–42, 51, 84. *See also name of specific person*

News: content of, 104–20; format, 117–23, 245–46n58; geography of, 89–103, 112–17, 134–42; planning, 24–26; purpose/function of, 85; selection of, 124, 125, 129, 251n43; similarity of, 87, 126, 217–18; television as the main source of, 31–32; and time devoted to subjects/ stories, 108–12. *See also* Fast-breaking news; *name of specific subject or type of news, e.g.* Domestic news

News agenda, 108–12; American,

96, 104–8; foreign, 129, 139, 141, 220; and the geography of news, 223, 241n14; and the public, 211, 224–25; and radio, 231n61; and salience of messages, 202, 219–20; Soviet, 88, 93, 99–100, 104–8, 113, 114, 119, 129, 139, 141, 223, 241n14. *See also specific subject or country, e.g.* Disasters/accidents; France

News bureaus, 92, 100, 103, 121, 135, 146, 213, 239–40n4, 244–45n56

News conferences, 49–50, 62–63, 67, 77, 117, 147, 228–29n20, 234n14, 237–38n46

News and public affairs programs, 8, 151, 159, 196, 207. *See also name of specific program*

Newsmakers, 39, 43–49, 51–56, 155–59, 162–64, 244–45n56, 249n23, 251–52n45, 251n43, 252n46, 252n47. *See also name of specific newsmaker*

Newspapers: and Communist Party policies, 184; and education, 196, 261n15; and entertainment, 233–34n4; and feedback, 195–96; and foreign political systems, 180; international news stories in, 32–34; local, 33–34, 57, 195–96; and official stories, 231n61; and planning, 25–26; and political doctrine, 213; and public opinion, 180, 184, 187, 195–96; readership of, 4, 180, 196, 261n15; regional, 33; as role models, 29; and the salience of the West, 32–34; and television columns, 25; volunteer correspondents on, 195–96. *See also name of specific newspaper*

Newsworthiness, 26–30, 69–84, 116–17, 146. *See also name of specific subject, e.g.* News agenda

Nicaragua: and Americans on Soviet television, 52; and contra aid, 71, 162; and the geography of news,

Nicaragua (*continued*)
   91, 96, 97, 100, 113, 135, 141; and
   the military as newsmakers,
   252n53; Soviet coverage of, 86, 96,
   97, 135, 141, 162; Soviet relations
   with, 96, 97
Nielsen ratings, 80–81
Nigeria, 90
"Nightline" [ABC program], 234–
   35n16
"Nightly News" [NBC program],
   122
Nomenklatura, 23–24, 145
North Africa, 102, 113, 248–49n22
North Korea, 129
North Yemen, 91, 99, 131–32, 223
Northern Ireland, 121–22, 129, 162,
   240n11
Novosti, 33, 159, 228n11
Nuclear weapons, 32, 35–39

Objectivity, 42–43, 55, 124, 134
Official observances. *See* Official stories
Official policies/publications/
   pronouncements. *See* Communist
   Party, directives/policies; Official
   stories
Official publications/
   pronouncements, 182, 197, 198
Official stories: and the American
   media, 104–5; Chernenko/
   Gorbachev regimes' coverage of,
   136; and education, 196; length
   of, 219; and the news agenda, 88,
   104; and the newspapers, 231n61;
   and newsworthiness, 28; and the
   Politburo, 49, 88; preeminence of,
   119; and radio, 231n61; and technology, 150; time devoted to stories about, 49, 88, 109, 110, 143–
   45; and weekday/weekend programming, 157–58. *See also* Communist Party, directives/policies;
   Official visits; Political doctrine
Official visits: as an example of

mixed signals, 224; coverage of,
   108–9, 113, 136, 141, 143–44,
   251n43; of Gorbachev, 49–50, 86,
   92–93, 99, 108–9, 224; as a legitimacy factor, 136; of Libya, 99–
   100; live broadcasting of, 251n43;
   and the news agenda, 99–100,
   104; of North Yemen, 99; and responsibility for events, 128
Officials: American, 76–77; American access to Soviet, 116–17; and
   feedback, 195; foreign, 50–51,
   221, 236n24, 236n26; and
   glasnost, 213–14; local, 58, 228–
   29n20; and multiple points of
   view, 50–51, 221, 236n24, 236n26;
   as newsmakers, 144–45, 252n47;
   Soviet, 58, 116–17, 195, 228–
   29n20; Soviet access to American,
   76–77. *See also* name of specific official
Ogarkov, Marshal, 49, 237–38n46
Ogonyok [Soviet journal], 66, 216
Older people, 18–19, 194, 205–6
Olitsky, Vladimir, 11
OPEC, 240–41n11
"Open Question" program [Britain],
   39–41
Opinion leaders. *See* Agitation
Opinionated writing/emotional col-
   oration, 114, 126, 130–34, 247n12,
   247n16
Orbita satellites, 14
Ostankino, 149–50, 174, 175
Ovchinnikov, Vsevolod, 236n26

Pack journalism, 87
Pakistan, 92, 127, 128–29, 132, 241–
   42n17
Papua, 91
Paraguay, 90, 132
Peltier, Leonard, 158–59
Pamyat [Russian nationalist organi-
   zation], 176
People meters, 80–81
People's Republic of China, 103,
   132–33, 135, 152–53, 223, 243n33

Pepsico, 75
Perm, 33, 206
Personal experience, 219–20, 221–22
Personal initiative, 74–75
Persuasion: and the assimilation of
    messages, 220, 221; and attitudes,
    202–3; as central to the Soviet me-
    dia, 3–4, 180–83, 189, 191, 193,
    196–97, 202–3, 213, 214, 225–26;
    and education, 196; and foreign
    broadcasts, 220; and the hypoder-
    mic effects model, 180–83; and
    public opinion, 180–83, 189, 191,
    193, 196–97; and salience, 202
Peru, 90
Petrovsky, Vladimir, 35–39, 234n14
Philadelphia, Pennsylvania, 168,
    169–71
Philippines, 87, 99, 132, 223
Pictures/graphics, 93, 117–20, 142,
    147–48, 213, 219, 243n30, 245–
    46n58
Planning and the Soviet media, 24–
    26
PLO [Palestine Liberation Organiza-
    tion], 87, 240–41n11
Pluralism, 232–33n83
Poland, 21, 46, 63–64, 99, 100, 135,
    141, 237n42, 241n14, 252n53
Politburo, 49, 88, 237n36
Political doctrine: and agitation, 210;
    and the assimilation of messages,
    221; and the brigade system, 192,
    257–58n28; and coherence, 125;
    and the Communist Party, 196,
    198–200; and economic issues,
    257–58n28; and education, 188;
    and the future, 198–99; impact on
    the masses of, 217; and the indi-
    vidual, 193–201; and official pro-
    nouncements, 144–45; and policy
    limits, 232–33n83; and political
    leaders, 144–45; preeminence of,
    199; and propaganda, 198–200;
    and public opinion, 179–203, 257–
    58n28; and scarcity, 28, 232n80,
    232n81; and socialization, 26–30,

57, 189–92, 198, 210, 212, 257–
    58n28; and stages toward commu-
    nism, 232n80; and television, 179–
    203, 209–11, 225–26
Political education. *See* Education
Political protest. *See* Protests/
    demonstrations
"Political Theater" [Soviet program],
    156
Political violence: definition of,
    243n34; and the news agenda,
    106–7; and responsibility for
    events, 127, 128–29; time devoted
    to stories about, 112, 113, 114,
    140, 244n42, 249n31
Poor people, 18–19
Popieluszko, Jerzy, 64
Popov, V. I., 82, 160
Pornography, 12–13, 168
Powell, Jody, 77
Pozner, Vladimir: audience criti-
    cisms of, 55, 117; and the
    Donahue space bridges, 43–48,
    55, 216, 234–35n16; and live broad-
    casting, 251n43; and multiple
    points of view, 43–48; preemi-
    nence of, 39; response to Reagan
    speech by, 79, 88; and the
    Schmemann interview, 41–43; as
    a spokesman for Gosteleradio, 39;
    and "The World and Youth" pro-
    gram, 39–43
Pozner, Vladimir, comments about:
    Chernobyl, 64; foreign programs
    on Soviet television, 53; interna-
    tional news stories, 39–46; multi-
    ple points of view, 39–46; nuclear
    arms roundtable discussion, 39; ra-
    dio, 18; responsiveness, 64; timeli-
    ness, 60, 64
Pravda: and the ambiguity of media
    policies, 67, 229n23; and
    Chernobyl, 62, 66; and multiple
    points of view, 29, 50, 67–68; and
    newsworthiness, 29; readership
    of, 67–68, 261n15; and salience of
    the West/United States, 34, 74;

Pravda (continued)
staff of, 239n67; and timeliness, 60, 67–68

Pravda, articles about: anchors, 123; corruption of Party members, 59; foreign officials' use of the Soviet media, 236n24, 236n26; international news stories, 34; media policy, 229n23; multiple points of view, 67–68, 236n24, 236n26; pictures in the news, 123, 142; rumors, 59; television in the Soviet Union, 7–8, 24–25, 225–26; timeliness, 67–68; the United States, 74

Pravda, letters to: and Chernobyl, 66; and multiple points of view, 50; quantity of, 81, 194; and responsiveness, 66; and timeliness, 60

Pravda, stories about: the brigade system, 192; the "Twelfth Floor" program, 176

President of the United States as a newsmaker, 142–44

"Program of Our Life" [Soviet program], 157–58

Programs/programming: audience impact on, 82, 229n26; length of, 88, 151; similarity of American, 87, 126, 217–18. *See also name of specific program*

Progressive, The [American newspaper], 84

Propaganda, 45, 181, 198–200, 210–11, 257n27

Propaganda Department [Communist Party Central Committee], 22–23

Protests/demonstrations: anti-American, 162; coverage of, 29, 73, 106–7; definition of, 243n34; in Great Britain, 86; and multiple points of view, 45; pictures about, 119; and responsibility for events, 127; time devoted to stories about, 112, 241n14, 249n31; in the U.S., 86; in the USSR, 7, 176, 208,

222; war, 44, 47, 158. *See also* Political violence

Pskov, 260n6

Public: and the Communist Party, 196; image of the, 79–83; as individuals, 193–201, 259n50; letters from Soviet citizens compared to the, 194; mass, 183–93; and the news agenda, 211; notions of the, 211; redefinition of the, 185

Public catering, 75

Public lectures, 257n27

Public opinion: and agitation, 180, 184–90, 192, 193; and American television, 219; and assimilation of messages, 182, 198–200; and the Communist Party, 194–90, 194–96, 257n27; and feedback, 187, 190, 194–96; and foreign political systems, 180; and gauging media effects, 201–3; and the hypodermic effects model, 180–83, 193, 196–97, 198, 259n50; ignorance of leadership of, 212–13; impact of, 212–13; individual as unit of, 193–201; and letters from Soviet citizens, 190, 194, 195; and model fitting, 180–201; and the news agenda, 224–25; and official stories, 198; and persuasion, 180–83, 189, 191, 193, 196–97; and political doctrine, 179–203, 257–58n28; polling, 200, 256n8; and the public as individuals, 193–201; role in foreign policy of, 49; and Soviet use of force, 52; and technology, 188; and television, 179–203; and the two-step flow model, 183–93; and work, 198

Pugachova, Alla, 63

Pushkin symposium, 73

Radio, 4, 16–22, 185–86, 195, 206, 220, 230n53, 231n61, 231n65, 233–34n4. *See also name of specific program or network/system*

Radio Free Europe, 231–32n66
Radio Liberty, 20, 22, 220, 222, 231n65, 231–32n66, 232n67, 262n40
Radio Moscow, 231–32n66
Raduga satellites, 14
Rambo [American film], 86
Rapidity of communication, 208–9
Rather, Dan, 93
Reagan, Ronald: Borovik interview of, 254n73; Pozner response to speech by, 79, 88; Soviet interview of, 50, 77; on Soviet television, 50; speech at the United Nations of, 95; Tripoli strike ordered by, 100
Red Dawn [film], 45
Redmont, Bernard, 241–42n17
Reed, John, 156
Regional newspapers, 33
Religion, 46–47, 52, 84, 106, 110, 168, 250n39, 252n54
Republic of Ireland, 129
"Respond, Buglers" [Soviet program], 154
Responsibility: for Chernobyl disaster, 66; and coherence, 126; collective, 190–93; of countries for events, 125–29; definition of, 246–47n8; and emotional coloration, 133–34; for events in the USSR, 66, 238n51; and glasnost, 215; and investigative reporting, 111–12; limits of, 69; and opinionated writing, 130; of the Soviet media, 221, 225; of youth, 174–75. *See also name of specific country*
Responsiveness, 60–68, 221
Reverse question, 253n58
Riga, 12
Rimashevskaya, N. M., 204
Rosenthal, A. M., 94
Roundtable discussions, 35–39, 52–53, 146, 151, 159
Rumania, 90, 130
Rumors, 59, 60, 66, 107, 207, 222
Rural areas, 19, 182, 187, 196, 206, 208, 209, 231n65

Ryazan, 19
Ryzhkov, Nikolai, 87

Sagalaev, Eduard, 172, 173–74
Sagdeev, Roald, 35–39
Sakharov case, 50
Salience: of messages, 219–20; need for, 202; of the USSR, 91; of the West/United States, 32–34, 43–49, 67–68, 74, 91, 97, 164, 178, 211–12, 219–20, 223
Samaritan [American film], 71–72
San Francisco, California, 70, 149
Saratov, 20
Satellites, 4–5, 13–16, 146, 186, 189, 244–45n56, 245–46n58. *See also* Space bridges
Saudi Arabia, 131–32
Saunders, Harold, 51
Sauter, Van Gordon, 105
Savimbi, Jonas, 73
Savitch, Jessica, 53
Sblizhenie, 182
Scarcity, 28, 232n80, 232n81
Schemas, 218, 225, 262n33, 262n48
Schmemann, Serge, 41–43, 117
Schramm, Wilbur, 240n5
Science/space stories: Americans on, 163; Chernenko/Gorbachev regimes' coverage of, 136, 138; and the content of the news, 105–6; and multiple points of view, 47, 236n26; and nature/environment issues, 109, 160; and pictures, 118–19; and the Soviet news agenda, 119; time devoted to, 108, 110, 136, 138, 249n31; and the U.S., 162; and weekend programming, 160, 163
Scientific socialism, 28–29, 125
Second Program, 5–6, 7–8, 48, 153, 154, 228n11, 229n23
Selection: of news, 124, 125, 129, 251n43; of non-news programs, 164–78
Self-criticism, Soviet, 58–59

Semiotic factor, 18–19
Senegal, 102
Sensationalism, 29, 107–8, 211, 225
Shalnev, Alexander, 25, 76, 115
Sharon, Ariel, 86
Shcherbina, Boris, 62
Sheen, Martin, 71–72
Shevardnadze, Eduard, 49, 95, 108–9, 200, 250n38
Shevelev, Grigory, 9, 229n26
Shultz, George, 50–51, 162
Siberia, 3, 14, 31, 115, 227n7
Singapore, 90
"60 Minutes" [CBS], 149
Snyder, Mitch, 71–72
Social issues, 59, 115, 178, 250n39. *See also* Alcohol; Drug abuse
Socialization: and agitation, 192; and the brigade system, 190–91, 192, 257–58n28; and the Communist Party, 189–90; and deviance, 27; and ethics/morals, 27–28; and political doctrine, 26–30, 57, 189–92, 198, 210, 212, 257–58n28; as primary mission of Soviet media, 26–30, 57; success of, 212
Sociodemographics. *See name of specific factor, e.g. Women; Youth*
Soft news. *See* Features/soft news
Somalia, 91
Sonnenfeldt, Helmut, 51, 52
Sound tracks, 146–47
South Africa: censorship in, 93–94; disasters/accidents in the, 112–13; and the geography of news, 91, 94–95, 96, 99, 110, 113, 134, 135, 138–39, 141, 223, 247–48n19, 248–49n22; newsmakers in, 252n53; and opinionated writing, 130, 132, 133; pictures about, 93, 102–3; political violence in, 87, 112, 113, racial policies in, 86; and responsibility for events, 127, 128–29, 246–47n8; Soviet relations with, 92; U.S. sanctions against, 86; and weekend programming, 159–60

South America, 98, 112, 113, 243n30, 248–49n22. *See also name of specific country*
South Korea, 128–29, 132, 149
South Pacific, 113, 248–49n22
South Yemen, 91, 131–32, 162, 223
Sovetskaya Rossia, 57
Soviet General Secretary as a newsmaker, 143–44
Soviet Union. *See* USSR
Soweto, 93–94
Space. *See* Science/space stories
Space bridges, 43–48, 49, 52–55, 163–64, 171–72, 234–35n16, 237n36
Space Science Institute, Soviet. *See name of specific person*
Spacek, Sissy, 163
Spain, 162
Spock, Benjamin, 76
Sports, 9, 47, 88, 108, 114, 151, 153–54, 157, 160, 163, 251n43, 254n69
"Sports for the Week" [Soviet program], 153
"Spotlight of Perestroika" [Soviet program], 111–12
Springsteen, Bruce, 76, 166
Spying/intelligence operations stories, 87, 127, 249n31
Standard of living, 53, 204, 220–21
Star Wars, 47, 162
State Cinematography Committee, 11–12. *See also name of specific person*
State Committee on Television and Radio Broadcasting. *See* Gosteleradio; *name of specific person*
Story length, 219, 239–40n4
Strategic Defense Initiative, 158, 159–60, 160, 162, 236n26
"Studio 9" [Soviet program], 9, 159, 162
"Studio 20" [Soviet news feature], 146
Summits. *See place of specific summit*
Supreme Soviet, 104, 234–35n16

Sverdlovsk, 33, 190, 191, 204
Sweden, 61, 75
Switzerland, 130, 132
Syria, 128–29, 139

Tadzhikistan, 136–37, 148
Taganrog, 186, 194–96
Tambo, Oliver, 94, 139
Tanzania, 91, 129
Tashkent, 12, 174
TASS, 25, 33, 84, 134, 200–201, 219, 231n61. *See also name of specific person*
Taubman, Philip, 237–38n46
Tbilisi, 206
Technical side of the media, 146–50, 251n43
Technology, 180, 188, 200–201, 213, 217. *See also specific type of technology, e.g. Satellites*
Tel-op. *See* Voice-overs
Television: American, 32, 79, 206, 207, 208–9, 217, 219, 220, 233–34n4; and the assimilation of messages, 217–24; availability of, 3–4, 6–7, 32, 186, 227n3, 227n7; centrality to official policies of, 5, 204, 217, 225–26; and contradictions, 224–26; credibility of, 208–9, 212, 217, 220, 233–34n4; development of, 179–80; educational function of, 56; impact/influence of, 31–32, 69, 201–3, 204–25; impact of international communications environment on, 180; as an integrative force, 207–8; as a major source of information, 32, 92, 188, 204–5, 209, 227n7, 233–34n4; negative aspects of, 209–16; and persuasion, 3–4, 180–83, 189, 191, 193, 196–97, 202–3, 213, 214, 225–26; and political doctrine, 179–203, 209–11, 225–26; political leaders' views about, 3–4; as a role model, 29; and sociodemographic characteristics, 205; status of, 180; trial

by, 111. *See also* Media; Media, American; Media, Soviet; *name of specific topic*
Teller, Edward, 236n26
Terrorism, 86, 87, 109, 110, 141, 162. *See also* Political violence; *name of specific act*
Thailand, 128–29, 132
Thatcher, Margaret, 54
Third Program, 9
Third World, 102
Time, elapsed, 89–90, 98–103, 120–23, 135, 140, 141–42, 239–40n4, 243n26, 251n42
Time [American magazine], 86, 114
Time devoted to stories: 103, 108–12. *See also name of specific subject*
Time slots, 110, 234–35n16
Timeliness: of communications, 189; importance of, 203, 213; and international news, 56–60, 68–79; and the legal system, 58; and live broadcasting, 251n43; and media coordination/planning, 24, 26; and newsworthiness, 30; and radio, 20, 231n61; and Soviet coverage of U.S., 75–76; and Soviet domestic news, 56–57, 60, 60–68; value of, 56–60, 192, 211, 221. *See also* Chernobyl
Tiumen, 174
"Today in the World" [Soviet program], 8, 151, 155, 229n23, 229n26
Tomsk, 175, 188
Trade unions, 12, 24, 169, 192, 195
Travel programs, 160
"Travelers' Club" [Soviet program], 160
Treml, Vladimir, 227n3
Trial by television, 111
Trud, 33, 58, 81, 82, 84, 135, 194, 261n15. *See also name of specific journalist*
Truth! and Nothing But the Truth!! [Soviet film], 156–57
Tunisia, 87, 129
Turkatenko, Nikolai, 76–77

Turkmen republic, 24
Tutu, Desmond, 252n54
TWA airliner story, 101
"Twelfth Floor" [Soviet program],
   172–78, 216, 257–58n35
Two-step flow model, 183–93

Uganda, 91
Ukraine, 5, 60, 191. *See also*
   Chernobyl
UNESCO, 15
Union of Cinematographers [USSR],
   23, 228n11, 260n6
Union of Journalists [USSR], 23
Union of Writers [USSR], 208,
   228n11, 262n31
Unions. *See* Trade unions; *name of*
   specific union
United Nations, 91, 95–96, 99, 135,
   141, 240–41n11, 241n13, 241n14,
   242n24, 243n30, 250n38
United States: coverage of the USSR
   by the, 98–99, 114–16, 117, 119,
   143, 241n12, 242n25, 244n52,
   250n38; crime in the, 114;
   disasters/accidents in the, 112–13,
   114; discrimination in the, 168; as
   a global actor, 128; as a model for
   emulation, 74, 75; and opinionated writing about the, 133; perceptions of the USSR in the, 41–
   43, 45–46, 48, 53, 55, 87–88, 115;
   pictures about the, 102; political
   violence in the, 112, 113; religion
   in the, 168; and responsibility for
   events, 92, 127–28, 162, 223, 246–
   47n8, 247n10; and salience of the
   West, 32–34, 43–49, 67–68, 74, 91,
   97, 164, 178, 211–12, 219–20, 223;
   USSR coverage of the, 68–79, 83–
   84, 98–99, 119, 134, 135, 146, 155–
   59, 162–64, 165–71, 211, 241n12,
   242n25, 244n52, 250n37, 250n38;
   USSR perceptions of the, 41–43,
   45–46, 48, 55, 69–84, 95, 119, 127–
   28, 155–59, 162, 165–71, 223. *See*

also name of specific person or sub-
   ject, e.g. Arms control
United States Information Agency,
   15, 231–32n66, 241–42n17
UPI [United Press International], 61
Uruguay, 90, 132
USA Today [American newspaper],
   101
USSR: American perceptions of the,
   41–43, 45–46, 48, 53, 55, 87–88,
   115; American/Western coverage
   of the, 98–99, 114–16, 117, 119,
   143, 200–201, 241n12, 242n25,
   244n52, 250n38; British perceptions of the, 40–41; coverage of
   the United States by the, 68–79,
   83–84, 98–99, 119, 134, 135, 146,
   155–59, 162–64, 165–71, 211,
   241n12, 242n25, 244n52, 250n37,
   250n38; perceptions of British in
   the, 155; perceptions of the U.S./
   West in the, 41–43, 45–46, 48, 55,
   69–84, 95, 119, 127–28, 155–59,
   162, 165–71, 223; and the salience
   of the U.S./West, 32–34, 43–49,
   67–68, 74, 91, 97, 219–20, 223;
   self-image of the, 120; and the
   stages toward communism,
   232n80. *See also* Media, Soviet;
   name of specific person, program, or
   subject
Utility of information, 222, 263n43

Values: differences in American/
   Soviet journalistic, 41–43; ethical/
   moral, 27–28, 33, 55, 110, 250n39
Vasilev, A. P., 174
Velikhov, Evgeny, 62
Vestiges of the past theory, 182
Video cassette recorders [VCRs],
   11–13
Vietnam, 129, 131, 251n42
"Viewer's Companion" [Soviet pro-
   gram], 10
Viewing patterns, 204–7, 260n6
Violence. *See* Political violence; Ter-
   rorism

Visnews [international service], 121–22

Vladivostok, 174

Voice of America, 20, 21–22, 220, 231n65, 231–32n66, 232n67

Voice-overs, 121–23, 146–47

Voitovich, Evgeny, 11–12

Volkogonov, Dmitri, 157–58

Volunteer correspondents, 195–96

Voronezh, 11

Voyager II story, 162

Vremya: audience size for, 8–9; average number of stories on, 88–89; and changes in Soviet leadership, 134–42; content of, 88, 104–8; legitimating sources for, 114; as a major source of information, 32; Molotov's preference for, 229n23; narrowing of perspective of, 141–42; persuasion function of, 123; preeminence of, 5, 87; role of, 9; story/program length for, 9, 88–89, 108–12; technical side of, 146–50; time slot for, 10. *See also* Vremya, stories about; *name of specific topic or country, e.g.* Anchors

Vremya, stories about: arms control, 108, 114, 136, 249n31; Chernobyl, 61, 63, 66, 237n45; civil rights/liberties, 110; crime, 114, 118, 249n31; culture/arts, 108, 119, 120, 138, 249n31; disasters/accidents, 107–8, 109, 113, 114, 119, 136–38, 249n31; domestic news, 106, 110, 114, 141, 142, 249n31; economic issues, 106, 109, 110–11, 113, 120, 136, 138, 249n31; elections, 108, 113; ethics/morals, 110; human interest, 71–72, 108; international politics, 106, 114, 119, 136, 138, 249n31; legislative processes, 136, 138, 249n31; the media, 114, 249n31; military issues, 114, 136, 249n31; newsmakers, 142–45, 252n46; official stories, 104, 108–9, 110, 113, 119, 136, 141; political violence, 106–7, 113, 114, 119,

249n31; protests/demonstrations, 106–7, 119, 241n14, 249n31; religion, 110; science/space, 108, 109, 118–19, 136, 138; sports, 108; spying/intelligence operations, 249n31; terrorism, 109; the United States, 71–72, 91, 98–99, 114–16, 144, 241n12, 242n25, 244n52, 250n37, 250n38. *See also name of specific country*

Wall Street Journal, 101

Wallace, Chris, 122

War, 44, 47, 158

Warnke, Paul, 162

Warsaw Pact countries, 99, 102, 112, 113, 114, 134–35, 240–41n11, 242n24, 243n26, 248–49n22. *See also name of specific country*

Washington Post, 84, 236n24

Washington Summit [1987], 50, 163

Washington Times, 83–84

Watson, George, 87–88, 100, 101, 107, 116

Wattenberg, Ben, 51, 52

Weather, 88, 108, 222

Weekday programming, 150–59, 253n61, 254n68, 254n69, 255n77

Weekend programming, 159–64, 206–7

West: characteristics of Soviet stories about the, 34; coverage of the USSR by the, 200–201; criticism in the, 196; and the hypodermic effects model, 181, 261n50; increase in Soviet coverage of the, 34, 139–40; influence on Soviet media of the, 47, 200–201, 210–12; influence on Soviet youth of the, 172–74; and multiple points of view, 47; purpose of Soviet coverage of the, 34; and the two-step flow model, 183–84, 188–89. *See also* Salience: of the West/United States; United States; *name of specific region, country, or subject*

West Africa, 102, 113, 248–49n22

West Germany, 44, 50, 91, 92, 128–
   29, 133, 135, 238n51, 251n42
Western Europe, 102, 112, 113, 134,
   248–49n22. *See also name of specific*
   country
Westin, Av, 80, 90, 253n58
What Is To Be Done? [Lenin], 184
White, Stephen, 186–87
Wierzynski, Maciej, 63–64
Women, 19, 74–75, 165, 186, 206,
   260n6
Work, 47, 111–12, 184–85, 186, 190–
   94, 197, 198, 209, 214
"World News Tonight" [ABC]: average numbers of stories on, 88–89;
   content of, 104–8; and in-depth/
   breadth coverage, 101; narrowing
   of perspective of, 141–42; and
   program/story length, 88–89, 108–
   12; and responsibility for events,
   127–29; salience of Soviet Union
   for, 87–88, 91. *See also* "World
   News Tonight" [ABC], stories
   about; *name of specific country or*
   subject
"World News Tonight" [ABC], stories about: arms control, 108, 114,
   118; citizenship issues, 114, 118,
   140; crime, 110, 112, 114, 250n39;
   culture/arts, 108, 112, 140;
   disasters/accidents, 107–8, 109,
   110, 112–14, 140; domestic news,
   89, 112, 113–14, 140–41; economic
   issues, 106, 109, 110–11, 118; elections, 108, 110; ethics/morals, 110,
   250n39; human interest, 108, 114;
   international/national politics,
   112, 114, 140; interviews, 245–
   46n58; the legislative process, 110;
   newsmakers, 142–45, 252n46; official government actions/visits,
   104, 108, 109; political violence,
   106–7, 112, 114, 140; protests/
   demonstrations, 106–7, 119; religion, 110, 250n39; science/space,
   105–6, 108, 109, 110; social issues,
   250n39; sports, 108, 114; terror-

ism, 109, 110; the USSR, 91, 98–
   99, 114–16, 144, 241n12, 242n25,
   244n52
"World and Youth, The" [Soviet pro-
   gram], 39–43, 154, 157, 172–78
Writers, Union of, 208, 228n11,
   262n31

Yakovlev, Alexander, 21–23, 217
Yakovlev, Egor, 54
Yale University, 86
Young, Andrew, 78
Young Communist League, 12, 24,
   175–77, 191, 192–93, 195
Young Pioneers, 160, 193, 195
"Young Voices" [Soviet program],
   10
Youth: and the Afghanistan war,
   160; Americans on programs for,
   163; British, 39–41; career choices
   of, 209; and the Communist
   Party, 175–77; criticisms of, 216;
   educational concerns of, 175–76;
   and glasnost, 173–74; impact of,
   177–78; impact of television on,
   31–32, 207; and international
   news stories, 34; and military issues, 163; and multiple points of
   view, 45, 47, 173; perceptions of
   the U.S. by Soviet, 158; and political education, 45, 160, 175–77;
   and propaganda, 45; responsibility of, 174–75; and the salience of
   the West, 34, 172–74, 211; viewing patterns of, 206; and
   weekday/weekend programming,
   154, 160, 163. *See also* Young Communist League; Young Pioneers;
   name of specific program
Yugoslavia, 130–31, 132, 251n42
Yurchenko, Vitaly, 87

Zakharov, Gennadi, 250n38
Zamyatin, Leonid, 165–66
Zhuravlev, G. T., 198–200
Zimbabwe, 91, 129
Zorin, Valentin, 169–71